What Your Colleagues Are Saying

"Collaborative Response has been instrumental in changing the lives of both staff and students. It has provided an explicit and collective framework for having conversations that lead to improved student learning outcomes and ensuring that the individual learning needs of all students are recognized as every person's responsibility."

Janeen Silcock, Principal
Ballina Coast High School
Ballina, New South Wales, Australia

"Our district in coastal, rural Maine has been actively implementing Collaborative Response for three years now, and each year we continue to grow and evolve through the implementation process. The Collaborative Response philosophy and approach served as the leverage that we needed after years of trying to get a district-wide RTI plan off the ground! It has been a transformational model for all of our teams through grade levels PK–12."

Nicole Chan, Director of Curriculum
Regional School Unit 24
Sullivan, Maine, United States of America

"The Collaborative Response framework has guided our school division to have deep and meaningful conversations around school-level data. All students deserve to be successful and by adopting the Collaborative Response framework, we will see it become a reality."

Joanna Landry, Superintendent of Education Services
Regina Catholic Schools
Regina, Saskatchewan, Canada

"Collaborative Response is based on a structure that enables professional learning communities in schools to develop for the benefit of student learning and well-being. That is because the approach includes a respect for the knowledge, idiosyncrasies, and experience of staff and students—all these are resources that can be used for the benefits and growth of all involved."

Ingileif Ástvaldsdóttir, Adjunct Lecturer
University of Iceland, Department of Education
Reykjavík, Iceland

"The positive impact of our revised meeting schedules, and our four-tiered intervention framework, is that all students are put in the spotlight, and none are left to fly under the radar. In addition, the collaborative team meeting has advanced the professional capacity of staff by providing the vehicle to engage in deep discussions of evidence-based teaching practices that assist in improving student achievement."

Leigh Toscan, Learning and Support Teacher
Southern Cross Public School
Ballina, New South Wales, Australia

"Through understanding the roles of assessment, collaboration, and a defined continuum of supports, Kurtis and Lorna Hewson lay out multiple entry points for schools, leadership teams, and senior leaders that will ultimately impact all students in achievement, inclusion, and well-being."

Joanne Pitman, Superintendent, School Improvement
Calgary Board of Education
Calgary, Alberta, Canada

"Collaborative Response provides a deeper model for collaboration and a way to be more intentional about supporting all our students. In addition, Kurtis and Lorna Hewson and the Jigsaw Learning team have been invaluable in providing informative videos, templates, articles, and learning opportunities that are guiding our leadership team in leading professional development for our staff."

Karen Currie, Principal
Kamloops Christian School
Kamloops, British Columbia, Canada

"Collaborative Response gave our school the focus and framework needed to change the culture around how we identify and support all of our students. Providing meaningful and strategic tiered systems of supports, along with an emphasis on relationships, totally changed the game for our collaborative teams. This philosophical shift from the 'Me' to 'We' in the work we do has empowered all staff to initiate more student-centered conversations and consistently highlight celebrations."

Chris Burris, Vice Principal & Behavior Support Teacher Coach
South Shore Regional Centre for Education
Bridgewater, Nova Scotia, Canada

"We have reimagined our student support structures, placing the Collaborative Response process at the heart of our practice. Long meetings focusing on deficits are gone, replaced by action-based collaborations focusing on classroom instructional strategies and learning dispositions. Collaborative Response is a key driver of our schoolwide collaborative culture and has been a major contributor to our strong growth in external assessments of literacy and numeracy."

Luke Bristow, Deputy Principal
Murwillumbah High School
Murwillumbah, New South Wales, Australia

"We all need to be on the same team when it comes to student success, and we are seeing huge benefits from Collaborative Response as it sets the table for increased student achievement at every grade level and subject area within our schools!"

Adam Murray, Superintendent
Peace River School Division
Peace River, Alberta, Canada

"Through the lens of intervention, our school has evolved notably in a short time span. Teachers now review their instructional practices more thoroughly, have a clearer understanding of student learning needs, and access recently created support structures to assist their students. Our Collaborative Response work has become a foundation to build upon to address a variety of concerns, both transient and long-lasting, and is now an essential part of our school growth processes."

Carolyn Jensen, Principal
Memorial Composite High School
Stony Plain, Alberta, Canada

"With the use of consistent, intentional structures such as the collaborative team meetings, data analysis, and continuum of supports, we have seen increased efficacy, confidence, and collaboration at all levels of our organization. We are embracing a culture where staff rely on the strengths of their colleagues in a student-centered approach to inclusivity."

Pamela Guilbault, Superintendent
Lakeland Catholic School Division
Bonnyville, Alberta, Canada

"Collaborative Response provides a well-researched, flexible framework from which to address and support individual student learning needs. Administrators and teachers will appreciate the structures and processes which can be easily integrated into their practice. With clear guidelines for everything from organizing student data, to planning efficient team meetings, this book is a fantastic resource for improving student learning."

David Dyck, Education Director
Calgary Board of Education
Calgary, Alberta, Canada

"Our structure for student support involves a wonderful collaboration from a large group that consists of Administrators, Teachers, Educational Assistants, Student Services Team, and Cree & Language Team with the help of Jigsaw Learning, their team, and our contracted Service Providers. Collaborative Response enables us as a collective to find solutions to create student success. This approach tailors to the needs of our organization, with Cree Language and Culture as the foundation of our school."

Lisa Thunder, Principal
Oski Pasiknowew Kamik School
Wabasca, Alberta, Canada

Collaborative Response

For our children, Cam, Kayty, Bobb, Marenn, Mikah, and Mia,
who inspire us daily to find joy in every moment
and to cherish each memory we make.

Collaborative Response

Three Foundational Components That Transform How We Respond to the Needs of Learners

Kurtis Hewson
Lorna Hewson

Foreword by Andy Hargreaves

FOR INFORMATION:

Corwin

A SAGE Company

2455 Teller Road

Thousand Oaks, California 91320

(800) 233-9936

www.corwin.com

SAGE Publications Ltd.

1 Oliver's Yard

55 City Road

London EC1Y 1SP

United Kingdom

SAGE Publications India Pvt. Ltd.

B 1/I 1 Mohan Cooperative Industrial Area

Mathura Road, New Delhi 110 044

India

SAGE Publications Asia-Pacific Pte. Ltd.

18 Cross Street #10-10/11/12

China Square Central

Singapore 048423

President: Mike Soules

Vice President and
 Editorial Director: Monica Eckman

Senior Acquisitions Editor: Ariel Curry

Content Development
 Manager: Desirée A. Bartlett

Editorial Assistants: Nancy Chung and
 Nyle De Leon

Production Editor: Tori Mirsadjadi

Copy Editor: QuADS Prepress Pvt. Ltd.

Typesetter: C&M Digitals (P) Ltd.

Cover Designer: Scott Van Atta

Marketing Manager: Morgan Fox

Copyright © 2022 by Corwin Press, Inc.

All rights reserved. Except as permitted by U.S. copyright law, no part of this work may be reproduced or distributed in any form or by any means, or stored in a database or retrieval system, without permission in writing from the publisher.

When forms and sample documents appearing in this work are intended for reproduction, they will be marked as such. Reproduction of their use is authorized for educational use by educators, local school sites, and/or noncommercial or nonprofit entities that have purchased the book.

All third-party trademarks referenced or depicted herein are included solely for the purpose of illustration and are the property of their respective owners. Reference to these trademarks in no way indicates any relationship with, or endorsement by, the trademark owner.

Printed in Canada

Library of Congress Cataloging-in-Publication Data

Names: Hewson, Kurtis, author. | Hewson, Lorna, author.

Title: Collaborative response : three foundational components that transform how we respond to the needs of learners / Kurtis Hewson, Lorna Hewson ; foreword by Andy Hargreaves.

Description: Thousand Oaks, California : Corwin, 2022. | Includes bibliographical references and index.

Identifiers: LCCN 2021049219 | ISBN 9781071862810 (paperback) | ISBN 9781071862827 (epub) | ISBN 9781071862834 (epub) | ISBN 9781071862841 (pdf)

Subjects: LCSH: Teaching teams. | Teachers—Professional relationships. | Individualized instruction. | School environment.

Classification: LCC LB1029.T4 H49 2022 | DDC 371.14/8—dc23/eng/20211116

LC record available at https://lccn.loc.gov/2021049219

This book is printed on acid-free paper.

22 23 24 25 26 10 9 8 7 6 5 4 3 2 1

DISCLAIMER: This book may direct you to access third-party content via web links, QR codes, or other scannable technologies, which are provided for your reference by the author(s). Corwin makes no guarantee that such third-party content will be available for your use and encourages you to review the terms and conditions of such third-party content. Corwin takes no responsibility and assumes no liability for your use of any third-party content, nor does Corwin approve, sponsor, endorse, verify, or certify such third-party content.

Contents

List of Figures	xi
List of Tables	xiii
Companion Website Contents	xv
Foreword by Andy Hargreaves	xvii
Acknowledgments	xxi
About the Authors	xxiii

Introduction: A Call to Action	**1**
Chapter 1: Examining a Culture of Response	**15**
Chapter 2: Envisioning Collaborative Response	**25**
Chapter 3: Collaborative Structures	**35**
Chapter 4: Collaborative Processes	**69**
Chapter 5: Collaborative Team Meetings	**87**
Chapter 6: Data and Evidence	**133**
Chapter 7: Continuum of Supports	**169**
Chapter 8: Putting the Pieces Together	**211**

References and Resources	217
Index	223

Note From the Publisher: The authors have provided web content that is available to you through a QR (quick response) code. To read a QR code, you must have a smartphone or tablet with a camera. We recommend that you download a QR code reader app that is made specifically for your phone or tablet brand.

The companion website may also be accessed at http://jigsawlearning.ca/collaborative-response

List of Figures

Figure I.1.	Visual representation of Collaborative Response	3
Figure 3.1.	Overview of collaborative structures	38
Figure 3.2.	Connecting district, school, and team priorities	50
Figure 4.1.	Robert W. Zahara School meeting overview	74
Figure 4.2.	Oski Pasikoniwew Kamik School collaborative team meeting agenda poster	76
Figure 4.3.	Crestwood School team meeting tent card	83
Figure 5.1.	Savanna School team CTM schedule (2018–2019)	105
Figure 5.2.	Pat Hardy Primary School team meeting roles	110
Figure 5.3.	Key issues flowchart	121
Figure 5.4.	Darwell School meeting discussion cards	124
Figure 5.5.	Corpus Christi Catholic Elementary/Junior High School key issues posters	125
Figure 6.1.	Sample calendar (January)	150
Figure 6.2.	Peace Wapiti Public School Division screen overview	151
Figure 6.3.	Literacy screen data overview	156
Figure 6.4.	Collaborative team meeting data overview sample	157
Figure 6.5.	Data overview for a large regional high school in New South Wales	159
Figure 6.6.	Sample visual team board	164
Figure 7.1.	Initial continuum of supports at Peace Wapiti Academy	177
Figure 7.2.	Continuum of supports overview	181
Figure 7.3.	Kildare School reading pyramid of supports	189
Figure 7.4.	Kisipatnahak School behavior continuum of supports	190
Figure 7.5.	Herald School continuum of supports (Tiers 3 and 4)	191
Figure 7.6.	Herald School continuum of supports (Tier 2)	192
Figure 7.7.	Continuum of supports visual wall	195
Figure 7.8.	Dr. Roy Wilson Detention Center, school meeting role tent cards	196

Figure 7.9.	Tier 1 before and after at Nipisihkopahk Elementary School	200
Figure 7.10.	Not a Tier 4 student visual	203
Figure 7.11.	Connection of collaborative structures with tiers of support	205
Figure 7.12.	Collaborative structures at Elmworth School	206
Figure 7.13.	Collaborative structure expectations for Medicine Hat Public School Division	207

List of Tables

Table 2.1.	Three essential components working together	30
Table 3.1.	Overview of collaborative structures	37
Table 4.1.	Team meeting participation overview	73
Table 5.1.	Collaborative team meeting role overview	108
Table 5.2.	Collaborative structures and processes not established	131
Table 6.1.	Data and evidence not established	168
Table 7.1.	Continuum of supports not established	208

Companion Website Contents

Visit our companion website at http://jigsawlearning.ca/collaborative-response to view and download all of the templates and tools from this book:

1.1—Essential Cultural Shifts, Change Index	24
1.2—Essential Cultural Shifts, Analysis	24
2.1—Collaborative Response Overview	31
3.1—Reflecting on Case Consult Team Meetings	41
3.2—Reflecting on School Support Team Meetings	42
3.3—Data Review and Team Goal Template	51
3.4—Data Review and Team Inquiry Question Template	51
3.5—Team Priorities and Actions	51
3.6—Team Planning Guide Template	53
3.7—Reflecting on Collaborative Planning	61
3.8—Team Meeting Overview Template	61
3.9—Collaborative Team Meeting Cycle	66
3.10—Embedding Time for Collaboration	67
4.1—Team Norms Template	71
4.2—Process for Establishing Team Norms	71
4.3—Unpacking Team Norms Template	72
4.4—Case Consult Team Agenda and Notes Template	78
4.5—School Support Team Meeting Agenda and Notes Template	79
4.6—Collaborative Space Planning Checklist	85
5.1—Collaborative Team Meeting Playlist	92
5.2—Collaborative Team Meeting Observation Organizer	92
5.3—Reflecting on Collaborative Team Meetings Template	94
5.4—Pre-Meeting Organizer	107
5.5—Team Meeting Role Cards	109
5.6—Reinforcing Norms Compilation Video	112

5.7—Strategies for Deepening Norms	112
5.8—Collaborative Team Meeting Agenda and Notes Template	113
5.9—Team Meeting Discussion and Question Cards	123
5.10—Key Issues and Tier 2 Supports Template	123
5.11—Locus of Control Visual	128
6.1—Reflecting on Data and Evidence	140
6.2—Criteria and Considerations When Determining a Universal Screen	145
6.3—Examining Potential Common Assessments	145
6.4—Potential Benchmarks/Screening Tools	145
6.5—Assessment Planning Template	149
6.6—Team Data Analysis Template	157
6.7—Data Overview Template	162
6.8—Data-Informed Pre-Meeting Organizer	162
6.9—Student Entry-Level Criteria Template	163
7.1—Reflecting on a Continuum of Supports	172
7.2—Continuum of Supports Template (General)	187
7.3—Intervention Description Template	193
7.4—Refining Continuum of Supports Template	201
8.1—Targets for Implementation	213

Visit the companion website at
http://jigsawlearning.ca/collaborative-response
for downloadable resources.

Foreword

It would be hard to find a teacher anywhere who would claim that what schools need is more meetings. So, when I got my chance to run a meeting or two, I overly embraced the insight, often attributed to Peter Drucker, that "culture eats strategy for breakfast."

Compare this with my experience of being a visiting professor, along with my colleague Dennis Shirley, at the University of Stavanger in Norway. The dean made a practice of inviting us for coffee with other members of faculty. Despite this feeling like an arcane ritual, Dennis and I eventually joined in, although we felt increasingly guilty that we were not working properly. But at the end of one of the first coffee mornings, one of the faculty members said, "Oh, I was going to email you about something, but we've discussed it now." Not only does culture eat strategy for breakfast, but it consumes a lot of coffee as well.

Culture doesn't happen spontaneously, even if that's what it seems like sometimes. Coffee occurred at a definite time and place. The dean made a priority of being there, and the room was provisioned with cups and spoons—and coffee. None of it happened by accident; there was a structure underpinning it. As Kurtis and Lorna Hewson demonstrate time and again, there are ways to go about designing a structure so that it works well, makes people feel motivated, and gets the job done. Many of the things the authors describe as they define what makes a good meeting seem obvious once pointed out. But meetings won't work without these things: having a clear focus, setting some kind of timeline, preparing things ahead of time to save getting bogged down in the meeting itself, having an agenda, knowing who does what, keeping time, documenting proceedings, and ultimately getting things done. Seems easy, doesn't it? But if it was, meetings would go swimmingly everywhere. Clearly, they don't.

Instead of supplanting the informal culture or even supporting it, the way a meeting looks and feels should exemplify what that culture is and aspires to be. Is it fun, at least some of the time? Do people get a chance to play? Does every meeting have explicit learning involved in it—looking at data, at children, or at research, for example (all of which are abiding themes in this book)? Do people get to stand up and do activities—walking around with manipulatives, flip chart paper, or sticky notes—rather than sitting still all the time? Does everyone come out of the room knowing something that they didn't understand or weren't aware of before they came in? Are solutions created by a group of people together, rather than originating from one individual? If good meetings are working well, they don't just exist to support the culture or even frame it—they become a vibrant part of the culture itself.

Suppose that when you're the chairperson, you find that you don't possess all the capabilities to accomplish everything meetings require. I have attention-deficit/hyperactivity disorder (ADHD), so this is personal. Without a clear plan, I can get to the end of a meeting having only addressed a third of the agenda. Then, many years ago, a counselor gave me some life-changing advice: "Stop trying to hide your disability." Show people what you can contribute that will advance their own interests and purposes and ask them to help you with the rest. So, although I often chair meetings, I ask someone else to keep an eye on the time. All of us need to be aware of our strengths and weaknesses and how to make the best of the first and mitigate the second—together. That's not just what makes effective meetings—it defines powerful groups too.

Good meetings need culture and structure. A positive *culture* is about deliberately building relationships, establishing trust, valuing diversity of identities and personalities, respecting people's contributions and opinions, hearing each other out, inviting clashes of ideas, managing conflicts, learning from mistakes, celebrating successes, and getting things done. *Structure* is about having protocols that improve the depth and quality of interactions, setting norms to guide those interactive processes, establishing clear roles and responsibilities, drawing up agendas, keeping to time, maintaining clear records, and working toward clear outcomes at the end.

Collaborative Response is about effective inclusion of all students and about the professional collaboration that is needed to make that happen. As a counterbalance to the many books that emphasize the informal aspects of collaborative professionalism, as expressed in high trust, positive relationships, and a shared vision, this book picks up the less fashionable, more formal, but equally essential aspects: meetings. Four kinds of meetings are described. But the pivotal ones perhaps are the collaborative team meetings: a kind of meeting of meetings. These are the subject of the most substantial chapter in this book—and with justification, because at their best, they draw everything else together and ensure that inquiry and discussion are followed by action and that students benefit.

This is a practical book as well as a programmatic one. For instance, in relation to the ubiquitous need for adequate teacher time outside of their own classes, the Hewsons set out clear practical strategies for protecting collaborative time—including asynchronous time, online. This book is chock-full of tools, processes, templates, and guidelines—for instance, how to define roles like recorder, interrupter, timekeeper, problem-solver, and so on—that have already been successfully implemented in the schools the authors have worked with.

A great strength of the book is that it encourages disagreement and even conflict, not about vision and direction, but about the best strategies for meeting the needs of every child. The norms, roles, and protocols are there not to avoid conflict, but to enable it to be professional and productive. This is not just a book that shows a need and points the way, and it is even more than a useful toolkit—example after example, this book illustrates how effective Collaborative Response teams really feel, what they look like, and how real students have benefited from them.

I've spent 30 years studying and writing about teacher collaboration. This book taught me that I still have some things to learn. Pick it up and use it, and it will do the same for you.

Andy Hargreaves
University of Ottawa
December 2021

Acknowledgments

We need to start our acknowledgments by recognizing all the passionate educators who are dedicated to the success of each and every child in their care.

We have had the privilege throughout our careers to learn from so many excellent educators. First, to the teachers who taught us throughout our school years, from whom we learned the importance of understanding and instilling hope. To the university professors who guided us through our learning in becoming teachers and leaders both at the undergraduate and graduate levels. To all the colleagues who supported us through the first years of teaching and beyond and who became our biggest cheerleaders. To all our leaders and mentors who acknowledged our passion for innovation and encouraged us to pursue change with our school teams. To all the teachers, school leaders, and district leaders who have joined us in envisioning and living out Collaborative Response and shared their challenges and successes along the way. We are humbled by the many people of influence and opportunities we have been privileged to interact with throughout our years in education. Thank you!

We would not be the people we are today without the love and support of our families. Our parents, Harry and Lynda Hewson, Jake and Mary Gerbrandt, as well as our siblings and their families, have always been our greatest advocates and teachers. Even when they were not always sure what it was we were trying to accomplish, they have always been curious, listened to our adventures and challenges, and encouraged us to pursue our dreams.

To our good friend, Jim Parsons, who mentored us and taught us through the writing of our first attempts at documenting our ideas. Jim shared his love of learning and passion for writing, which has greatly influenced our ability to share our ideas. Thank you, Jim, for your coaching and friendship over the years.

As we established Jigsaw Learning as a support for schools and districts, beginning first in our home province of Alberta, Canada, and now extending beyond those borders, our growth has been substantial over the past few years. As a result, we have had the privilege of creating a team of educators with a wealth of experience and expertise who have expanded the work that began through Collaborative Response. This team provides unwavering, responsive, and dedicated support to every classroom, school, or district that has reached out in partnership. We have learned so much from our team, and we thank them for their patience and persistence as we've experienced the aches and pains of a growing organization. They continue to push our thinking and expand our awareness to ensure success for all.

To the staff at Corwin, we thank you for your support and patience as we worked through the process to arrive at this final product. We are grateful for your expertise, guidance, and belief in *Collaborative Response*.

And finally, to every student who persistently voices their needs explicitly or implicitly to their teachers. We hear you! You are the reason we have dedicated our lives to ensuring every student has their needs met, to pledge equity for all and that every child is the focus of the dedicated teams that convene to determine next steps. Our passion is fueled by our belief that every child deserves a team!

About the Authors

Kurtis Hewson has been an award-winning teacher, vice principal, and principal as well as taught at the postsecondary level. With more than a decade of experience as a school administrator, Kurtis has championed the call for collaborative structures in schools to ensure success for all students. In addition to two finalist awards from the Alberta Excellence in Teaching program and an Edwin Parr award recipients for excellence in his first year of teaching, Kurtis was an honoree for the ASCD Outstanding Young Educator Award in 2010. Kurtis is one of five Alberta principals featured in *Reflecting on Leadership for Learning: Case Studies of Five Alberta Elementary School Principals*, addressing exemplary leadership practices in elementary schools in Alberta. He is the co-founder of Jigsaw Learning and currently works with districts and schools nationally and internationally establishing Collaborative Response frameworks and interacting with thousands of educators annually.

Lorna Hewson is a passionate educator who is co-founder and Lead Learner of Jigsaw Learning, a Canadian consulting company that provides support for educators. She is an engaging presenter, facilitator, coach, and mentor and has served to support classrooms, schools, and districts nationally and internationally. An Alberta Excellence in Teaching Award winner, Lorna has served diverse roles in schools and districts and has a wealth of experience in essentially every area of development in supporting the needs of districts, schools, staff, and students. She has served in district leadership roles in curriculum, learning, and inclusive services; has experience in curriculum implementation and design at the provincial level; and has had the privilege to serve as the chair of the Alberta Assessment Consortium. Lorna engages in a variety of support structures with systems, including coaching, mentoring, leading, and facilitating schools and districts in Collaborative Response, designing and coordinating teams throughout systems, and building inclusive frameworks that ensure that every child has a team to identify and meet their needs.

Introduction

A Call to Action

This book is not a silver bullet.

It is not a step-by-step guide for improving schools. It will not share a magic formula or a quick fix for school leaders to ensure high-quality learning and success for students. We recognize "the inherent dangers in efforts to simplify complex tasks" (DuFour, 1998, p. 57), and as a result, we embark with a full disclosure. This book introduces an approach that is simple in design but complex in execution. It is more than a little messy, . . . but it is an organizational framework that can have a profound impact on student success and educator collective efficacy!

What this book will do is examine what we call *Collaborative Response* and bring attention to basic tenets, elements, and ideas we have shared across schools and districts, beginning in our home province of Alberta, Canada, and extending beyond our provincial and national borders. Our goal is to help schools make sure that all students are engaged learners and that no child slips through the cracks, with educator expertise honored, maximized, and extended throughout the process. Traditional schools, in our experience, fit some children better than others. These fortunate students who fit our commonly understood mold of schooling are the benefactors of teaching, according to what Rose (2016) would refer to as "the hidden tyranny of the average" (p. 9). These children have found success in the past and will continue to succeed in traditional classroom models.

To truly achieve equity across all systems, we believe that all children deserve the best we have to offer. We know that teachers and schools do not purposely disregard some students; the teachers we know care that all children learn. Yet the individualistic teaching and learning models common to our schools create a system that makes individual and, often, isolated teacher responses to children's needs either next to impossible or an exhausting personal martyrdom.

We believe that schools can and should change so that, as the old saying goes, "It takes a village to raise a child." Or, in the case of schooling, we believe that the entire school should teach and raise up all learners. Here, we propose a model that we know can move us toward this goal.

Implementing the approach presented in this book will not make life in schools any less busy or demanding. In fact, as the culture of your school is addressed, articulated, and likely challenged through ideas and concepts we share here, things may get harder before they get better. Although "harder before better" is consistent with what we know about engaging in meaningful change, it doesn't mean that some difficult discussions and resulting tensions are not part of the short-term forecast. By putting the needs of students at the forefront of school conversations, we will potentially place some long-held teaching practices and educational beliefs in direct conflict with traditional schooling. We will also raise some conversations perhaps left dormant out of a desire to avoid uncomfortable and challenging conversations.

The schoolwide approach presented in this book will place a direct focus on quality classroom instruction and, in time, an open conversation about what is not working and what we could try in order to see success for each and every child. Our experiences have shown that transitioning to a school-based Collaborative Response will result in a greater focus on students in the classroom, an increased individual teacher awareness of student needs, and powerful conversations that become the impetus for shifts in classroom teaching and learning. In time, it will bring together general and specialized approaches for all, with fewer learners needing to be moved to more intensive special education processes.

DuFour, DuFour, and Eaker (2010) remind us, "It would be a huge mistake to assume a system of interventions can solve the problems created by poor instruction occurring on a wide-scale basis. Schools need both skillful teachers and a system of interventions" (p. 256). Our experience working with schools and districts across Alberta and beyond has shown us repeatedly that the conversations and laser-like focus placed on students through Collaborative Response brings with it substantial shifts in individual teacher practice and collective communities of practice that recognize, reinforce, sustain, and celebrate highly impactful pedagogy. In short, this book will provide a systemic framework that consistently examines exceptional classroom learning, through the identification and response related to the needs of students, and will provide examples of schools that have successfully experienced the emergence of systemic, highly impactful classroom instruction, as well as schoolwide response, through the use of this approach.

Finally, although this text relies on and expands tenets of response to intervention (RTI), multitiered systems of support (MTSS), positive behavior intervention support, and other similar models, Collaborative Response is not synonymous with these approaches. They are not interchangeable. Shortly, we will examine the distinctive features that we believe set Collaborative Response apart from the contemporary tiered support models. Although several elements may be recognizable for leaders previously engaged in a typical three-tiered approach to supporting students, it is important to establish at the outset that this is not a book about establishing a system of multitiered support. What we are sharing is different.

What This Book *Will* Do!

So, why begin with a disclaimer? We believe that it is important that readers engage with our text without any misconceptions about the book's purpose or content. We recognize that school improvement and reform is an exhausting subject matter, susceptible to ever-changing educational movements and the latest "fad of the day." However, we do feel that our work holds immense promise by providing a framework on which schools can build on their ongoing efforts, striving for and ensuring success for every child.

This book will share and dissect a schoolwide approach for addressing the individual needs of students, founded on equal portions of educational research and practical application. Our model has evolved for us in our own school experiences and subsequently deepened in our experiences working with other schools and districts throughout Alberta and abroad. This work has involved not only individual school conversations, but also districtwide frameworks to support effective school structures and processes. Throughout the text, we share examples from schools and districts that are framing their work in accordance with the foundational graphic shared in Figure I.1.

Figure I.1 Visual representation of Collaborative Response

This book will break down the three foundational components of this responsive framework, providing schools with resources, templates, and narrative examples that help your school or district purposefully and collectively respond to individual student needs. Because we recognize and celebrate the uniqueness of every school's diverse community, we present Collaborative Response as a flexible framework, without strict adherence to specific features of each component. In other words, we believe that this approach provides a framework that helps each school create its own specific path toward Collaborative Response. This said, we strongly believe that all three components need to be established if schools are to provide the best possible set of structures and processes critical for student success. What each component looks like will be (and should be) unique to the context of each educational environment. We also recognize that we are not speaking to a specific geographical audience—we believe and have seen evidence that Collaborative Response can transcend multiple unique global approaches to education.

We also recognize (and have witnessed) the reality that establishing a responsive model into schools can be potentially fraught with high tension, disillusionment, and considerable efforts at the outset. In short, some school cultures do not provide fertile ground in which a responsive model, such as the one presented in this book, will grow and flourish. We know that simply adding or revising structures won't have an impact on underlying culture. In fact, the superficial act of introducing a structure without changing the culture often gives organizations license to avoid problems that must be confronted and addressed (Collins, 2009).

Our collective work in schools has identified characteristics of traditional cultures focused on teaching or learning for *most* students and helped us recognize the shifts needed to establish a responsive model focused on truly achieving the aspiration of learning and success for *all* students. Simply stated, we believe that traditionally structured schools can no longer meet the diverse and varied needs of all students. As Buffum et al. (2012) point out,

> We know one thing for certain: we are never going to get there doing what we have always done. Our traditional school system was created in a time when the typical educator worked in a one-room schoolhouse and served as the only teacher for an entire town. Today it is virtually impossible for a single teacher to possess all the skills and knowledge necessary to meet the unique needs of every child in the classroom. (p. 1)

We know and celebrate teachers who go above and beyond the call of duty for their children, working tirelessly to support and ensure success for all. Pfeffer and Sutton (2000) suggest, "It is impossible for even the most talented people to do competent, let alone brilliant, work in a flawed system" (p. 96). Our intention in this book is to establish the collective capacity to support the great day-to-day work of teachers happening in schools and ensure that it can be a reality throughout an entire system. *Our ultimate vision is to transform teaching from an isolated to a collective endeavor* while *supporting each and every child in our charge.*

This book also builds on the diverse research base and practical application of the diversity of thought flooding our educational landscape. It can be difficult for schools (and more specifically school leaders) to bridge educational thought and theory. Throughout this text, we bridge the findings of researchers and the work of educators with the practical structures, processes, and direction of Collaborative Response.

Finally, although the context in which we originally established our thinking was an elementary setting with a primary focus on literacy, the essential components of this model are relevant for all schools, regardless of size, location, grade focus, or subject area. We have helped schools utilize the framework with a focus on student behavior and social-emotional needs. We have seen its implementation make a difference for schools focusing on numeracy success for students. We have seen the model adapted in small rural schools with a wide range of grades and combined classes and have helped large schools with multiple classes at each grade level. Junior high and senior high have successfully used our model to create flexible programs, with an unwavering focus on student success, and enhance student engagement. We are now seeing the impact of district initiatives and directions that subscribe to this framework of response, ensuring that support at the district level is ultimately driven by conversations centered on students at the school level. Throughout this book, we highlight some of these efforts and provide additional links and direction so your school can connect with others engaging in this fundamental work.

Essentially, our book is a call to action for schools and districts that want to make a difference for children. We hope to encourage educational leaders to honor current best practices while building new perspectives and insights about how schools can address success for all students. And, because we don't believe the work is done yet, we are encouraging you to join with us in building research-engaged schools that can respond quickly and effectively to children's needs as these needs present themselves.

We know that schools significantly affect student achievement and that the most effective schools can transcend the effect of student backgrounds (Marzano, 2003). Ultimately, we hope that this book will be a starting place for great conversations and cultural transitions, as schools work to become increasingly effective responders to the needs of *all* students.

What We Have Learned

Throughout our journey, we have definitely lived the mantra of "Ready, Fire, Aim." As we have shared these ideas with hundreds of educators across the educational landscape, we have been learning alongside all our partners. Since we first self-published the concept of Collaborative Response (initially termed a *Collaborative Response Model*) in 2015, we have learned a lot from a number of exceptional educators and leaders, and it has deepened the understanding and implementation of the Collaborative Response approach. We have brought that learning into this text as a way of moving the literature to align with our current thinking. We are truly learners, excited to continue to extend and enrich our understanding of how systems can best structure themselves to ensure high levels of student success while attaining increasing levels of collective efficacy among the staff team. While some of the core concepts we explored in our first self-published book will be familiar for those who engaged with that text, there are a number of learnings that we have embedded throughout this text to reflect a deepening understanding that will and has been significantly transforming collective practice in schools. For those readers who previously engaged with the 2015 text, we hope that this book will provide a number of confirmations as well as a number of substantial shifts to truly deepen and extend the work.

Examining Our Core Beliefs

At the outset, it is important to share the core beliefs that serve to guide the discussion within this text and can serve as the foundation of Collaborative Response for schools and districts. Essentially, four core beliefs lie at the heart of our efforts to re-envision how schools and districts organize to collectively respond to students.

Core Belief 1: All Students Can Succeed

We believe that all children can learn and have success in our schools. This belief should ground any discussion about how education is organized and how schools are structured. Some variation of this statement appears in countless school authority mission statements and serves as a rallying cry for most educational initiatives. Sadly, as we discuss further in Chapter 1, the phrase may be present but is not always truly ingrained in schools. We have observed and worked in schools where the collective, long-standing policies and practices are actually counterproductive to this core belief—even as they post the words "all children can succeed" on their walls. However, as you will see throughout this book, we are unwavering in our goal that all students can learn and have success, although we recognize that success is going to look different for each learner. If we truly believe that all students can succeed, then it demands that we provide flexible responses and adaptive environments that allow students to succeed. We have to walk the talk. This philosophy must be both stated and lived at the core of any school or district's Collaborative Response efforts.

Core Belief 2: Teachers Make the Greatest Impact on Student Learning

This belief acknowledges that classroom teachers ultimately know what is best for their students' learning. Central to a Collaborative Response is the deep recognition that teachers' professional judgments must be sought, honored, and thoughtfully accessed in any discussion about how to respond to students' needs. Furthermore, because we believe that the school educates the child, we also believe that all other staff members working with students in schools must also weigh in on students' needs. We believe that schools should seek and consider a diverse collection of insights from across the organization, from general and specialized teachers, thus living the mantra of "it takes a village to raise a child."

Do we want to ensure success for our students? Listen to the professionals closest to the child and build on the priceless professional capital that exists in schools and that can be drawn on in thoughtful and timely ways. As we discuss in Chapter 5, schools simply cannot function unless we believe that teachers know their students best, that they develop deep and meaningful relationships that endure, and that they ultimately make the greatest impact on student success.

However, this core belief does not necessitate a blind or unquestioning reverence to "teacher knows best." As we will explore throughout the text, the belief that teachers make the greatest impact is paralleled by the understanding that we are all learners and that, collectively, teachers are constantly learning throughout the process. Truly being professional means that we as teachers are constantly reflecting on our practice, seeking out additional insights or perspectives, challenging our assumptions and current pedagogy, and aspiring to improve each and every day. As we will see through a Collaborative Response approach, this becomes a collective process that is honed and deepened through each conversation about a student. Teachers make the greatest impact on student learning, but truthfully, they *may be the most affected as learners themselves through the process.*

> *Teachers make the greatest impact on student learning, but truthfully, they* may be the most affected as learners themselves through the process.

Core Belief 3: Schools Cannot Achieve High Levels of Success When Adults Work in Isolation

Our second core belief actually becomes a detriment if those teachers who know best continue to work in isolation. Although this is not likely a factor that is within teachers' control, it is an essential component that requires structures and processes envisioned and implemented by school or district leadership—a core belief to examine next. We believe that working together should be not just an aspiration but an organizational requirement. In Chapter 1, we examine rich, impactful collaboration in depth, discussing the educational paradigm shift that must happen if we truly desire a Collaborative Response to the diverse needs of our students. Collaboration is simply not a "nice to have;" it is a moral imperative that must be purposefully established in every school and school authority. However, it is critical to understand that we can't wait until we have a collaborative culture before we begin to engage in this work. It is *through the work* that we come to learn and deeply recognize that teachers working in isolation is substantially inferior to us working together as a team.

Core Belief 4: Leadership Is Responsible for Ensuring Structures for Collaboration

Leadership in schools and districts has a critical role to play in the establishment of Collaborative Response. In fact, we would argue that Collaborative Response has limited impact for staff and students without a strong and intentional focus on the role and involvement of leadership. We believe that the number one priority for school and district leaders is to ensure that those working closest to students have the time and structures to collectively examine and collaboratively determine how best to respond to students' needs. If how time is to be used is not strategically planned, Collaborative Response becomes just another burden on the already exhaustive role of the teacher and other professionals working in our organizations. If leadership is not deeply involved in the work of Collaborative Response, it is not likely to take root in a school's organizational DNA.

Chapter Overview

Collaborative Response: Three Foundational Components That Transform How We Respond to the Needs of Learners is written for school and district leaders and those interested in restructuring educational systems to identify, respond to, and support learners and the teachers working with them.

There is good news. We are almost certain that elements of this framework are already in place in your organization. We encourage readers to take time to read through this text and thoughtfully consider where your school and school authority currently are in your journey and the next phases of implementation you should be pursuing, potentially using the resources we provide to assist with your evaluation and subsequent planning. The chapter structure will assist in this process.

Chapter 1, *Examining a Culture of Response*, starts by examining two schools. Each vignette shows a classroom teacher striving to make a difference for a student, but trying to accomplish it in two very different cultures of response. Chapter 1 sets the stage for the introduction of Collaborative Response by examining why a collaborative culture of response is critical when considering how best we can organize our efforts to ensure success for all.

Chapter 2, *Envisioning Collaborative Response*, provides an introduction to the student response framework explored in the remaining chapters. This chapter briefly reviews the foundational components that comprise Collaborative Response. Collaborative Response simultaneously complements but differs from contemporary RTI, MTSS, and other tiered response frameworks, and this chapter indicates what can result when any one of these foundational components is not present in schools. Chapter 2 examines the role of a Collaborative Response in an inclusive framework, focusing on how schools can ensure that structures and supports are in place to respond to unique student needs as well as supporting the needs of all learners through collaborative capacity building in ways that value an individual school's context and ultimately affects collective efficacy across the organization.

Chapter 3, *Collaborative Structures*, focuses on the first foundational component of Collaborative Response. To clearly articulate this complex component of Collaborative Response, we have intentionally dedicated three chapters to this explanation. Chapters 3, 4, and 5 are dedicated to defining collaborative structures and processes in detail. As the visual implies, the collaborative structures (Chapter 3) and collaborative processes (Chapter 4) along with the collaborative team meetings (described in detail in Chapter 5) are the most important and impactful components of the model. Chapter 3 defines four foundational layers of collaborative structures that pave the way for an inclusive system of supports where no child can fall through the cracks:

- Case consult team meetings
- School support team meetings
- Collaborative team meetings
- Collaborative planning time

Chapter 4, *Collaborative Processes*, expands on the belief that teams are only as successful as the processes that they have defined to guide their practice. Essential to the functioning of each team and the communication between teams are the consistent, clearly articulated processes that will be described in this chapter, which include:

- Team meeting norms
- Team meeting agendas
- Celebrations
- Defined involvement
- Roles
- Action focused
- Meeting space

Chapter 5, *Collaborative Team Meetings*, is central to a school's Collaborative Response and capitalizes on the collective knowledge and expertise of adults in schools, with a laser-like focus on student needs, identified through key issues and resulting actions. In essence, Chapter 4 embodies what Mike Schmoker writes in the foreword to Richard DuFour and his associates' text, *Whatever It Takes*: "What schools most need now [is] to begin harnessing the power of collective intelligence that already resides in the school to solve problems" (DuFour et al., 2004, p. xiii). If Collaborative Response is the vehicle that drives the school forward, the collaborative team meeting is its engine. This chapter will highlight the processes that are essential to collaborative team meetings and that make this level of team a unique and essential element of providing a Collaborative Response. Nine key elements for collaborative team meetings will be explored:

1. Maximum adult involvement
2. Focus and timeline for meetings
3. Pre-meeting processes
4. Defined roles

5. Team norms

6. Meeting agenda and notes

7. Celebrations

8. Focus on key issues

9. Action focused

Chapter 6, *Data and Evidence*, describes the critical role that the identification of universal screens, diagnostic assessments, and progress monitoring assessments play and the intentional organization of data that can effectively provide evidence to inform conversations. This is the second foundational component of Collaborative Response. Common schoolwide assessments provide a shared language essential for successful collaborative conversations and collective problem solving, which can augment the relational knowledge that we hold for students within our care. Assessments are no longer used to sort and classify children but to help teachers "inform and improve their practice and respond to the needs of their students" (DuFour, DuFour, Eaker, & Karhanek, 2010, p. 10), essentially "flagging" students to focus on first in the collaborative team meetings and then potentially in subsequent structures. The data provided are important, but how that evidence is organized, accessed, and then used is absolutely critical. Rather than focusing on implementing specific assessment tools, using the assessment data wisely becomes the emphasis in Collaborative Response. Nine key elements of the data and evidence component are defined and discussed:

1. Flag students for discussion

2. Universal screens

3. Diagnostic assessments

4. Progress monitoring assessment

5. Assessment schedule established

6. Intentional organization of results for team analysis

7. Intentional organization of results for collaborative team meeting

8. Student entry level

9. Data-informed planning

Chapter 7, *Continuum of Supports*, focuses on answering the third critical question of a professional learning community: "How will we respond to students who aren't learning?" (Eaker et al., 2002, p. 12). This chapter articulates the importance of establishing a multitiered framework *of supports* and stresses the need for schoolwide articulation and identification of interventions, strategies, and accommodations to be accessed when responding to the individual needs of students. This framework must be shaped by each school's unique context and organized to support students with increasing levels of intensity and intervention. Essentially, when we ask the critical and empowering question, "So what should we do?", in reference to a student's identified needs, the continuum of supports should provide a starting place for a response. Nine key elements will be shared to guide schools and school leaders in developing their own continuum of supports:

1. Honor current practices in areas of focus

2. Articulation of tiers of support

3. Articulation of interventions, strategies, and accommodations

4. Development of a menu of supports

5. Intentional utilization in team meetings

6. Refinement of Tier 1 instruction

7. Inform professional learning

8. Connection to visual team board

9. Alignment with collaborative structures and processes

Chapter 8, *Putting the Pieces Together*, simultaneously concludes the book and signals new beginnings as schools work to realize their own Collaborative Response framework for meeting students' needs. Three final thoughts for school communities are explored, with a closing message of hope for all those dedicated to ensuring success for all learners.

Features of the Book

Throughout the text, a number of features are included to assist schools and provide further insights and reflections:

▶ *Starting Steps*: These sidebars and connected interjections share potential first steps to consider when just getting started. They provide initial entry points, so that leaders can establish specific aspects of Collaborative Response.

▶ *Potential Pitfalls*: These notes for leaders are related to potential hazards to consider and potentially avoid. These hazards are based on our experiences working in and with schools to plan, establish, and sustain a Collaborative Response approach.

▶ *Recommended Resources*: A number of templates and resources are shared throughout the text and are available through our accompanying online Companion Website. Information about accessing and navigating the Companion Website is shared below.

- *In the Field*: Throughout the text, thoughts and ideas from schools and districts that are working to establish and refine their own Collaborative Response will be shared. These offerings are not intended to define "how it should be done" but rather offer illustrative examples of what the components of Collaborative Response can look like in a variety of unique contexts and organizations.

- *Substantial Shifts*: Over the past number of years, we've engaged in deep learning related to Collaborative Response as we've engaged with hundreds of schools and districts establishing the framework. These sections will identify shifts we've made in our thinking in relation to Collaborative Response that we consider substantial to early iterations of the framework shared in our 2015 self-published text, *Envisioning a Collaborative Response Model*.

Accessing Additional Samples and Resources

http://jigsawlearning.ca/collaborative-response

To read a QR code, you must have a smartphone or tablet with a camera. We recommend that you download a QR code reader app that is made specifically for your phone or tablet brand.

Throughout the text, we will share selected samples, templates, and other resources to assist schools and districts in establishing their Collaborative Response structures and processes, and we reference these resources and samples, which are organized and available in the Companion Website. A full listing of all resources available is also given following the Companion Website contents at the front of the text.

To access the Companion Website, please scan the QR code or visit https://www.jigsawlearning.ca/collaborative-response. The Companion Website also includes a book study guide to assist teams engaging in the text and looking to further explore the ideas and processes that we describe throughout the book.

However, the text and the companion website would be massive if we included every resource we've collected or developed over the years; also, they do not reflect the new learning we are continually engaging in related to Collaborative Response. We encourage you to visit our website at http://jigsawlearning.ca to not only access versions of the templates, additional resources, and the current growing library of samples from a myriad of schools and districts, but also to connect with a flourishing community of educators engaging in Collaborative Response work in their organizations.

Every Child Deserves a Team

As you set forth to envision a Collaborative Response for your school or district, we leave you with a driving message we share as central to this work—a message that speaks to equity, inclusion, and the need for collaborative structures surrounding our learners:

Every child deserves a team!

In the end, every child deserves a team of caring adults who are hypervigilant in recognizing and providing for their needs. We support every child through thoughtfully designed structures and processes and do whatever it takes to create a supportive environment for all!

Examining a Culture of Response

CHAPTER #1

Here is Edward Bear, coming downstairs now, bump, bump, bump, on the back of his head, behind Christopher Robin. It is, as far as he knows, the only way of coming downstairs, but sometimes he feels that there really is another way, if only he could stop bumping for a moment and think of it.

—A. A. Milne, *Winnie-the-Pooh*

Two Schools, Two Cultures of Response

Milne's (1972) classic introduction of *Winnie-the-Pooh* speaks volumes, serving as a poignant metaphor for teachers and leaders knowing there must be a better way than continuing to "bump along." This is not an attempt to criticize the great work of teachers and leaders in the past, but rather illustrate that a new way of looking at how we structure schools is imperative to meet contemporary demands. Let's take a moment to dive right into a narrative portrayal of two teachers' experiences attempting to meet the needs of a single struggling student. Although the teachers and students bear a striking resemblance, how the school in which they teach and learn responds is notably different.

> As you read, consider the following questions:
>
> 1. In the scenarios, does one *teacher* demonstrate greater instructional proficiency or care for students than the other? Would you characterize one teacher as "more effective" than the other? How do you know?
>
> 2. What do the schools in each scenario do to identify, respond to, and support struggling students and teachers?
>
> 3. How would you summarize the culture of each school?

15

Supporting Students at Castaway Elementary

The first two weeks of the new school year had been going well in Mrs. Hart's third-grade classroom, one of four third-grade classes at Castaway Elementary. Like most primary classrooms, she had been focusing a great deal of her initial classroom time on getting to know her students, establishing routines, and laying the foundational work for a safe and caring classroom community. Things seemed to be going smoothly with her new group of students.

Prior to the start of the school year, Mrs. Hart had bumped into one of her second-grade colleagues in the staff room and had found out a few details about some of the students who would be entering her room. Although she was thankful for the insights offered, she believed that every student deserved to have the "slate wiped clean" and didn't want to enter the new school year harboring preconceived notions about her new batch of children. She typically didn't preview student files prior to getting to know them. Everyone deserves a "fresh start" in her classroom.

During the first two weeks, she had already started some small preliminary reading groups in her classroom and had begun to notice that Philip, Akina, and Dante did not have reading skills comparable to those of their classmates. Mrs. Hart was already beginning to plan for small-group instruction with those students. She also noticed that Jackson and Henry were not that excited to read, with no library books checked out yet this year and little reading happening for them during the class independent reading time. She would need to work with both boys to try to hook them on a book series or topic that may appeal to them. She was also noting other little concerns during the first few weeks, but felt that this class "was going to be alright."

Then Alex arrived at the school.

He had a smile on his face and new sneakers on his feet. However, it didn't take long for Mrs. Hart to recognize that Alex was coming into the class well below where he should be. He seemed lost during independent reading time, and when Mrs. Hart found a moment to sit down and read with him, he could barely sound out the most basic of words. It only took one reading to determine that Alex was by far her class's weakest reader.

Over the next few weeks, Mrs. Hart added Alex to her already-established lowest reading group, but it was clear that he was not even at their level. She found ways to carve out time in her classroom to work with him one-on-one, but that was incredibly difficult without neglecting other children or small groups of children in the classroom. She began to find times outside of the classroom, during recess and lunch, to work with Alex to provide him with additional time, but after a few weeks, she realized that this plan was not sustainable. Alex seemed to be slipping further behind the other students, and she was feeling overwhelmed with the amount of recess and

CHAPTER #1. Examining a Culture of Response

lunch times she was devoting to him, sometimes creating tension for Alex, who just wanted to play during these break times. She tried to contact his parents, but it became obvious early that this was not productive, with Alex's parents working full-time, and despite wanting the best for their son, they were not equipped to meaningfully assist him.

Mrs. Hart continued to grow more frustrated with Alex's lack of growth. She had talked with the school's learning support coordinator about Alex several times, and that teacher was now pulling Alex from Mrs. Hart's Language Arts class three times a week for intervention. Although this decision allowed Mrs. Hart a reprieve from worrying about Alex, who was unable to engage in most of the learning activities his classmates could, she saw little improvement on the days he was part of her class. She also struggled to find out what he was doing during the times he was pulled out for the additional support, with little connection to what was happening in her classroom during those missed times. Although he was improving, the gap between Alex and the rest of the class was widening as most of his classmates were venturing into the exciting new world of chapter books.

Mrs. Hart sought the assistance of a second-grade colleague whom she had taught with previously and whose input she trusted immensely. Her colleague offered a few suggestions, but these didn't really "fit" Alex's needs. In fact, nothing seemed to fit Alex's needs. Finally, in exasperation, Mrs. Hart approached the school's administration team to seek additional support for her student. Following that conversation, Alex was placed on the school's waiting list for psychological testing to try to determine why he was struggling and if there may be a reason to provide him with a learning disability code, which might help secure additional resources. All in all, Mrs. Hart, who cared for each child in her classroom, felt like she was failing this student.

Supporting Students at Robinson Elementary

The first two weeks of the new school year had been going well in Mrs. Gonzales's third-grade classroom, one of four third-grade classes at Robinson Elementary. Like most primary classrooms, she had been focusing a great deal of her initial classroom time on getting to know her students, establishing routines, and laying the foundational work for a safe and caring classroom community. Things seemed to be going smoothly with her new group of students.

(Continued)

(Continued)

Prior to the start of the school year, Mrs. Gonzales and the rest of the third-grade team had met with the second-grade team, learning support staff, and administration to find out more about the students coming into their classrooms for the new school year. She was also provided with data related to her incoming group of students, including reading levels, benchmark assessment scores, supports put in place for them during their second-grade year, and even their library circulation statistics, all contributing to a student profile for her to better understand every one of her students. She also took some time to review the second-grade collaborative team meeting (CTM) notes from the previous year to gain a richer sense of the needs of the students and the support that had been put in place for them. Although she believed that every student should have a chance to "start fresh," this information allowed her to prepare for her incoming group of students and have supports in place early in the school year. As the principal in her school explained it, "We can ensure that students who left a grade with training wheels can still use those training wheels when returning from a two-month classroom hiatus."

As a result, Mrs. Gonzales had prepared for the students who would be entering her classroom. She had her initial small reading groups established, with Peter, Destiny, and Juanita in the smallest group, because they were the readers reported by the second-grade team to be entering third grade the furthest behind. Mrs. Gonzales had initial reading resources ready, attending to the students' interests, and had spent time reading about instructional strategies that would assist in addressing the phonetic needs that the previous teachers had indicated would need to be the initial focus for these three students. During one of their first collaborative planning times, the third-grade team were already starting to set up their intervention reading groups for the 30-minute block that was scheduled every day prior to lunch time in the timetable. The plan was to get started next week teaching the students the routines and processes for moving to their cross-class groups during this time.

Her classroom library included several new baseball titles that she had scavenged from a secondhand bookstore and her own son's home library, because the second-grade team indicated that Francisco and Julia were reluctant readers but baseball fanatics: this subject material had finally turned them on to reading late in the school year (although the team predicted that they may have lost momentum during the summer break). Overall, she was noting other little concerns and connecting students to the anecdotal notes and data she had on them. And, she felt this class was on the right track.

Then Arthur arrived at the school. The day prior, Mrs. Gonzales and the rest of the third-grade team received an email from the school's learning support coordinator stating that a new third-grade student would be arriving tomorrow. The school's practice was for the student to meet with the learning support team on their first day of arrival, so the email served as a heads-up for teachers. Mr. Jordan, one of the third-grade teachers, volunteered one of his students, Gurheet, to be Arthur's "Robinson Rover" for the day, another practice the school had implemented last year.

Arthur arrived the next day, a smile on his face and new sneakers on his feet. At the office, Arthur was introduced to Gurheet, and after having a chance to meet the learning support coordinator and the principal of the school, the two boys embarked on a tour of the school, following the tour map Gurheet had learned to use for a morning just like this. After the half-hour tour, Gurheet returned to his classroom and Arthur joined the learning support coordinator (along with two other students who were also new to the school that day). There, the teacher did some fun activities with the new students, answered questions about the school, and did a short benchmark reading assessment with each of them. For the remainder of the day, Arthur engaged in a mix of activities in all four third-grade classes (with Gurheet at his side), including an art lesson in Mrs. Gonzales's classroom.

At the end of the day, the learning support coordinator met with the third-grade team, and together, they determined Mrs. Gonzales's classroom to be the best placement for Arthur. His reading assessment indicated reading issues similar to those of Peter and Destiny (although Arthur was still below those students), and like Francisco and Julia, he enjoyed baseball and had formed a connection that day at recess with Jujar, a boy from Mrs. Gonzales's room. Although Mrs. Gonzales currently had one more student than the other third-grade classrooms, it was the best fit for Arthur overall. The learning support coordinator shared the assessment data, some notes she collected from a conversation with Arthur's previous school that she contacted in the afternoon, and some other notes on his student entry form. She let Mrs. Gonzales know that she would check in with her at the end of the week during her weekly inclusive education prep to see how things were for Arthur during his first few days.

The next day, Arthur entered class, assuming his new seat next to Jujar. It didn't take long for Mrs. Gonzales to confirm what the learning support team had discovered: Arthur was by far her weakest reader. Although he was interested in the baseball book she helped him get from the classroom library during independent reading, it was far above his reading level; she made a note to seek some lower-level baseball-related materials from the school library. Mrs. Gonzales placed Arthur with Destiny and Juanita for small-group reading instruction, and although he had some of the same phonetic difficulties as the group, he was still significantly below their level and clearly lacked the basic skills necessary for forming letters into words. She immediately started him into several of the Tier 2 supports established in her classroom, including fluency passages during independent reading time (along with four other students Mrs. Gonzales worked with), everyday small-group reading instruction, and sight word practice for home.

At the end of the week, the learning support coordinator met with Mrs. Gonzales to see how things were going. Mrs. Gonzales communicated what she was seeing but wished to continue with what she had in place

(Continued)

(Continued)

until the first CTM, which was scheduled two weeks from then. She did, however, wish Arthur to be placed on the progress monitoring assessment schedule for the school to provide her with additional data about Arthur's reading. They agreed on this plan of action, and Mrs. Gonzales continued with the supports she had initiated for Arthur. Any time she had to work one-on-one with students, her first stop was typically Arthur, who had fit nicely into the classroom; but it was clear that he was reading at a level below his classmates.

Two weeks later at the first third-grade CTM, Mrs. Gonzales was quick to celebrate the transition Arthur had made into the school. The team facilitator asked why she thought he might be doing so well. Mrs. Gonzales responded that she had connected him with peers to play together on the playground and that was going very well for him. As well, Mrs. Gonzales knew that he liked baseball, so she had found some baseball books at his level that he was very excited about reading. When it came time to begin discussing students in need, as the focus of this team meeting was connected to literacy, she immediately indicated Arthur. Through a brief discussion, with her team asking clarifying questions, it was determined that the key issue to address was "identifying letter sounds in words." The team identified two other students with a similar concern from the other classes, and after a short brainstorming session, identified a number of strategies to consider. Although Mrs. Gonzales committed to trying letter tiles in her small-group reading time with Arthur (with one of her colleagues committing to providing her the resources for this), she also noted for herself to connect with Mr. Littlechild following the meeting to learn more about the Elkonin boxes strategy he mentioned. Mr. Littlechild's previous background was in kindergarten and first grade, and this was a strategy he used often at those levels. The team also agreed to use their next collaborative planning time to further explore other classroom strategies and ideas for students significantly below grade level, particularly lacking skills to attack letter formations in words. To conclude, Mrs. Gonzales shared that, although his parents were nice people and truly wanted to support Arthur, their full-time work schedule did not equip them to assist Arthur meaningfully. As a result, her use of sight word practice cards for home had been a bust.

As a next step later in the meeting, it was decided to also include Arthur at the next School Support Team Meeting happening the following Tuesday to begin looking at some additional school supports to put in place immediately. The learning support coordinator quickly mentioned having him join her after-lunch reading group, focusing specifically on phonetics with one other third-grade student and two other second-grade students. It seemed like an easy next step as she felt she could handle another student in that group. The principal, Mr. Martin, also offered to include Arthur immediately in "Mr. Martin's Mob," a group of second- and third-grade students who met with the principal every morning in the 15 minutes before school to listen to a story, where Mr. Martin systematically pointed out reading strategies he employed when reading. Mrs. Gonzales thought that this might be beneficial because Arthur was at school early and could benefit from more modeling of reading strategies in addition to the focus on basic letter sounds in words. It would also be great for him to form a relationship with the principal, as a new student to the school. In addition to the other students and key issues discussed in the CTM, Mrs. Gonzales felt good about the emerging plan being put in place as well as some of the new ideas generated with her colleagues in the meeting that she was looking forward to trying.

Over the next five weeks, Arthur participated in the supports that had been put in place for him. As determined at the subsequent School Support Team Meeting, the learning support coordinator also visited the classroom twice a week during Mrs. Gonzales's Language Arts instruction time to sometimes work individually with Arthur in the classroom or to sometimes work with other students, so Mrs. Gonzales had a chance to work with Arthur. By the time the next CTM came, Mrs. Gonzales celebrated the progress Arthur was making with the team. His progress monitoring scores supported this celebration, showing steady growth toward his target. Although he was still below grade level, he was closing the gap. She felt that another five-week round of continued supports both in the classroom and at the Tier 3 level would provide Arthur the extra instructional care he needed to return to primarily Tier 2 classroom supports. All in all, she felt positive that he was on the right track to becoming a reader!

Obviously, both vignettes portray teachers who care deeply about their students and work hard to provide for all learners. However, the school's response differs significantly in each scenario. Specifically, how the school's culture and system of supports collectively respond to students is markedly different.

Focus on Culture

Culture affects all aspects of a school. It influences informal conversations in the faculty lunchroom, the type of instruction valued, how professional development is viewed, and the shared commitment to assuring all students learn. (Deal & Peterson, 2009, p. 12)

Typically, schools assert (often publicly in a school mission statement) their belief that "all students can learn." However, an institution's traditions, practices, policies, and procedures, both written and implied, may not always align with this assertion or, in some cases, may work in direct conflict with the claim of ensuring success for *all* children. Indeed, long-held practices and policies (some of them unexamined) may directly contradict the very beliefs they claim to hold dear. This is not an indictment on the work of teachers and leaders, but rather points out a growing awareness of the need to reexamine the way schools have been organized to support students, a topic on which this text will respond.

McLaughlin and Talbert (2001) described "educational lotteries" where student learning depends "heavily on the teachers they draw, from class to class and from year to year" (p. 64). This reality is still prevalent today and is not congruent with a culture of Collaborative Response. Teachers, burdened by a growing list of classroom tasks and responsibilities, continue to resemble Winnie-the-Pooh, repeatedly taking the same bumpy journey down the stairs, attempting to do all they can for their students but engaging in school cultures that are not truly collaborative and do not have the structures and processes required to support each teacher in each classroom.

Like Mrs. Hart at Castaway Elementary, we repeatedly see effective, dedicated teachers striving to help students learn in organizations that provide few systemic structures to support students as a collaborative endeavor. Unfortunately, educators in these school cultures "readily acknowledge that the fate of a student who is not learning will depend on the randomness of the teacher to whom he or she is assigned rather than any collective, coherent, systematic plan for meeting the needs of all students" (DuFour, DuFour, Eaker, & Karhanek, 2010, p. 39). This is not a formula to ensure equity and access for all learners.

Consider Barth's (2001) simple definition of culture: "the way we do things around here" (p. 7). The way we do things has, over time, often led to educational pessimism and cynicism about the possibility of positive change. Professionals sometimes, and with good reason, become resilient to change, and schools, as institutions, are not stepping back to thoughtfully examine long-standing practices that sometimes are incongruent with improving student learning and rely heavily on the skill and expertise of a single, isolated teacher. Despite substantial funds being spent each year on professional development to ensure that individual teachers remain current and up-to-date on best practices, we seem to fall short of our ultimate goal of improved student learning and success systemwide because we need to move to a different way of seeing our work. As we suggest throughout this book, we subscribe wholeheartedly to Hargreaves and O'Connor's (2018) assertion in relation to professional collaboration:

> The evidence that, in general, professional collaboration benefits students and teachers alike has become almost irrefutable. Professional collaboration boosts student achievement, increases teacher retention and enhances the implementation of innovation and change. The big questions are no longer about whether teachers *should* collaborate. No profession can serve people effectively if its members do not share and exchange knowledge about their expertise or about the clients, patients, or students they have in common. The big

questions, rather, are about *how* and *how well* teachers and other educators collaborate. (p. 4)

When we attend to the questions focused on *"how"* and *"how well,"* we focus on the ways in which we are structuring effective collaboration in our organizations. Without attention to the purposeful crafting of collaboration, we reinforce an underlying mindset where teachers have been led to believe that they are, and should be, alone to contend with the growing diversity of needs of their students. For good research reasons, we disagree.

In this book, we hold a simple belief: we believe that children learn when all the caring adults in their lives come together with the intention of knowing them well and working together in clearly aligned structures to address their individual and collective needs so they might experience high levels of success. We believe that children are treasures: we believe that their uniqueness and diversity grow as they become successful learners, and we believe that, if we can help children find a home (in schools) where they might express their growth and shine through owning their own learning through equitable opportunities, we will all benefit as people and as a society. For real change to occur, we need more than just the introduction of new structures, processes, and practices. As Fullan (2007) notes,

> most strategies for reform focus on structures, formal requirements, and event-based activities involving, for example, professional development sessions. They do not struggle directly with existing cultures within which new values and practices may be required . . . *restructuring* (which can be done by fiat) occurs time and time again, whereas *reculturing* (how teachers come to question and change their beliefs and habits) is what is needed. (p. 25)

Reculturing is needed to bring to the surface the fertile soil necessary for Collaborative Response to take seed. It involves questioning conventional, and sometimes outdated, beliefs and practices that have long governed and ultimately shaped teachers' practices when responding to students. In far too many schools, isolation and insulation are the expected conditions, not the anomalies (Lieberman & Rosenholtz, 1987), an observation that often still holds true today. Although this isolation and insulation has been culturally ingrained in the name of professional autonomy, it is not a prevailing mindset in tune with today's classrooms. "As the student population grew more diverse and more complex," Hargreaves and Fullan (2012) lament, "individual classroom autonomy became a liability" (p. 49).

However, we don't believe autonomy and collaboration need to be viewed as polarized concepts, consistent with an "either/or" perspective. They can both be fostered and attained through envisioning a Collaborative Response across the educational landscape.

Potential Pitfall

It is important to recognize that a focus on reculturing is not a prerequisite "step" *before* starting to establish the essential components and key elements related to Collaborative Response discussed in subsequent chapters. We want to assist school and district leaders in understanding the cultural shifts that will be addressed *through* the establishment of a Collaborative Response framework. The focus on reculturing will happen *through* the work of introducing Collaborative Response, its essential components, and key elements over time. Leaders should not fall into the trap of believing that they must attend to cultural elements before ever moving into engaging in the work. Reculturing happens over time and through the process. In many cases, it *is* the work.

Companion Website Resources

1.1. Essential cultural shifts—change index: A reflection tool for leaders to consider minor to major shifts for their school to move from a traditional culture to one responsive to the needs of students.

1.2. Essential cultural shifts—analysis: A survey tool to use with staff teams, identifying cultural shifts that staff believe versus their current reality in the school.

Both these tools allow leaders and school staff to reflect on their current culture of response and can help identify areas of focus that can be addressed through Collaborative Response.

Access all online resources via the QR code, or at http://jigsawlearning.ca/collaborative-response

Envisioning Collaborative Response

CHAPTER #2

In his book *Simplexity*, Kluger (2008) dissects the nature of complex and simple concepts, exploring the duality of trying to overcome the complexity inherent in seemingly simple tasks and recognizing that simple concepts are fraught with complexity. The desire to ensure learning for all students may be simple in its intent, but the network of supports, structures, and factors that influence highly effective instruction and allow that desire to become a reality can be incredibly complex. As Sharratt and Fullan (2012) remind us, "It's all well and good to say 'Let's start with shared beliefs and understandings,' but operationalizing those beliefs and understandings requires definitions of each that result in goals, and we need structures through which we accomplish our work toward those goals" (p. 29). Kruger's theme of "simplexity" aptly applies to the development of Collaborative Response.

Over the past decade, we have witnessed that the greater educational community, in response to societal shifts, have engaged deeply in the research and implementation of equity and inclusion and the philosophical shift that is necessary to truly support the needs of all students.

The first step in designing and implementing an authentic inclusive education mindset requires deep understanding, recognition, and dedication for attending to the fair and respectful treatment of all people. While we recognize that every child is unique and is deserving of an environment that not only promotes their individuality, but also responds to their individual needs, it then goes without saying that we also need to acknowledge the factors that have contributed to this uniqueness. Children are entering our buildings every day who have experienced discrimination on multiple levels. Racism, religious intolerance, homophobia, and gender-based violence are a reality for many of our children, and the resulting trauma affects their ability to engage emotionally, socially, and academically. As educators, we sometimes set those factors aside to attend to academics because "that's what schools do." We recognize that in today's society, accompanied by the medical and brain research we now have access to, we can no longer just attend to academics. Equity is established when we recognize and acknowledge the atrocities and intergenerational trauma that our students and families have endured, and only then can we focus on establishing an inclusive education mindset and responsive system of supports.

The endeavor to address equity and focus on inclusive education has supported the movement away from the historical tradition of labeling students for the purpose of funding. This has always been accompanied with the challenge that once children are assigned a diagnosis by a doctor or psychologist, it is extremely difficult to have that coding removed. It is a label that sticks and can ultimately define who that learner is as a person. We sometimes have seen specific populations of students (based on race, ethnicity, gender identity, religion, health, and more) restricted through this process, which leads to variations of explicit or implicit streaming resulting in the limitation of opportunities for a student's future. The good news is that schools are shifting from strictly relying on a cycle of identifying a student, coding through testing, accessing funding, and then implementing individualized support to now reflecting on the observable needs of a student while taking into consideration their strengths and interests and providing what is necessary in the classroom or throughout the school regardless of the absence of a code or a diagnosis. Every child deserves a flexible and responsive support system.

Without a deep understanding or purposeful thought given to implementation, schools and districts moved to inclusion and equity education in two general ways. First, by replacing the language of special education with the word inclusion and then continuing on with their practices of segregation of students for the purpose of programming and meeting the myriad of local, state/provincial, and federal funding requirements. Second, at the other end of the spectrum, schools and districts interpreted inclusion to mean placing students with complex needs into classrooms without necessarily providing them with the additional support to ensure that those children were receiving meaningful experiences throughout their education or specialized supports and services that could also extend beyond the classroom.

All these changes have resulted in schools and districts attempting to provide support for students with complex needs under the guise of equity and inclusion but without the realization that this philosophy is not about time or place or funding but is central to determining a student's strengths, identifying their needs, and providing programming to address their challenges, which may include the classroom teacher, specialized teachers, paraprofessionals, schoolwide programming, and/or external partners. The primary reason this has been such a struggle for schools and districts is because they have lacked the structures and processes that are required to ensure that all levels of support are implemented at the right time by the right people for the right reason. Collaborative Response provides schools with the opportunity to examine their structures and processes to ensure that *all* students, including but not limited to only those with a diagnosis, are provided with what they need, when they need it, through layers of support and collaboration intentionally designed and articulated throughout the school. In essence, Collaborative Response is the process through which the vision of inclusion is realized.

Tiered systems of response have been a primary approach introduced to actualize and operationalize the premise of equity and inclusion. Whether that is described as response to intervention (RTI), positive behavior interventions and supports (PBIS), multitiered systems of support (MTSS), interconnected system framework, or comprehensive, integrated, three-tiered models of prevention, each of these approaches provides a system for students to access increasing levels of support (Lane et al., 2019). So let's be clear at the outset. As suggested in the introduction, Collaborative Response owes a great deal to the research and literature related to tiered systems of response. However, Collaborative Response is not exclusively synonymous or interchangeable with these approaches. We believe that a Collaborative Response framework encompasses everything in a school connected to student learning, becoming a practical marrying of many elements, and includes some subtle but fundamental shifts. Collaborative Response explicitly connects the complex work of providing support for all students, but through a purposeful framework of collaborative structures and processes to ensure high levels of collective efficacy, determined by Hattie (2016) to be the number one factor positively affecting student achievement (as cited by Donohoo, 2017).

We are also deeply influenced by long-standing work related to professional learning communities because we feel that learning communities are at the heart of schools reculturing to ensure success for all students. Effective instruction grounded in best practice and differentiated to meet the diverse needs of learners is foundational to the success of any school. After all, "no matter how good the instructional support programs may be, they cannot overcome weak or unfocused classroom instruction" (Allington & Walmsley, 2007, p. 261).

The good news is that schools that have engaged in tiered systems of response, as well as professional learning communities, have an advantage. They will be exceptionally well positioned to see many connections between their current work and Collaborative Response. In fact, those implementing these approaches with high degrees of fidelity will be able to easily envision the subtle shifts necessary to truly engage in Collaborative Response.

It goes without saying that there is a critical need to envision these concepts through a collaborative lens. All our efforts in supporting students are enhanced when a team regularly collaborates to problem solve and engage in "what if" conversations in order to provide the best possible opportunities for all our students. We need to be intentionally focused on building capacity throughout our staff team through the responses we are providing students beginning at the classroom level. This is accomplished not through *training* but through ongoing engagement, interaction, and dialogue, which builds capacity and enhances our professionalism over time. Topics for professional learning surface through collaborative conversations as teams identify gaps in their understanding. Providing training is simply not enough.

Dissecting the Terms

Let's begin with the name. True to its title, Collaborative Response can be defined by a targeted investigation of each individual term.

Defining "Collaborative": The old adage "two heads are better than one" is really at the heart of Collaborative Response. We know that "leadership decision making is more accurate and less risky when entrusted to a diverse group than to a single individual, even when that individual has significant expertise" (Reeves, 2006, p. 25). School leaders need to ensure that structures and processes exist that encourage staff members to work together to address the learning needs of students and foster the ongoing development of what Hargreaves and Fullan (2012) describe as professional capital:

> To sum up, collaborative cultures build social capital and therefore also *professional capital* in a school's community. They accumulate and circulate knowledge and ideas, as well as assistance and support, that help teachers become more effective, increase their confidence, and encourage them to be more open to and actively engaged in improvement and change. Collaborative cultures value individuals and individuality because they value people in their own right and for how they contribute to the group. (p. 114)

We have observed schools that have adopted a multitiered response framework that endeavor to establish teams at each tier but place their focus on labeling then tiering and moving students up the tiers to the next team to respond. This can restrict a truly collaborative focus between general and special educators and possibly remove the responsibility of the classroom teacher in implementing day-to-day programming for students who require ongoing support. When collaboration is rich and purposeful, everyone walks away stronger from the conversation at every level, not only with a plan to implement for a child but with a focus on building everyone's collective toolbox through the process. Multilayered collaboration changes us.

Defining "Response": Teachers can tell you which students are struggling. Reporting procedures in schools are focused on identifying students who are not learning. When examining students at risk in Grade 3, kindergarten teachers lament that they knew that those students would not be successful. Often, we can track struggles in the early years as a strong correlation for later high school graduation (Pingault et al., 2011). So if we "know" which students we need to support, then it is essential to craft a response. As Allington (2009) shares,

> In most cases these students were recognized early, often on entry to Kindergarten. The most typical scenario has been that

CHAPTER #2. Envisioning Collaborative Response

these students were given the "gift of time." In other words, we waited for them to develop. When they didn't, we referred them for more testing and typically for placement in an intervention program (Title I, special education, English language learners, etc.). Sometimes we simply held them back to repeat a grade level in the hopes they would catch up. Yet most never caught up, whether they were provided an intervention or retained in grade. They became the bottom group of students who forever lagged behind their on-level peers. (p. 7)

What schools have traditionally lacked is the *response* to this real question: "What do we do when at-risk learners are identified?" This response must be proactive, strategic, systematic, and responsive. We know that without that response, our at-risk students are in real danger of seeing the gap widen between their current level and their realized potential as a learner and ultimately affecting their trajectory for life beyond school. When asked, "What happens when a student is struggling?", schools, through a systematic approach, need to be able to provide an answer.

Furthermore, when we look at student success through a broader lens, we see that *every* learner is in need of some type of response throughout the course of their education. All of us, adults and students alike, have a jagged profile where we excel in some areas, are competent in other areas, and need additional support in still other areas. Students cannot be easily relegated into a clearly defined "box" that labels them as "at-risk," "normal," "gifted," "on track," or the myriad of other labels, formal and informal, that we can attach to students. If we truly believe in the success of *all* students and true equity across our educational systems, it comes with the understanding and inherent belief that *all* students will be in need of a response from the school team at different points in time, and in different areas. The intention to provide a response is simply the recognition that every discussion about a learner needs to be attended to and that response is first viewed through the lens of the classroom.

So, let's turn our attention now to the foundational components that are the essence of Collaborative Response.

> Every *learner is in need of some type of response throughout the course of their education.*

Foundational Components of Collaborative Response

Collaborative Response consists of three foundational components as shown in Figure I.1. We would argue that each component is essential when considering how schools coherently respond to the needs of students. However, we also agree with Hargreaves (2009) when he states, "The challenge of coherence is not to clone or align everything so it looks the same in all schools" (p. 32).

Collaborative Response and the foundational components that undergird it provide a clear framework for ensuring that a sustainable network of support is in place for students, done in a manner that places primary focus on examining collective classroom practices. It is not, however, a color-by-number process in which a school follows a prescriptive legend and produces a lovely picture that is exactly the same as everyone else's lovely picture. Rather, you hold the blank canvas, and the elements discussed and shared are the tools, supplies, and materials required to paint the intricate landscape. Each school needs to consider its unique culture, cohort of students, community, and staff to paint the desired results—a one-of-a-kind work of art unique to your school that is a living entity as it shifts, adjusts, and morphs through collective learning and organizational adjustments. Although we know that each component will look fundamentally different in each school, all three components must be present in some shape or form, as illustrated in Table 2.1.

It is also important to consider each component represented in the visual as connected, as shown in Table 2.1. We are sometimes challenged in sharing these ideas as it is difficult to discuss one component without referring to another. In a highly organized and effective Collaborative Response, each component is integral and intimately connected to the next. As you can see in Table 2.1, when any one of these components is missing, the result is a poor system of support for students.

Table 2.1   Three essential components working together

COLLABORATIVE STRUCTURES AND PROCESSES	DATA AND EVIDENCE	CONTINUUM OF SUPPORTS	RESULT
Established	Established	Established	A comprehensive framework that ensures that every child receives the supports that they require to be successful while systematically cultivating collective efficacy throughout the organization
Not established	Established	Established	Supports established based on scores from assessment or determined by a single person. Does not take advantage of multiple viewpoints and collaborative problem solving. Knowledge of a child limited to a few

COLLABORATIVE STRUCTURES AND PROCESSES	DATA AND EVIDENCE	CONTINUUM OF SUPPORTS	RESULT
			and less collective accountability present. No structures to ensure collective efficacy
Established	Not established	Established	Conversations about the needs of students lacking data to inform—based primarily on observation or assumptions. Limited ability to determine the impact of formalized supports. Lack of consistency in determining students in need of collective response
Established	Established	Not established	Informed conversation about the needs of students but an unclear action plan of next steps—response inconsistent and individualized depending on specific teacher skills and may have limited impact

Companion Website Resources

2.1. Collaborative response overview: A one-page overview of Collaborative Response, complete with the chart identifying what happens when components are not present as well as core beliefs and distinctive features.

What's Missing in Many Tiered Approaches?

Goal displacement, the phenomenon of a reform goal becoming more important than the reason for the reform, is not uncommon when examining the structures being established by schools and districts. We have seen goal displacement phenomena arise with the growing popularity of some tiered models. We have sat through conference presentations that shared lengthy referral forms developed by districts for teachers to complete when identifying students for "Tier 2 support." We have visited schools that had lock-step approaches that they stringently followed when moving through their pyramid of interventions, much to the dismay of teachers trying to navigate them. We have visited websites of districts with prescribed "PBIS programs" that are followed in each of their schools. We have walked the exhibitor halls, traversing through the myriad of vendors promoting their company's MTSS solution or instructional intervention systems. With growing acceptance and popularity, perhaps best exemplified by "the notion that one can become a 'fan' of RTI on Facebook" (Fisher & Frey, 2010, p. 15), the theory of goal displacement is increasingly evident. Although we know that success can be seen through any of these approaches when followed with fidelity and with a commitment to maintain the approaches over time, if schools are not focused on the *why*, they can become focused on the hope of discovering a set of resources or lock-step approach that holds the elusive answer for student success. But ensuring success for *all* students is complex and requires a focus on mindsets, culture, building professional capacity, and the interconnectedness of structures and processes.

We believe that a truly effective framework of response includes all three foundational components of Collaborative Response. We need data and evidence, a responsive continuum of supports, and perhaps more than anything, we need teachers who are dedicated to working together toward solutions to problems and meeting children's needs, with a desire to continually deepen their craft through each and every conversation. We need layers of collaborative structures and processes that are aligned, purposeful, and clearly connected.

Distinctive Features

Seven distinctive features of Collaborative Response provide the platform for unique and systematic supports for an educational organization, features that we believe lay the foundation for an equitable and inclusive system of supports. These features are explored in more depth in subsequent chapters.

1. Collaboration is at the heart of all student examination and response, ensuring that the *professional capital* present in schools is maximized.

2. *Layers of collaborative teams* are established, each with a different purpose and focused on a different level of support accessible for each and every learner at their time of need.

3. Value is placed on *varied perspectives and expertise* when examining the unique, complex, and diverse needs of students.

4. Capacity building is a natural by-product of collaborative discussions related to supporting students in the classroom, with an emphasis on the value of *distributive coaching* for staff members.

5. An intentional review of assessment data ensures that students are *flagged* for discussion, placing emphasis on collective professional judgment when examining students and the purposeful use of evidence to *inform* next steps.

6. The development of a continuum of supports is a *fluid*, ever-changing organization of interventions, strategies, and accommodations that explicitly emphasizes action taken in the classroom as the first locus of response for students.

7. *Supports are tiered*, not the students. In Collaborative Response, supports are provided when needed and are not dependent on coding, labeling, or a student failing in order to access the next level of support.

Recognizing the danger inherent in pulling apart the foundational components for further exploration and analysis, we encourage you to consider their interconnectedness. How do various aspects of the approach support and mesh with other aspects? By examining each component in depth, we trust that school leaders will be able to reassemble the model into a coherent and interdependent framework, achieving "simplexity" in their schools and districts that is developed over time. This work is a process, but we can assure you that the journey is well worth taking!

The following chapters dig into Collaborative Response, exploring the three foundational components in more depth. The vignettes, resources, potential pitfalls, starting steps, significant shifts, and field examples that we share show how those working in schools might use or have used a Collaborative Response approach to build a responsive culture within their schools and districts.

Collaborative Structures

CHAPTER #3

If schools are to work well, those working with them must be collaborating. Almost 20 years ago, Kouzes and Posner (2003) reinforced the belief that "collaboration is a social imperative. Without it people can't get extraordinary things done in organizations" (p. 22).

Collaboration is essential when attempting to address the diverse individual needs of each and every student. Traditionally, teachers have been trained by universities to focus on the curricular outcomes as laid out in programs of study and curriculum documents or learn a process based on which to develop their curriculum and then implement effective instructional strategies to bring that curriculum to life for their learners. At the same time, a number of educators were trained through a separate "special education" stream to provide extensive supports for students who had exceptional needs. In essence, our "training" led us to believe that we had a responsibility to ensure that students were learning what was intended, and if they didn't, there was someone else who had more intensive training who would step in and fill the gap. In this way, a great divide was formed that assumed that we had two tracks for learning, consisting of those who fit the typical mold for classroom success and those who needed something else or something different, most often provided by someone else. This dual track set the trend for teachers to move students who were not able to meet the typical standards to the "special education" department or other specialists as needed. In essence, we had jumped from classroom supports to extensive individualized supports without considering what could be taking place in between (we will discuss this further in Chapter 7 in relation to a continuum of supports). The system paved the way for exclusion and segregated supports, but this was not any fault of teachers or schools as they were only doing what was provided in their current structures.

Fast forward to today, and the reality is that "most students with disabilities spend the majority of their time in school in the general education classroom" (Bateman & Cline, 2016, as cited in Bateman & Cline, 2019). We understand that there are a number of things that we can ensure through inclusive structures and processes to support the needs of every student regardless of what challenges they may face and begin down the road of ensuring equity for all learners. It is not just students with disabilities who require our attention. As stated at the outset, we believe that *all* children deserve a team!

We also have come to understand the value and importance of Universal Design for Learning, which articulates that the concept of a flexible support designed for one student may be a support that could be accessed by others or perhaps all. Meyer et al. (2013) contend that a "teacher can plan for expected variability across learners and can provide a curriculum that has corresponding flexibility. The lesson or curriculum should then have the flexibility and affordances to amplify natural abilities and reduce unnecessary barriers for most students" (p. 10).

This concept of variance and flexibility has led to a number of traditional specialized supports being accessed by any student who may feel that they are beneficial for their learning. A simple example of this is a wiggle cushion. Early in our careers, wiggle cushions were provided only to those students who required regulation and were often suggested and provided through an occupational therapist, noted specifically in a child's individualized education plan. Today, we see varied seating in most classrooms, which include wiggle cushions, stand-up desks, bean bags, and much more. While this has had a physical impact on the environment of our classroom, the conceptual impact is also significant. The supports that we design with one student in mind may be beneficial for many more.

> *The supports that we design with one student in mind may be beneficial for many more.*

In addition to the realization that we face a gap in the supports that we have been providing, we also understand that in order to ensure that all students receive what they need, we need to create a layering of collaborative teams that communicate with each other, but with each serving very distinct purposes as part of an inclusive system of supports. The remainder of this chapter is dedicated to describing a fluid system of teams, which through effective structures and processes, can provide support for any and all students to ensure their individual success. Although we recognize that these layers of teams may be referred to by different names in different educational organizations, it is essential that a version of each layer exists that reflects the processes and focuses that we describe.

Within Collaborative Response, four specific collaborative structures are critical to provide a layered and comprehensive approach that ensures that the needs of all students can be met. These four structures are as follows:

1. Case consult team meetings

2. School support team meetings

3. Collaborative team meetings (CTMs)

4. Collaborative planning

Table 3.1 provides a brief overview of the purpose, frequency, and potential participation of the four meeting types. Please note that across educational systems, various titles are used for these positions. Figure 3.1 shows a visual representation of the four layers.

CHAPTER #3. Collaborative Structures

37

Table 3.1 Overview of collaborative structures

TYPE OF TEAM	PURPOSE	FREQUENCY	POTENTIAL PARTICIPATION
Case consult team meetings	Focus on an individual student requiring intensive and responsive wrap-around supports, often involving specialists beyond the school	As needed	Dependent on the situation: • District inclusive coordinator • Director of special education • Director of curriculum and instruction • External providers • Police or school resource officers • Social services • Medical professionals • Administration • Learning support teacher • Counseling services • Reading specialists • School social worker/family school liaison • Teacher and EA team • Parents/guardians • Indigenous cultural advisors (elders and knowledge keepers)
School support team meetings	Focus on students who require additional supports beyond the classroom level, typically referred by the collaborative team meeting	Weekly/biweekly	School-level roles: • Administration • Director of special education • Director of curriculum and instruction • Learning support teacher • Counseling services • Reading specialist • School social worker/family school liaison • Indigenous cultural advisors (elders and knowledge keepers) • Teachers invited as needed

(Continued)

(Continued)

TYPE OF TEAM	PURPOSE	FREQUENCY	POTENTIAL PARTICIPATION
Collaborative team meetings	Focus on all students designated for the team (grade level, multigrade, advisory group, etc.), with support focused primarily on the classroom level through an examination of key issues	Every three to five weeks	School-level roles: • Administration • Teachers • Director of special education • Director of curriculum and instruction • Learning support teacher • Reading specialist • Counseling services • School social worker/family school liaison • Paraprofessionals (educational assistants)
Collaborative planning	Regular collaborative time focused on classroom planning for teams	Weekly, biweekly, or monthly	Classroom-level roles: • Teachers • Others as requested

Figure 3.1 Overview of collaborative structures

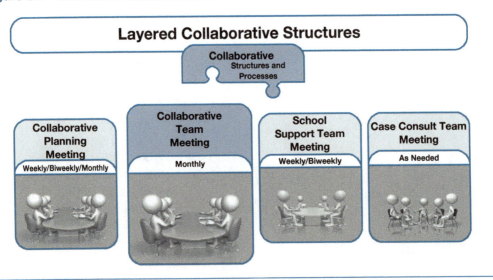

ClipArt Source: PresenterMedia

Examining Layered Teams

Establishing layered structures demands thoughtful and intentional planning. It is highly likely that your school already has a number of these layers, or versions of these layers, in place. We often find, due to the establishment of special education processes in the past, that most schools have the case consult team and school support team in place as these were designed traditionally as the teams that respond to crisis as well as the specialized needs of individual students. As you well know, these two structures are integral to providing individualized supports for students with intensive needs.

In addition, due to the seminal work of Richard DuFour and his colleagues, it is highly likely that you have a structure for collaborative planning, possibly with adherence to the extensive body of professional learning communities' literature and resources. This is another structure that is integral to the examination of teaching and learning and to the growth and development of teachers as they work together to share current practice and develop new understandings as a team.

The most critical structure to implementing Collaborative Response is the CTM. This structure is unique to Collaborative Response, and we've had several instances over the past number of years where participants in overview sessions, at an initial glance, mistake CTMs for collaborative planning or school support team meetings, as those are familiar structures. On deeper examination, you will find that this structure is uniquely designed to enhance instructional practice while developing supports for students at the classroom level. It is a bridge between universal classroom practices and specialized supports, generalist teachers, and special education teachers. The CTM is a critical component of Collaborative Response and is described in detail in Chapter 5.

Let's take some time to unpack the layers of collaborative structures, recognizing that many of the procedural elements for the case consult team meeting and the school support team meeting will be further examined in Chapter 4, focused on collaborative processes.

Case Consult Team Meeting

The most intense level of support is a structure that is typically firmly established in most schools and focuses primarily on one student at a time. This structure is referred to as the *case consult team meeting*. There are two situations that initiate this team meeting. First, we convene this team when we have a student with complex needs who requires much more support than we are able to provide on our own. In this case, the case consult team is convened to determine the most appropriate programming, external supports, and specialized equipment that may be needed for a particular student.

The second situation in which we engage the case consult team is in the case of an immediate crisis and/or a situation where students themselves or others are at risk. This team serves as the problem-solving body that navigates intensive circumstances that sometimes occur in schools. This may require the involvement of other organizations such as the district or state administrators (associate superintendents, supervisors, directors), the police department, and/or other partners such as health services or social services. We will not be exploring this particular situation in depth in this text as this has already been well defined by organizations that provide leadership around trauma response.

Regardless of the reason for convening the team, it is a highly specialized meeting that focuses on the academic needs, health, and well-being of a *single student*. This team engages the family and activates supports at home as well as what is needed at the school. Essentially, we "wrap-around" one learner. When the team is convened, it may include classroom teachers, paraprofessionals, administrators, special education leads, support teachers, and most often school counselors. In addition, it also potentially involves external roles such as psychologists, therapists, and clinicians that support the specialized needs of one individual student. This wrap-around meeting may also involve parents and/or guardians as this structure is intended to ensure a common understanding of support on all levels, including the home context. It could involve the student especially if they are of an age to contribute to the decision-making in regard to their supports and their engagement in those supports. This is an intensive support team that is needed to ensure safety and wellness for all involved, and membership fluctuates depending on the student and their needs, either ongoing or emergent.

Companion Website Resources

3.1. Reflecting on case consult team meetings: This reflection organizer is designed to assist schools in reviewing the key elements found in case consult team meetings and determine next steps to refining the collaborative structure. A number of the considerations listed will be examined in the subsequent chapter on collaborative structures.

CHAPTER #3. Collaborative Structures

School Support Team Meetings

The next level of team that is frequently found in schools to support the specialized needs of students is the *school support team meeting*. This school team structure provides ongoing support to classroom teachers in regard to individual students and perhaps small groups. Administrators, special education leads, support teachers, and counselors or social workers typically make up the team roster. Ideally, this team meets weekly or biweekly to engage in conversations regarding programming for students, schoolwide supports, and referrals to district or external services.

Starting Steps

We have engaged with schools that have asserted that they have a team that meets to review students needing supports beyond the classroom but that it convenes on an as-needed basis. We would contend that establishing a consistent time (weekly or biweekly) for that team to meet is essential for two reasons:

- It ensures that the review of emerging needs of students is not a reactive process, only initiated when a referral is made or a need has emerged. Establishing a consistent time and process for this team meeting not only communicates its importance but ensures regular, and often proactive, review of students accessing supports beyond the classroom level.

- It communicates to staff that there is a consistent structure to attend to the needs of students requiring schoolwide supports, in addition to classroom-based supports. This becomes critical to the CTM if teachers know that there is a consistent structure in place to examine and scaffold support for students needing more specialized attention. Without a consistent school support team meeting structure in place, the CTM could become less than impactful (a concept explored further in Chapter 5).

At times and when appropriate, teachers and paraprofessionals are invited to participate when a student for whom they are responsible will be discussed at the meeting. Teachers have the greatest understanding about the students in their classroom and should be invited to contribute to the discussions in regard to setting up the necessary supports. However, some of the determined supports may not require a teacher's direct involvement if information is included in a referral that is gathered through a conversation or shared in a CTM (discussed in Chapter 5). In some situations, next steps or supports established can be communicated to the classroom staff following the school support team meeting.

The school support team also provides an organizational venue for the development and implementation of schoolwide programs to support the needs of small groups. As the team convenes to discuss students who require additional supports, it may become apparent that there are some similar concerns coming forward, and perhaps rather than dealing with one student at a time, the most efficient response is to provide small-group support. Some examples of small-group, schoolwide support (that could also be cross-graded) would be small-group counseling sessions for grief, small-group intervention focused on phonemic awareness, a small group for study skills, or a small group developing social stories for behavioral concerns.

Both the case consult team structure and the school support team structure are primarily focused on individual students in an attempt to ensure that intensive individual needs are met. These structures have been in schools most certainly throughout our careers. The primary focus has been to collaborate with multiple partners when a student has clearly defined academic, medical, or social-emotional needs. These teams are the connection between classroom supports for students and external partners that can provide specialized service for students and families.

Companion Website Resources

3.2. Reflecting on school support team meetings: Reflection organizer to assist schools in reviewing the key elements found in school support team meetings and determine next steps to refining the collaborative structure.

Collaborative Team Meetings

A third and absolutely most critical structure is the CTM. CTMs are the one team structure that is not typically prevalent in schools, and it is the structure that ensures that we've done everything we could at the classroom level prior to accessing more intensive supports requiring specialized roles, services, and resources. This structure is intended to provide an avenue for discussing students who are experiencing challenges in the classroom and might benefit from a boost in terms of differentiating strategies to support their needs. Their needs, however, may be needs that have surfaced for other students and could be used to design unique strategies that would not only support that particular student, but many more in other classrooms as well. We refer to this as focusing on key issues (a topic to be expanded in Chapter 5).

This unique team meeting structure provides an avenue to explore and expand classroom practices while surfacing concerns for students. During this team meeting, all individuals around the table are both experts and learners, and the intentionally designed processes begin with students whose progress we are concerned about and then shifts to an examination of strategies currently employed and sharing those practices across classrooms, cohorts, and/or grade levels. As educators, we are compelled by identifying needs for our students and then finding ways to meet those needs. It is what drives our work.

When the CTM structure is not in place or is not functioning to support classroom instruction, we find that the people and resources in the other two layers (the school support team and the case consult team) become stretched and overwhelmed with the number of students for whom they need to provide individualized support. We also recognize that without the CTM layer, teachers have no recourse when struggling with the needs of a student but to reach out to these more intensive structures.

Due to the pivotal role the CTM plays in Collaborative Response, we have dedicated Chapter 5 to unpacking it in depth.

Collaborative Planning

Throughout our careers, we have seen many versions of what could be described as *collaborative planning*. The collaborative planning structure operates parallel to the CTM, providing teaching staff with the opportunity to work in teams creating the resources, materials, lessons, and strategies that would support teaching and learning in their classrooms. Collaborative planning time is an integral structure that ensures that the supports that we are initiating through the CTM have dedicated time to be actualized in the classroom.

Leaders can make a difference (Parsons & Beauchamp, 2011) by creating the space for collaboration; however, "perhaps the biggest mistake leaders make in attempting to create a collaborative culture is to assign teachers or principals into groups and encourage them to collaborate—with little other direction or support" (DuFour & Marzano, 2011, p. 79). In these situations, "collaboration is about sharing resources, sharing anecdotes and war stories and sharing beliefs about why or why not something might work in my context" (Hattie, 2015, p. 23). Unfocused or informal collaboration is not likely to produce the systemic results we are intending. Essentially, school leaders must seek to answer two crucial questions when exploring collaborative planning for their staff teams. The first question is, "When do we collaborate?" This question necessitates a considerate examination of the master timetable and calendar to creatively determine that time is carved out for teams to meet, a concept explored later in this chapter. The second question is, "How do we collaborate?" When teams come together, what do they do? What structures and processes, goals and plans, and aspirations and expectations are in place to ensure that time is being used in a way that truly will make a difference for student, staff, and school success?

Consider the following portrayal of two grade-level teams that have had embedded time provided in their school for professional collaboration to occur. As you read, consider the following questions:

1. Does each scenario demonstrate a commitment from school leadership to provide time for educators to work together?

2. What expectations have been communicated to teams when coming together for their embedded time?

3. What supports have been established for teams in each of the scenarios?

4. What role has leadership taken in each school to ensure that collaborative time is successful?

5. How does the collaborative planning time connect to the CTM?

Grade-Level Time at Collegial Academy

This year, Collegial Academy has emphasized grade-level teams working together, contrary to the culture of isolation that previously permeated the school. Every grade level has an hour embedded weekly into their schedule that allows the teachers to meet as a team, with every fourth or fifth meeting being scheduled as a CTM, where the team is joined by an administrator and other specialized staff members. Today marks the fourth time that the sixth-grade team has met as a collective group. At the start of the year, examples were presented to the entire staff during a 10-minute section of their staff meeting, sharing things that they could be doing during this collaborative time, such as developing common assessments, mapping their curriculum, developing units of study, and other activities.

CHAPTER #3. Collaborative Structures

This week, only three of the four sixth-grade teachers are meeting. After starting 15 minutes late, as team members went to grab a coffee and use the washroom, they discussed the increasing number of disagreements that seem to be occurring on the playground in relation to informal soccer games. Following this discussion, where they all agree to talk to their students about the issue and help establish an organized soccer intramural program, time is devoted to planning the upcoming grade-level field trip to the local museum, including the group creation of the permission letter to go home. One teacher shares a copy of her latest science unit test with her team members while another makes copies to share an outstanding lesson she did in mathematics.

As their collaborative time comes to a close, the team agrees to bring poetry resources to their next meeting to share with one another, as it was mentioned during their last CTM that some students were going to struggle with an upcoming focus on poetry. They depart, excited about the completion of the field trip note, their planned soccer intramurals, and the great resources they continue to share with one another. Why had they not been working collaboratively in years past?

Grade-Level Time at Focus Elementary

This year, Focus Elementary has emphasized grade-level teams working together. Every grade level has an hour embedded weekly into their schedule that allows the teachers at each grade level to meet as a team, with every fourth or fifth meeting scheduled as a CTM, where the team is joined by an administrator and other specialized staff members. Today marks the fourth time that the sixth-grade team has met as a collective.

At the start of the year, the entire staff engaged in a workshop focused on the review of the school's core goal related to literacy, and grade-level teams were presented with literacy data from their students of the previous year and incoming students of the current year. They began the work of crafting a grade-level goal, related to the school's core goal. The staff also worked to establish norms for their grade-level teams and reviewed the expectations for team embedded time, which included focus on their priorities (related to the team goals), as well as the completion of a team planning guide, which is saved in the school's shared drive.

Two weeks ago (at the team's second meeting), the school's principal met with the sixth-grade team to review the team goal, priorities, and norms

(Continued)

COLLABORATIVE RESPONSE

(Continued)

and worked with them to help develop strategies to meet their goal of "By the end of the year, the sixth-grade team will ensure 70 or more of their 80 students were proficient in the area of vocabulary, as determined by their literacy assessments." When the team reviewed their data, they determined vocabulary to be an area their previous sixth-grade students most struggled with (and through discussion, the team admittedly felt that they collectively could improve on their vocabulary instructional strategies related to reading). They also identified that 50 students were coming into grade 6 demonstrating proficiency in reading vocabulary (meaning that 30 students were going to be considered at risk in this area entering grade 6—the team noted the names of those 30 students). With the principal's involvement, the team determined two priority areas (explicit instruction and enhanced assessment in vocabulary) and several strategies related to their priorities and overall goal.

Today, the team arrived with an article that they had all agreed to read related to effective vocabulary instruction. In their team norms, they had determined that the first 15 minutes of every meeting would be related to other grade-6 issues, so they set a timer for 15 minutes, so as not to go over. One teacher brought up the concerns her students were expressing relating to soccer at recess time. After a short discussion, teachers agreed to talk to their classes, and one teacher agreed to approach the vice principal to investigate a soccer intramural program. The team then focused on the upcoming grade-level field trip at the local museum. They determined that they still needed to develop a permission form, which one teacher agreed to do and then email a draft to the team within the next two days.

Following these discussions, which concluded prior to the 15-minute timer going off, the team turned to the article and compiled a list of 5 practices suggested in the article that they could be exploring related to their vocabulary instruction. The ones that piqued their interest most were the development of word walls related to cross-curricular vocabulary terms and the use of peer editing and thesaurus applications to enhance vocabulary usage in writing. The team decided that each of them would take a core subject area and develop a list of what they considered "essential vocabulary" in that subject's unit of study for the sixth-grade year. This would be the master list, and they would add to and revise it at future meetings to eventually develop their quintessential list of key vocabulary terms for the grade level, which they could then start focusing on, particularly in establishing classroom word walls (a concept to come back to at a later meeting). They also decided to use some of the funds given to each grade level to support their collaborative work to purchase 10 thesauruses for each classroom as well as download a thesaurus app to their class iPads, to support the exploration of peer-editing practices (a subject for a future meeting). One teacher agreed to chat with the principal about this.

The team used the remainder of their team meeting time to begin individually crafting the start of their essential vocabulary list. One teacher agreed to complete the notes in the team planning guide. Once finished, he quickly shared it with the group.

After examining the team meeting record, the group agreed that it would be more effective to complete these records during the course of the meeting. One teacher agreed to be the recordkeeper at subsequent meetings. The team departed, excited about the progress they were making in their goal. At the CTM happening during grade-level time the following week, they knew that they would have some early student celebration stories to share! They also had in mind some students to bring forth to the CTM conversations, whom they would individually identify in their pre-meeting organizers on their own time prior to next week. Why had they not been working collaboratively in years past?

The vignettes portray two grade-level teams coming together, with embedded time provided, but at very different levels of functioning and focus. We are reminded of DuFour and Marzano's (2011) commentary that "a collaborative team is more than a group of random people who meet periodically to see if they can discover a topic of conversation" (p. 70). This accurately describes the work of the sixth-grade team at Collegial Academy! At Focus Elementary, collaboration is not an end in itself; rather, collaboration is the structure that allows teams to move closer toward their shared goal. Although collegial relationships are important in schools, "collaborative relationships are about teachers supporting teachers in order to promote success for students. Unlike collegial relationships, in which emphasis is on supporting teachers on a more personal and social level, collaboration is all about the professional side of teaching" (Martin, 2008, p. 150). By moving from informal to focused collaboration, educators harness the power of the team—and team is an important concept in establishing the conditions for Collaborative Response.

As shared in the Focus Elementary vignette, it is important to intentionally focus on refining structures and processes, so that the time intended for collaboration is used effectively. Without clarity, expectations, and structure, the valuable time for teams can become misaligned, unfocused, and at worst, frustrating or lack any true value for those involved. However, this must be effectively balanced with an increasing level of intrinsic motivation for teams to engage in collective work that attends to what Pink (2009) refers to as the four drivers of motivation:

1. Purpose (doing what matters to us): Teams must be *invested* in what they see as a primary focus, based on an analysis of their data and evidence. They must be able to feel that their work will make a substantial and meaningful impact on their pedagogy and student learning.

COLLABORATIVE RESPONSE

2. Autonomy (freedom to self-determine): Teams must have the *freedom to determine* the goal or inquiry question they wish to focus on that they feel will make a difference for their practice.

3. Mastery (getting better over time): Teams must have the *time and support* to refine their collaborative practices over time, recognizing that collaborating effectively takes time and practice. As teams gain experience and identify successes produced by their collaborative efforts, they will continue to refine the skill sets necessary to work and engage together at optimal levels.

4. Connectedness (engaging with others): In addition to the professional results attained through collaboration, the heightened sense of connectedness between team members must be nurtured, identified, and celebrated. Teams will reach a place where they will go to the wall for each other, not because their norms prescribe particular behaviors but because they genuinely care about their colleagues' well-being and professional growth.

The challenge for leaders in regard to collaborative planning is to strike an intentional and evolving balance of loose/tight leadership (DuFour, 2008) that honors the drivers essential for intrinsic motivation for the team while setting clear parameters and expectations that can effectively guide their work.

Potential Pitfall

It is no secret that "collaboration can be messy, complicated, and difficult" (Ferriter et al., 2013, p. 1). However, school leaders can err if they assume that, by providing time and structure for collaboration, staff members will be able to collaborate effectively to meet the needs of students. For many of our staff members, this type of work is a departure from *collegial* work.

We have worked with many staff teams in schools that were collegial. They shared resources. They laughed together in the staff room and cried together through personal tragedies. They enjoyed working together. However, collaborating effectively is different. It involves a great deal of professional trust because staff members critically examine their (sometimes long-held) instructional practices about how they meet the needs of students in classrooms and throughout the school. Gaining experience and confidence in collaborative teams takes time, careful structure, purposeful processes, and intentional coaching.

School leaders might also err if they assume that certain individuals will not be able to work well in a collaborative setting. They may have

CHAPTER #3. Collaborative Structures

witnessed staff members purposefully isolate themselves, reluctant to share or work with others in the traditional school setting. However, these teachers might actually be looking for a reason to work collaboratively.

Heath and Heath (2010) address this issue, instructing that what might be perceived as a *people* problem may actually be a *situational* problem. Having potentially not engaged in formalized collaborative structures, some staff members may not seem to have the skills necessary; however, in actuality, these teachers may have never been placed in a situation that required collaborative skills to be used and developed.

Understanding that effective collaborative work takes time, patience, and guidance is important for leaders as staff begin to interact in collaborative structures and processes. In fact, a wise leader might engage the elephant in the room by talking through their teachers' experiences with collaboration, both as a teacher and as a learner.

Central to the layering of collaborative team structures is the development of embedded time for collaboration. That will be a primary focus in the next section of this chapter. However, once the time is established, there needs to be consideration given to the processes integral to the collaborative planning time established for teams. Although overall collaborative processes will take center stage in Chapter 4, it is important to discuss some of the foundational considerations that need to be taken specifically when establishing collaborative planning time for teams. These include the following:

▶ Establishing a team focus

▶ Developing team planning guides

▶ Aligning to CTMs

▶ Establishing a review process

▶ Engaging in schoolwide sharing

These foundation considerations align largely with what Ericson and Pool (2016) describe as purposeful practice, which includes the key elements of narrow goals, specificity of focus, a clear plan to reach those goals, and ways to monitor progress. It starts with establishing a team focus.

Establishing a Team Focus

As collaborative planning teams are convened, a focus for the team needs to be established to ensure that the time is targeted on areas of need as identified through data.

It is critical that the focus for a collaborative team is directly aligned to the identified priorities of the district and the school. Consider a nested approach shown in Figure 3.2, where the district priorities inform the school priorities, which in time inform the team focus areas.

Figure 3.2 Connecting district, school, and team priorities

District Priorities

School Priorities

Team Focus Areas

Although not every school system adopts a district approach as a way to organize schools, the same premise applies if priorities are set from a ministry, state, provincial, or federal level. Clear alignment of priorities should help guide focus areas established for each team within a school, as shown in the Focus Elementary vignette. Essentially, all oars should be paddling in a common direction if we truly want to see movement in relation to school improvement priority areas.

Consider the following example. A ministry has established key priority areas for schools, which include a focus on student engagement in learning. The school then develops a school goal connected to student engagement, including key measures that will inform growth in that particular area. We should then be working with teams within the school to focus on some aspect of student engagement that will drive their work during their collaborative planning time.

When Kurtis was principal of a southern Alberta elementary school, the district had established one of their priority areas to focus on literacy success for students. The school then adopted a core goal related to reading success, with an ambitious target that every student would be reading at grade level by the end of third grade over the next three years. From that, each grade-level team examined the key literacy data available at the beginning of the year to determine a team goal explicitly linked to the core goal of reading success for every student. One grade focused primarily on phonemic awareness strategies for students, while another determined through an examination of their data that more robust vocabulary instruction was an area in which to devote time and energy. This alignment ensured that every team was working in unison to make a substantial impact on an identified need, not just for the school but for the district as a whole.

A possible variation to the development of a team goal is the development of a team inquiry question, such as "What impact will the cocreation of essential questions at the outset of units of study with students have on student engagement?" In this example, an inquiry question can guide the work of the team engaged in cocreating questions with students in relation to curriculum and could include strategies for the team such as the development of a student engagement survey to measure their impact, professional reading related to the topic, creation and sharing of templates and lessons connected to their aspiration, and more. The question, similar to a goal, is still informed by data, is connected to the larger school priority, and must be viewed as a compelling question that inspires exploration, potential shifts in practice, and seeking evidence that can help support possible responses.

Companion Website Resources

3.3. Data review and team goal template: Organizes initial team planning when reviewing data to determine strengths and gaps for students, to then help establish a SMART (specific, measurable, achievable, relevant, and time-bound) goal on which to focus, and potential strategies to consider.

3.4. Data review and team inquiry question template: Replication of the team goal template, with a focus on the development of a team inquiry question.

3.5. Team priorities and actions: Once a team goal or inquiry question is determined, this template assists teams in the development of priorities related to their focus as well as establishing timelines and responsibilities. This could be a useful initial planning document that should serve as a potential thought organizer to help when developing a team planning guide, discussed in subsequent pages

Regardless of a goal, inquiry question, or some other semblance of a team focus area, examining existing student data should be undertaken to help with the formulation. When teams work together to examine the data in connection to overarching school priorities, such as literacy, numeracy, student engagement, social-emotional well-being, executive functioning, or other, it provides a foundation on which team focus areas can be data informed and directly related to the identified needs of students. Focusing on three primary questions can assist teams when determining an area of focus:

- What are the strengths as demonstrated in the data?
- What are the interesting elements that surfaced in the data?
- What appear to be the common challenges in the data?

The next step is to review the common challenges list and determine as a team the area of greatest need to support students within that particular cohort. The area identified then becomes the focus of the learning for the collaborative planning time. Establishing a process for ensuring that the team goals or inquiry questions are data informed, as well as the determination of key measures that will indicate progress and/or success in relation to their goal, is valuable to develop over time for teams.

Starting Steps

Establishing an area of focus for teams, based on an examination of data, can seem like a daunting task if teams are new to this process. It can be a process that can be introduced once the team's collaborative process is already established, to help further refine and narrow the focus areas. A comfortable starting step may be establishing an area of focus based on dialogue related to questions such as the following:

- What is an area in which we observe our students as a whole struggle?
- What is an area about which we as a team would like to learn more deeply in order to best meet the needs of our students?
- What is an area on which we could focus our collective practice that would have an impact on student learning?

Although we want to reach a place where the priorities of our teams are data informed, this shouldn't be viewed as a massive undertaking when first establishing an area of focus for collaborative teams.

Developing Team Planning Guides

Documenting the collective work of the team, as it relates to their goal(s) or inquiry question(s), is an important aspect of collaborative planning, which all too often is not recognized. This can not only assist in focusing the efforts of the team, but also provide evidence of team growth and the work they have accomplished collectively. Furthermore, it can be useful for administrative review to be apprised of the work of individual teams without needing to be present for each team engagement. Documenting the ongoing work of each individual team also allows teams to review the work of other teams to identify additional opportunities for connection and sharing of ideas and resources.

Substantial Shifts

When we first engaged in structuring focused collaborative processes for teams, team members would have a binder to collect individual documents: a page documenting norms, a page for a team goal or inquiry question, and a page for priorities and possible strategies, followed by a separate notes document for each time the team met. Although the binder (and shared digital folders) kept the team's work together, we have learned that it is much easier to have it all compiled in a team planning guide, a single digital document that can be added to regularly. Also, an individual template, such as the data review and team goal, can be valuable as a rough planning organizer, but having the team's norms, goal/inquiry question, review of key data, and ongoing notes in a single, ongoing document can be powerful. For schools with regularly structured collaborative time for teams, it also allows for the collaboration dates to be determined and then allows for aligned planning of a number of infused team processes throughout the year, such as administrative reviews, data analysis times, and coordination of CTMs. Having the team planning guide as a shared online document allows easy access and overall transparency of team endeavors.

Companion Website Resources

3.6. Team planning guide template: The planning guide template includes the key elements discussed as well as the ability to preestablish dates for collaborative planning time during the course of the school year.

When establishing team guides, there are a number of key features that should be considered in their design:

- *Infusion of team norms*: As will be discussed in Chapter 4, team norms help provide a common understanding of how we interact with each other when engaged in collaborative endeavors. Once established, the team norms should be included in the team planning guides as well as referenced regularly by the team.

- *Team focus area*: Whether presented as a team goal, an inquiry question, or in some other format, documenting the focus area for the team allows continual reference and revisiting, should the focus need to be adjusted throughout the year, particularly in connection to the ongoing conversations in CTMs (a connection described in the next section).

- *Articulation of the importance of the focus*: Reflecting on and then articulating the *why*, what Sinek (2009) would refer to as the center of "The Golden Circle" (p. 39), is important when teams are establishing a focus area for their ongoing collaborative efforts. It can serve as a reminder of why the focus area was initially established, communicate the urgency or need for the work to be viewed as important for the team, and help infuse a level of commitment and possibly greater purpose for the future endeavors of the team.

- *Current reality*: At the onset of a school year, having the team assess and communicate the current reality in relation to their focus area can not only support the *why*, but also encourage the recognition of data that support the need for their focus area. Consider the two current reality statements in relation to a team inquiry question such as, "What impact will the integration of gamification elements in our instruction have upon student achievement and engagement, specifically in mathematics?"

  1. "Currently, a number of students in our math classes are not as engaged as we would like and we suspect that they would be more interested in mathematics if we explored a gamification approach. We also have a number of students that fail math classes that have the ability to be more successful."

  2. "Currently, only 52% are reporting somewhat engaged or highly engaged in surveys of our math classes. In the school student interest survey, 92% of students reported video games as an interest outside of school. We are collectively wondering if infusing gamification elements in our math classes would increase engagement. We also currently have 62% of students achieving 60% or higher in our math classes, although our

numeracy screen data shows 74% of students with acceptable numeracy skills. We intend to see growth both in the engagement data and the percentage of students achieving 60% or higher through our focus on gamification infusion."

Both statements declare an examination of the current reality and provide support for the *why* underlying their team inquiry question. However, the introduction of data examination, with some key data measures in place, establishes another level of clarity for the team and, in time, sets clear targets the team is striving for through their collective work. An assessment of the current reality helps "open our eyes" to the need for refining our practices and engaging in rich professional learning and exploration, to ensure higher levels of overall student success.

- ▸ *Possible strategies*: Including an area for possible strategies allows the team, at the onset, to envision some possible directions that they could be taking during the course of the year to affect their area of focus. This collection can also be added to, as the team grows, learns more about their students' needs, and engages in learning with each other. Possible strategies could include the following:
  - ○ development of assessment tools or data collection instruments in relation to their area of focus, if none currently exist, to help determine student growth;
  - ○ engagement in professional learning (book studies, article reviews, engagement in webinars or professional development sessions, etc.);
  - ○ classroom observations or school visits (in-person or virtual);
  - ○ development of common units, lessons, assessments, or classroom practices; and
  - ○ creation of home materials or resources for supporting student learning.

Two other key features illustrated in the team planning guide template—referencing a team goal review and indication of CTM dates, with related team tasks—are discussed in the following sections.

Whenever possible, establishing the dates for collaborative planning in the planning guide at the start of the year can ensure a number of things. First off, it allows teams to "look forward" and plan when appropriate next steps can be established, taking into account the bigger picture of upcoming activities important for the team. It can, in time, reflect key data administration and analysis timelines (to be discussed further in Chapter 6) that correspond with CTMs, to help ensure that these meetings have students brought forward through a prior examination of data. It also allows coordinated planning in relation to key events happening in the school that could affect elements of the collaborative work. Ensuring a less-intensive planning time in the week prior to report cards being due may seem irrelevant, but ask any teacher their mindset and propensity for deeply engaging work when in the midst of demanding times at points during the school year!

Aligning to Collaborative Team Meetings

As we will explore in depth in Chapter 5, the CTM is the engine that drives Collaborative Response and, in time, comes to inform and influence strategic directions in the school in relation to team focus areas, data collection tools and processes, development of responsive supports, and more. Simply put, the needs of the students unearthed during CTMs drive the response of staff and the overall school community.

Although entirely dependent on how collaborative time is established, ideally, a CTM is infused into the cycle of collaborative planning time every three to five weeks. Within the CTM, it may inform team tasks (as noted in the team planning guide template) for the team to return to in subsequent collaborative time. Essentially, it becomes a way for the team to have focus and time to act on any ideas or suggestions that may arise from the CTM. Although this will be further described in Chapter 5, it should be a consideration when establishing a team planning guide and attempting to ensure a clear alignment between the collaborative planning time and the CTM.

Starting Steps

It may be too ambitious for a school first engaging in Collaborative Response to introduce a highly formalized set of structures and processes for collaborative planning or develop a timetable that can guarantee regular embedded time for teams. Recognizing that the CTM is essential, many schools introduce a simple cycle of CTM, followed by collaborative planning, followed by CTM, and so on. On one hand, this can mean that the time needed for collaboration is less frequent. On the other, it also can establish a cycle where the CTM determines team tasks that are then focused on during the subsequent collaborative planning time, effectively simplifying the need for teams to have areas of focus connected to data or other elements already described. We have worked with schools, when first starting, that infused the collaborative work into days established in a divisional calendar and then created a schedule within that day that included CTMs, followed by dedicated time for the teams to attend to the collective actions determined during the CTM discussion. Creating this alternating cycle can be effective and clearly shows the explicit alignment between the CTM and the subsequent collaborative planning time.

Establishing a Review Process

There is great benefit in creating a school timetable where the principal is not scheduled for teaching or other responsibilities during teams' collaborative time. This schedule allows the principal to join and support teams during their collaborative time, as deemed necessary or as invited by the team. Consider Moller and Pankake's (2006) advice:

> Principals are unable to attend every scheduled meeting. However, they can, with a little planning, "stop by" to check in on how things are going with most meetings. Finding time to stop by . . . allows principals to be in tune with what's going on and who is involved with what's going on. As brief as stop-bys might be, they still provide an opportunity to gather information about the focus of the meeting and the participants. (p. 80)

This emphasis on involvement and supervision of teams has numerous benefits for principals and can often provide a richer indication of teaching and learning practices happening in the school than a traditional classroom observation routine (Hewson, 2013). As discussed earlier, the meaningful involvement of the principal in these team structures and conversations has immeasurable benefits.

However, we advocate that leaders not micromanage the work of teams. Establishing a regular review process is a powerful way for leaders to not only engage with teams and offer support, but also ensure school-wide alignment of team areas of focus with overall focus areas for the school. By establishing an initial review, a midyear check-in, and an end-of-year review, an administrator can join the team to help refine, guide, and support their work. Ideally, having these review periods clearly identified in the team planning guide communicates their importance and allows teams to prepare for the conversation. Being transparent about the questions to be asked can ensure that intentional leadership practices are infused into the collaborative planning process. The work of the team can then also be integrated into classroom walkthroughs and observations because principals provide individual guidance to teachers, aligned with their team goals.

Establishing the first administrative review within the first two to three weeks of teams engaging in their collaborative planning time allows the team to engage in the development of their team focus area, and team norms and administrative involvement early in the process allow for adjustments or refinements to be made. As a principal, Kurtis employed the following process for his teams:

▶ *Final quarter of the school year*: During a professional development half-day workshop, teams would review current student data, analyze their current team goals, and begin drafting a very rough potential area of focus for the next school year. This work was in alignment with the school's improvement planning process.

▶ *Prior to school beginning*: On teachers' return for a new school year, administration led a half-day workshop to have teams revisit their student data (with some further data presented that may not have been available in May/June of the previous year) and refine their team goal as well as establish norms for each team. This was an opportunity to reinforce key priorities for the school at the onset of the new school year and ensure alignment between school priorities and team focus areas. It was also an opportunity to revisit the importance of the norms, team structures, and processes and reinforce the overall alignment of collaborative structures throughout the school. During the session, teams shared through gallery walks and reporting out strategies, so teachers could view the work of other teams and further ensure connections and commonalities among the individual teams.

▶ *Third week of school*: During weekly embedded collaborative time, Kurtis joined teams, with the communicated expectation that norms and a draft of a team goal would be prepared for review. Following a review of their team norms and any adjustments needed, the draft goal was examined using four key questions to guide the discussion:

1. *How did you arrive at your goal?* The intention of this question was to elicit the *why* behind the team goal and what evidence was apparent in the student data that necessitated the development of the particular area of focus for the team.

2. *How will you know if you've achieved your goal? What impact will it have?* These questions helped establish a target for the team to aim for in connection to student data. They also revealed the need to develop some time for common assessment tools to collect some data in relation to their area of focus, if nothing was currently in place. They also helped the team envision what change they expected to see if achieving their goal, establishing optimism, and forecasting a preferred future for their students and their instructional practices.

3. *What challenges do you anticipate in accomplishing your goal?* This question was intended to preidentify issues that may arise and begin planning how to potentially address them should they occur. It could also forecast potential challenges that administration could attend to in order to support the team and develop further shared commitment to the collective direction of the school.

4. *How can leadership support you in achieving your goal?* Asking this question demonstrated leadership's commitment to the work of the team and helped the administration play a role in the team successfully meeting their goal.

▶ *Midyear*: Kurtis once again joined the team for a midyear review. Although informal conversations were ongoing, with opportunities embedded through staff meetings, professional development days, and ongoing communication for teams to be sharing their progress with other teams and the wider school community, this formal review again reinforced the importance of the team goals and focused on another set of questions:

1. What have you accomplished in relation to your goal?

2. What are your next steps to accomplish your goal?

3. What have you learned in relation to working effectively as a team?

4. How can leadership support you in achieving your goal?

▶ *End of school*: Kurtis joined the teams for a final review, in alignment with the aforementioned work, to examine data and start crafting a new team goal in May/June. This conversation was guided by three questions and set the stage for the transition into a new school year:

1. What did you accomplish in relation to your goal?

2. What did you learn this year in relation to your goal?

3. How did your goal affect student learning? What evidence do you have?

By creating a regular and transparent cycle of administrative review and connected support, a leader communicates, both in messaging and in deliberate action, that the work of the team matters, that their professional learning in collaborative teams is valued, and that the collective focus remains on seeking evidence of our success through the continual examination of data-informed priorities operating in synchronicity across the school.

Engaging in Schoolwide Sharing

In the establishment of collaborative planning time, leaders should simultaneously reflect on ways to have teams continuously sharing the work of their team, their learning and gathering feedback, or considerations from colleagues outside of their team in relation to next steps. Through sharing, learning is celebrated and the growth of the team is recognized, providing the opportunity for teams to perhaps lead learning for the rest of the staff, sharing their collaborative work and the impact they are seeing for their students. Collective sharing ensures that accountability of the team is evidenced, creating publicly observed standards to continually drive teams to perform at high levels through positive peer pressure. Finally, it ensures a continued and collective focus on the school priorities on which team focus areas are based.

Consider the following ways to continually be reinforcing the importance of the collaborative work happening for teams across the school.

- *Staff meeting*: Staff meetings provide an exceptional space to maintain ongoing focus on school priorities, as evidenced by the work of the teams within the school. Some possible ideas for infusing sharing in staff meetings could include the following:
  - regular practice of teams reporting out their progress since the last meeting—potentially consider an ongoing structure of each team sharing: "What did you do? What did you learn? What will you do next?"
  - teams bringing artifacts or evidence of their team's collaborative work to share and potentially post in a staff space;
  - teams come ready to share their progress in relation to their focus area. As a leader, when it is determined that a team has accomplished something significant in relation to their area of focus, it is a powerful way to recognize their accomplishment by sharing what it is that they did with the larger staff team; and
  - team members jigsaw into cross-team groups to share, promoting more intimate discussions that could lead to further exploration and collaboration across teams.

- *Professional development days*: Infusing team sharing during professional development day agendas can provide longer blocks of time for team sharing. It could provide an opportune time to gather feedback from colleagues outside of their team in relation to questions that could promote deeper thinking or lead to unimagined next steps in relation to their areas of focus. It can provide the venue for teams to lead professional learning for their peers, in relation to the collaborative learning they have engaged in as a team. Classroom visits can be infused, allowing team members a chance to evidence the impact of their collaborative work directly in their classroom and instructional practices.

- *Asynchronous sharing platforms*: Creating collaborative digital spaces for teams to share, pose questions, gather feedback, reflect on questions prompted by leadership, and so on, can potentially provide one more avenue for teams to be learning from each other.

Through the intentional infusion of schoolwide sharing for teams, leaders communicate strong messages in relation to the importance of the collaborative planning time as part of the greater school strategic plan. It sends a clear message that the work teams are engaging in matters!

Companion Website Resources

3.7. Reflecting on collaborative planning: The following template provides an opportunity to reflect on the elements necessary to ensure the effectiveness of the collaborative planning time for teams.

3.8. Team meeting overview template: This is a template for planning to determine the types of collaborative structures already happening in the school and the purpose of each, who is involved, the duration, and the frequency. This overview assists in reflecting on meetings already happening in the school and begins the alignment to the layering of team meetings we've described thus far in this chapter.

Time Embedded in the School Timetable and Calendar

If working collaboratively with a variety of team structures established to support and respond to the diverse needs of all students is truly a mission for schools, it must be embedded into the school's timetable and calendar. As DuFour and Marzano (2011) pointed out more than a decade ago,

> It is perplexing to see the number of districts that proclaim the importance of staff members working collaboratively that provide neither the time nor the structure vital to collaboration. It is disingenuous to assert that working together is an organizational priority and then do nothing to support it. (p. 73)

Reeves (2009) further supports this argument, asserting that "effective leaders must provide more time during the school day. Asking teachers to 'work smarter' without giving them more time is not a sufficient solution" (p. 65). Although providing this time can be a challenge, it cannot become a barrier to establishing the four layers of collaboration essential for an impactful Collaborative Response in schools. Our education system is overflowing with examples of schools adjusting schedules, calendars, and timetables to allow staff members to collaborate. Acquiescing to the statement "we just can't find the time to collaborate" is simply unacceptable.

When it comes to timetabling collaborative structures, the time for the case consult and school support team meetings is typically quite easy, which could be why these structures are usually already in place in a large majority of schools. With case consult team meetings, their very nature requires flexible scheduling, due to the number of individuals that are required and the reality that the team meeting participation is going to vary based on each individual student. Generally, these meetings happen

- before or after school
- at lunch or break times
- during the school day, with the release of teachers if they need to be involved in the team meeting.

For school support team meetings, the primary participants (administrators, special education leads, support teachers, counselors, etc.) typically have flexibility in their timetable to allow for the establishment of a consistent meeting time during the school day. As these meetings should be happening on a consistent basis weekly or biweekly, it takes some moderate coordination to set a consistent time that then should be honored by those staff members expected to be part of the team. Many schools we engage with set this time against a natural break in the school day (first thing in the morning, end of the day, or up against a break time during the day) so that their conversation could invite a teacher in without disrupting anyone's teaching schedule. For example, a team may determine their meeting time to be from 8:00 to 9:00 a.m. every Wednesday morning, to allow them to bring in a teacher to their conversation prior to the start of the school day (assuming a start time is 8:30 a.m. for this particular example) but also continue their meeting into the school day, knowing that many conversations may not need the direct involvement of a teacher.

However, embedding time for the CTM and collaborative planning takes more focused and concerted efforts. Before exploring different ways in which leaders and schools can envision time for these structures, it is important to note the frequency of the CTMs focused exclusively on the needs of students.

Creating a Cycle for Collaborative Team Meetings

The overarching intent of CTMs is to examine the needs of students through the lens of classroom practices and develop appropriate

CHAPTER #3. Collaborative Structures

responses to address those needs, both for individuals and through a more universal instructional approach. However, there must be appropriate time between these meetings to allow the proposed practices and supports to be implemented as well as time for progress to be made by the student before reexamining what adjustments are necessary in the ongoing response. Keeping the idea of appropriate time between meetings in mind, we believe that CTMs should happen every three to five weeks, as determined by each individual school calendar. During a typical 10-month school calendar, these formalized meetings would happen 6 to 10 times per school year.

Ideally, the first meetings should happen by the third or fourth week of the school year, after allowing teachers time to learn about their students' needs coming into their grade level and adjusting supports that might have been carried over from the previous school year.

Potential Pitfall

Occasionally, leaders and their staff may misinterpret the three- to five-week cycle to mean that this is the *only* time that we talk about students. That is not what we suggest. Rather, this cycle determines the *formalized* timeline for CTMs, with the understanding that conversations about students will be ongoing, guided by the work of each classroom teacher.

Typically, CTMs are scheduled in three primary ways in schools. The following list is intentionally numbered from least effective to most effective, recognizing that not all schools may be at a place where option number 3 is a possibility—at least, they are not there yet. However, if CTMs and the connected collaborative planning time are truly an essential component of a school's Collaborative Response, they need to be established now, with the understanding that in time, schools will develop ways to more effectively embed them into the school timetable.

Scheduling Collaborative Team Meetings

1. Before/after school
2. During staff meetings/school planning days
3. Embedded into the weekly timetable

Before/After School

Although we do not promote the overscheduling of meetings outside of school hours, we recognize that for some schools, where the will of the staff team is great but the timetable proves to be a substantial initial hurdle, starting with CTMs outside of school hours may be the only option. We encourage school leaders to work diligently to find ways to plan these meetings during regular working hours, but such a schedule can be a suitable (and hopefully temporary) solution to ensure that CTMs are established (particularly if piloting the meetings with a particular team). We have worked with schools where after-school planning was the only way to initiate CTMs, with the school administration dedicated to ensuring that this configuration was only temporary. Setting and sticking to a time limit for after-school meetings is important in respecting staff members' willingness to attend and will increase the buy-in and commitment to these meetings.

During Staff Meetings/School Planning Days

We have worked with some schools that embed CTM times into the regular staff meeting schedule. For instance, in a school where one-hour staff meetings happen every two weeks, a school could determine that every third meeting will be reconfigured as time where CTMs occur, with multiple teams meeting at the same time. Although this schedule takes a more coordinated effort for those team members typically in attendance for all team meetings (i.e., administration, special education leads, counselors, etc.), it demonstrates a whole-school commitment to ensuring time to talk about the specific needs of students. Where multiple meetings are happening at the same time, administrators, special education leads, counselors, and others, who are normally involved in multiple team meetings but now spreading to the various meetings, are assigned to meet with a particular team and then meet afterward to share information and coordinate their efforts.

Some schools have utilized staff planning days, either determined by the district or the school. In these situations, schools either developed a schedule similar to the structure shared previously for staff meetings (multiple meetings occurring simultaneously) or a rotating schedule, where one team met, followed by another, and so on. This structure has two advantages:

1. team members, such as administrators, special education leads, counselors, paraprofessionals, and so on, could attend multiple meetings, providing insight and support for each team; and

2. during times when teams are not scheduled for a CTM, members can engage in the collaborative planning efforts described previously in this chapter.

With intentional planning, CTMs can be embedded into the existing staff meeting and planning day calendar for the school. However, this option still lacks the much greater benefits found when team meeting processes are embedded into the weekly timetable.

Potential Pitfall

While scheduling time for CTMs would appear to be relatively simple on staff meeting or staff planning days, there are a number of disadvantages. During these two dedicated spaces of time when all staff are available and are not dedicated to serving students, there are a few things to consider:

- There are many competing priorities that may sometimes take precedent over CTMs, such as district professional learning initiatives, timelines for school planning demands, or even regular school priorities such as report cards and individualized education plan timelines.

- The timing for staff planning days may not be frequent enough to create a consistent schedule to provide for responsive conversations about students and classroom practice.

- Emergent issues that require full staff awareness or participation can trump the time dedicated for CTMs.

Despite these potential complications, dedicating time during staff meetings or staff planning days can provide an opportunity to follow up on actions determined during CTMs and possibly provide an opportunity to prepare materials for supports suggested at the meetings.

Embedded Into the Weekly Timetable

It should come as no surprise that embedding time into the normal school timetable for teams to collaborate is the most effective structure for regular team collaboration, with CTMs happening every three to five weeks. The most common question is not related to the *why* but rather the *how*. Before exploring the latter part of this statement, let's examine how the CTM cycle operates when team time is established directly in the weekly timetable.

Cycle for Team Meeting Times

As discussed earlier in this section, CTMs are intended to occur every three to five weeks, dependent on the individual school calendar. So what happens during the other weeks? When time is embedded for weekly team planning time, alternate weeks (weeks where CTMs do not happen) become time for collaborative planning, taking a more instructional focus as described earlier in this chapter.

Companion Website Resources

3.9. Collaborative team meeting cycle: This document provides an overview of the team meeting cycle, sharing expectations about how teams utilize their collaborative time.

With embedded meeting time in the school's timetable, it becomes easier for administration to determine an annual schedule for CTMs. For instance, the annual school calendar may indicate that the first CTMs happen in the third week of September, during each team's meeting time that week. School leaders then ensure that whoever needs to be at each CTM is able to attend during that time.

Embedding Time for Teams

Few would argue the merits of providing time for collaboration during the school day. However, determining how to provide that time is not a simple task. We also have to be very mindful that student learning is not dismissed to create time for teachers to collaborate. The good news is that many schools have found ways to embed time for teacher collaborative teams while ensuring that the activities students were engaged in during that time were still robust. We acknowledge that creativity is needed when looking to create time for teams; however, so many schools have found collaborative time during the school day that we believe it can be done with some creativity.

Starting Steps

On our Jigsaw Learning website (http://jigsawlearning.ca), there is a Resources and Samples section titled "Collaborative Structures and Processes," where a section on "Embedding Time for Collaboration" can be found. Within that section, a number of resources are available, including the following:

- an online form, where we encourage schools to share how they currently provide time for teams in their school;
- a database of the submissions from schools, sharing how collaborative time is being provided;
- templates for planning and designing collaborative time in school timetables; and
- school samples sharing how time has been provided in their timetables for collaboration.

CHAPTER #3. Collaborative Structures

Essentially, embedding time for teams requires flexibility, creativity, and a willingness to try something new. In our experiences, we have just as many "bombs" in relation to creating team time as we do successes. It is all about taking risks as a staff team and finding what is effective for your school.

We had an opportunity to benefit from one of those moments of flexibility and staff creativity with a grade-level team during our work at our school in the initial stages of Collaborative Response. Concerned about the time being lost with their students as a result of current team structures in our school, this team suggested that they could, one day a week, use their lunch time, recess time, and after lunch sustained reading time at their grade level to meet, which actually amounted to increased time for the team. During this time, they would meet, have a working lunch, and engage in the formalized team processes we had established at the school. It would only involve having someone supervise their classes while eating and during the sustained silent reading time (a relatively easy problem to find a solution, as the classes could be easily combined for both these activities) as well as ensure that they did not have recess supervision during this time (an even easier problem to contend with).

Although this solution would not have been initiated by administration (due to impact on contractual time), it was imagined by a group of teachers who valued collaborative time together and were eager to find solutions that honored that time but also had limited impact on their students. If we truly believe in the need for professional, formalized collaboration in schools, school leaders must work with their staff teams to make it happen during the course of the school day. Ultimately, one of the greatest rewards in engaging in Collaborative Response is when your staff begins to value their collaborative time to a degree that they will engage in problem solving and inventive solutions to barriers that impede them from accessing their collaborative time through a regular and predictable schedule.

Companion Website Resources

3.10. Embedding time for collaboration: This thought organizer is intended to be used by a staff team when examining how they currently provide time for collaboration and other ideas they may have. Often, accessing the staff team for ideas can open other possibilities not previously explored by administration.

Potential Pitfalls

Reeves (2009) contends that "one of the least popular actions any teacher or school leader can take is to change the schedule" (p. 93). Many school leaders are hesitant to take steps that may be deemed initially to be undesirable or unpopular. Reeves agrees and concludes that change "inevitably represents risk, loss, and fear—a triumvirate never associated with popularity" (p. 93).

Making adjustments to the timetable is a bold move, but one that school leaders must be willing to make to ensure real change in how a school is structured to respond to students. Often schedules are steeped in tradition and may not necessarily provide the best use of time or ease in function but rather focus on how things have always been done. Once staff members are able to see how these changes can ensure that their daily work makes a meaningful contribution to the overall success of students, they will be more willing to give (Senge et al., 1994). This revelation may not be clear at the outset, and leaders need to be resilient, not opting for complacency to maintain popularity.

Providing time for collaboration is an essential first step. What happens during that valuable time is the next area that requires intentional focus, which is the focus of our next chapter.

Collaborative Processes

CHAPTER #4

Although the previous chapter concluded with a message regarding the importance of establishing time for collaboration, simply providing the time is not enough. Time for staff to be collaborating, particularly in relation to the needs of students, needs to be focused and purposeful, with a clear direction and succinct set of processes.

In the last chapter, we dedicated a significant amount of time to a number of structures, particularly collaborative planning time for teachers. Although we will expand on some elements that we only alluded to in relation to collaborative planning time, many of the processes we address in this chapter are most directly related to the collaborative team meeting (CTM), school support team meeting, and case consult team meeting layers. The formalized processes established when specifically examining the needs of students and potential responses are absolutely essential, so that time is most effectively used to discuss and plan with high levels of efficiency and purpose. Not only must the meeting be efficient, but it must also be positive, focused, and always moving toward answering the question, "What should we do?"

In this chapter, we turn our attention to seven processes to be attended to in the established collaborative structures, previously described:

- Team norms
- Defined involvement
- Agendas and notes
- Defined roles
- Celebrations
- Focus on action
- Collaborative meeting space

Team Norms

As described earlier, schools have traditionally been characterized by isolation, where teachers and staff members often shut their classroom doors to teach *their* class of students. Staff members may converge at staff meetings, share resources or consult with one another but on a collegial level. As teachers, if we seldom collaborate meaningfully with each other about individual student learning, we fail to move from the "me" to "we" mentality central to the success of Collaborative Response. Coming from this mindset, it would be unreasonable to expect that staff members would intuitively know and collectively agree on how they will work together. Schools can't assume that teachers will simply know how to work together when they first introduce collaborative structures. They can't believe that, if they provide the time and place where people meet together, this time will be immediately productive for each and every team or that productivity that could be experienced initially is sustainable over time. Simply put, we need to do more. In addition to the protocols and processes we have described thus far to guide the structures of layered collaboration, establishing, reviewing, and adhering to team norms is critical.

Lencioni (2002) shares an element of effective collaboration that points to the need for team norms. In his book *The Five Dysfunctions of a Team*, he posits that teams need diverse ideas and thoughts, but they also require productive conflict to continue to enhance what we call their collaborative efficacy. When teams work to build trust on a shared foundation, they are more prepared to engage in critical discussion that promotes problem-solving but not always immediate consensus. "They discuss and resolve issues more quickly and completely than others, and they emerge from heated debates with no residual feelings or collateral damage" (p. 203). Healthy conflict, coupled with defined relational expectations and norms for behavior, results in active, energetic collaboration that has the ability to solve problems and address critical topics that make a real difference in the lives of students. However, this productive conflict does not typically happen naturally, without the guidance of ground rules to govern interactions within the team.

> *If we seldom collaborate meaningfully with each other about individual student learning, we fail to move from the "me" to "we" mentality central to the success of Collaborative Response.*

Boudett and Lockwood (2019) provide us the following description of team norms:

> Norms are shared agreements about how a group will work together. They help us answer questions like: How will we treat one another? How will we engage with challenging content? What will we do if we disagree? Without having an explicit conversation about these questions, collaborative work tends to reinforce inequitable patterns that exist within an organization or society. (p. 12–13)

Team norms bring to the forefront and intentionally articulate what the team collectively agrees to do and how they will interact during their meeting times. Once established, these norms should be reviewed regularly and can be referred to when team members stray from their established purpose.

Companion Website Resources

4.1. Team norms template: This template not only records the norms developed by the team but provides guidance for teams when developing their norms with examples and areas on which to focus.

4.2. Process for establishing team norms: This one-page overview details a process for establishing team norms with the larger staff team in order to honor the voice of all staff members. Although it is important that a single set of team norms exist for all CTMs, it may be a consideration when first starting out to develop a shared set of school norms that function in all layers of collaborative teams. In time, individual teams may want to further refine to reflect their specific context, and teams may want to define their own norms when meeting regularly for collaborative planning time. However, living with a single set of schoolwide norms at the start may provide multiple opportunities to practice and refine these shared commitments across the entire staff population.

In the Field

In the Resources and Samples section of our website (http://jigsawlearning.ca), a large number of sample norms from schools have been shared for reference when developing norms within your own school.

Once team norms are established, it is important to review them regularly within the teams. We have worked with schools who have also made these norms visually accessible during their team meetings, through posters on the wall, embedded in their team meeting records, or even displayed on table stands. Each meeting, one norm can be selected to "practice" or discuss, to ensure that over time, the norms are living and constantly being referenced to support team conversations as they become more professionally challenging. When truly being lived, we can engage in productive debate or even conflict, as Lencioni (2002) suggests, as long as we remain true to our established norms that describe *how* we interact during these conversations.

These norms also become the document referenced if leaders need to directly address individual behaviors that may not adhere to a team's collective norms. In short, team norms describe, "This is how we will behave when we meet, and this is what we agree to do." The norms purposefully articulate what we may assume is understood but, in actuality, may not be the case for staff inexperienced with working in truly collaborative teams.

Potential Pitfalls

It is easy for school staff (and leadership) to assume that, as adults, teams already know how to work collaboratively and that team norms may not be necessary for their school. After all, we get along so well together already! In our experience, we have generally found that beginning conversations usually lack depth or critical inquiry, as team members get used to the concept of being vulnerable. However, as teams become more comfortable in these meetings and start to really critically analyze their collective practices in relation to student success, hard conversations will emerge and true collaborative work will lead to some levels of discomfort, which is good.

When discomfort does occur, team norms are a critical component for collaborative structures. Not planning to establish or review them with teams can slow the evolution of a school's Collaborative Response. It is easier to engage norms as a natural part of the initial introduction of team structures than to introduce them as a Band-Aid when meaningful and critical conversations emerge.

Companion Website Resources

4.3. Unpacking team norms template: This organizer can be used for schools and their individual teams to examine their team norms, making them explicitly relevant and identifiable as well as collectively articulating how we will respond when a norm is broken. This further process of unpacking the team norms can be done over time but allows the school community to understand the *why* behind our norms, what it specifically looks like and does not look like when being lived, and what we can expect as a response when broken. Many schools, when engaging in this final step, infuse a degree of levity to the response, such as someone breaking the norm of "arrived on time and prepared" is required to bring snacks the next time the team convenes!

Defined Involvement

It is not enough to simply state, "We are having a meeting." It is incredibly important that we clearly communicate who is expected to be involved at each layer of collaboration and who is expected to be around the table for each conversation. Because each layer of collaboration that we've described has a different fundamental purpose, participation of specific staff members or external partners may vary. When reflecting on collaborative planning time, CTMs, school support team meetings, and case consult team meetings, Table 4.1 articulates participants to consider for each structure (as an extension of the overview first shared in Table 3.1). Please note that when we refer to "learning support," we are referencing a role (or roles) that takes a lead in coordinating and facilitating additional supports for students with exceptional needs, recognizing that the role takes on many titles in schools, such as "Student Services," "Director of Special Education," "Inclusion Coach," "Inclusive Education Facilitators," "Intervention Coordinators," "Instructional Coach," and many, many more!

Table 4.1 Team meeting participation overview

MEETING	REQUIRED PARTICIPANTS	ADDITIONAL CONSIDERATIONS
Collaborative planning	Teachers	• Administrator as requested, when engaging in review, or when support is necessary • Educational assistants (depending on classroom role) • Other participants as requested or needed by the teachers in relation to their team focus
Collaborative team meeting	• Teachers • Administrator(s) • Learning support • Instructional coach(es)	Further exploration of additional participants is found in the "Maximum Adult Involvement" section in Chapter 5
School support team meeting	• Administrator(s) • Learning support • Counselor(s)	• Teachers and/or educational assistants, as needed • Depending on the school, there may be a number of other specialized roles, focused on coordinating support for students, involved in this team meeting
Case consult team meeting	• Administrator(s) • Learning support • Classroom teacher(s)	A large number of other participants may be involved, based on the student being discussed. This could include school staff, external partners, family members/guardians, and the student on whom the meeting is focused

COLLABORATIVE RESPONSE

Clearly defining the expected involvement for each layer of collaborative meeting accomplishes two things. First, it ensures that staff are aware of which meetings they are expected to attend and can plan for accordingly. Second, it not only communicates to the rest of the staff team who is involved in each conversation, ensuring overall transparency and coordination of meaningful structures, but also how each role within the building is contributing to the complex layering of support that maximizes staff expertise to best attend to the needs of our learners.

In the Field

At Robert W. Zahara School in Sexsmith, Alberta, Canada, leadership has developed a visual overview of each meeting in their school, in relation to Collaborative Response, demonstrating a coordinated approach to supporting the needs of students and a strategic alignment of their collaborative efforts. The visual, shown in Figure 4.1, defines the frequency, purpose, and expected participation for each structure. Some further related samples are shared near the end of Chapter 7, focused on a continuum of supports.

Figure 4.1 Robert W. Zahara School meeting overview

Collaborative Response Model Structure

Weekly Collaboration Time (Weekly)

Who's Involved?

- Grade Cohort

Purpose

- Review Date
- Create Common Assessments
- Make Team Goals
- Share Expertise
- Prepare for CRM Meeting
- Share Resources
- Develop New Programs
- Complete Actions in CRM Software

CRM Meeting (Monthly)

Who's Involved?

- Administration
- Grade Cohort
- Educational Assistants

Purpose

- Identify key issues related to students at Tier 1 and 2
- Focus on classroom instructional strategies and adjustments
- Reinforce practices consistent with QLE

CHAPTER #4. Collaborative Processes

Student Support Meeting (Wednesdays)

Who's Involved?

- Administration
- Inclusive Education Support
- Teachers and Educational Assistant as needed

Purpose

- Focused on individual students requiring Tier 2 and 3 supports

Team Meeting (as needed)

Who's Involved?

- Outside Agencies
- Classroom Teacher
- Administration
- Inclusive Education Coordinator
- Family/Parent
- Educational Assistant
- Inclusive Education Support

Purpose

- Focused on wraparound plans
- Necessitated by Student Support Meeting

Inclusive Education Preps

Who's Involved?

- Classroom Teacher
- *Inclusive Ed. Support

Purpose

- Scheduled time to discuss individual students and individual student needs
- Discuss ongoing supports or temporary supports needed

Source: ©2021, L. McKeith, Robert W. Zahara School, Peace Wapiti Public School Division, AB. Used with permission.

Agendas and Notes

Communicating a clear, formalized process, through the form of an agenda, is absolutely essential for each collaborative structure established within the school. It communicates a clear path forward for the conversation along with expected time intervals to help guide the productivity of the team and maximize efficiency for every participant involved. As Graham and Ferriter (2010) remind us,

> Team minutes are helpful because they document discussions and decisions. Too often participants leave a meeting thinking

one decision was agreed upon, only to find out later that something entirely different was implemented. By creating documentation, minutes allow teams to function without confusion or misunderstanding. (p. 100)

The agenda for each layer of team is going to be adjusted slightly to align with the purpose of the meeting, but there are some general guidelines to be considered when constructing an agenda and related notes document for any team meeting:

- *Consistent agenda format*: Establishing a consistent, predictable format for each team meeting is critically important for building familiarity, routines, and shared understanding for how the meeting should progress. We have seen many schools establish posters, such as the sample shared below, that communicate the consistent flow and timeline for the team meeting that can be replicated over and over again. The predictability of the agenda contributes to trust in the process and eventual intensification of vulnerability for meeting participants, which opens the door to deeper learning and willingness to consider alternate approaches.

Figure 4.2   Oski Pasikoniwew Kamik School CTM agenda poster

Agenda for
Mamaw-Ohpikihawaso'miskawasowihtowina
(Collaborative Team Meeting)

Prior to the Mamaw-Ohpikihawaso'miskawasowihtowina, teachers should come prepared with a celebration, 2–3 students they wish to discuss, and a KEY ISSUE for each identified student.

10 minutes
- Norms and Celebrations

45 minutes
- Key Issues and Tier 2 Supports

15 minutes
- Additional Students (Student Services)

10 minutes
- Identify Team Tasks

Source: ©2021, C. Auger, Oski Pasikoniwew Kamik School, Bigstone Cree Nation Education Authority, AB. Used with permission.

CHAPTER #4. Collaborative Processes

In the Field

At Oski Pasikoniwew Kamik School in Wabasca, Alberta, Canada, a poster that is displayed in team meeting spaces has been developed for their CTMs, which they have renamed in Cree, "Mamaw-Ohpi kihawaso'miskawasowihtowina." The poster, shown in Figure 4.2, articulates each section of the meeting, with time guidelines to help structure their conversation.

- *Infusion of team norms*: Infusing the team norms not only brings attention back to them on a continual basis for teams, but it also provides an opportunity to select one to focus on in each team meeting, which leads to deeper shared understanding and adherence to the collective commitments over time.

- *Agenda integrated into the notes document*: For each notes template we share for the different layers of collaboration, the agenda has been integrated into the document, with times indicated throughout. Structuring the notes document to reflect the agenda further strengthens adherence to a preestablished format and allows easy taking of notes by a recorder.

- *Projecting the notes*: We have seen time and time again that projecting the notes during a meeting for all participants to view is a powerful practice, to not only ensure that everyone is aware of the notes and ideas being recorded, but to also remain true to the designed process for the meeting. If the notes document has been constructed to carefully follow the intended agenda format, the projection of the notes can contribute to the overall flow of the meeting for all parties involved.

- *Explicit recording of actions*: As we will discuss later in more depth, key to any collaborative meeting structure is a driving focus on staff action. Discussion is not sufficient. We need to be constantly voicing the question, "So what are we going to do?" and ensuring that the actions we intend to take are documented, with clear indication of who is responsible and a timeline they intend for initiating and/or completing the action.

The specific agenda format for collaborative planning time was described in relation to the team planning guide earlier in Chapter 3, and we will dive deep into the uniqueness of the agenda and notes document for the CTM in Chapter 5. However, let's take a bit of time to focus exclusively on the meeting process, as reflected in the agenda and notes template for the case consult team and school support team meeting.

Case Consult Team

The agenda for the case consult team differs slightly from the other collaborative structures due to the complex nature of the meeting as well as the multiple participants. We would suggest that a very thoughtful process for the meeting be engaged through the agenda that might proceed as follows:

1. *Introductions and student celebrations*: This provides an opportunity for everyone to understand who is contributing to the discussion as well as specifically identify positives for the student being discussed. It is important not to assume that everyone around the table knows each other, particularly when family/guardians are part of the conversation.

2. *Student strengths and interests*: Focusing on the student's strengths and interests early in the meeting will provide a starting place for supports to be designed for the student later in the conversation.

3. *Student medical and/or diagnostic updates (if needed)*: For students who have intensive medical needs, it is important to update the team on current diagnosis, medications, and medical procedures.

4. *Area(s) of need or concern*: Consideration must be given to the order of voice when presenting and examining area(s) of need or concern. Parents/guardians should be given the opportunity to speak first in this area as they may be intimidated or be less willing to participate if they are requested to comment following the specialists or educators. Second, therapists or specialists should be given the time to speak on areas of need or concern. Finally, the educators bring forward their needs or concerns. This will allow the school and district personnel time to reflect on what is needed, respond to parent/guardian and specialist comments, and perhaps adjust or add to their areas of need or concern based on what they've heard.

Actions are captured throughout the discussion, including who is responsible and a timeline to support the commitment to the action, consistent with documentation recorded in all other team meetings.

Companion Website Resources

4.4. Case consult team agenda and notes template: This template includes the sequence and key elements for the case consult team meeting, along with space to include notes.

School Support Team

Similar to the case consult team, the agenda for the school support team is also somewhat unique and differs slightly from the other collaborative structures due to the focus on individual students, in addition to school-wide programming and supports. This agenda may include the following:

1. *Norms and last meeting review*: Focusing on one of the norms, each meeting provides the team with a reminder of "how we function together as a team." A quick review of the last meeting ensures that the committed-to tasks and actions have been accomplished.

2. *Student celebrations*: Identifying specific celebrations for the students sets the tone for the meeting and recognizes that students are making progress, often as a result of focused dedication of the teams in the school.

3. *Students from referrals*: If a school support team determines that it is appropriate for the school to complete a referral in order to engage the school support team, then the referral becomes the initiating factor for discussing students at this level.

4. *Additional students of concern*: Time is dedicated to emergent issues arising for students that may lead to additional supports required. This ensures that the school support team has a pulse on what is happening throughout the school and could possibly lead to proactive support being initiated.

5. *Review and closure*: Time is dedicated in the agenda to review actions and add any additional steps that should be taken as a school.

Actions are captured throughout the discussion, including who is responsible and a timeline to support the commitment to the action.

Companion Website Resources

4.5. School support team meeting agenda and notes template: This template includes the sequence and key elements for the school support team meeting, along with space to include notes.

Regardless of the meeting type, a clear and consistent process—reflected through the intentional design of the agenda and connected notes document—functions to keep team members focused and contributes to proficiency, flow, and productivity for everyone involved.

Defined Roles

In team meetings, a role describes the responsibilities and actions a particular team member will take on for the discussion in the particular collaborative structure. The use of roles serves three primary functions:

1. It creates an environment of shared responsibility, as each team member takes on leadership or supporting roles to ensure that the conversation is focused and productive rather than having that expectation rest on a single leader for the meeting. Once capacity is developed and the process for the meeting is clearly understood by all team members, the roles developed for the meeting can fluctuate, allowing shared leadership and opportunities for each team member to take varying levels of responsibility. Although it takes time for the process to be so deeply embedded that the leadership of each role can rotate, this level of distributed leadership is truly the hallmark of a strong professional community.

2. It ensures team attendance to the structures and processes established to enhance the productivity and effectiveness of the team meeting. The development of roles is intended to put structures in place, so that everyone is focused on the conversation, and has clearly understood mechanisms to ensure that it does not go offtrack.

3. It ensures engagement for multiple members of the team as they attend to their specific roles.

Although the defined roles will fluctuate depending on the type of meetings, three roles are particularly important in every meeting structure.

1. *Facilitator*: The facilitator essentially "chairs" the meeting, attending to the progression of the agenda and ensuring ongoing adherence to the established norms and setting the conditions that lead to "psychological safety," a key determinant of team success (Edmondson, 2019). As described by Duhigg (2016), two elements discovered by Google's Project Aristotle (a project focused on team effectiveness) that are seen as central to the creation of psychological safety are equality of conversational turn-taking and ostentatious listening. An effective facilitator endeavors to bring all team members into the conversation and ensures, through modeling and attendance to the norms, that their voices are being heard by all. Without explicitly establishing this role, it is entirely possible that the conditions that lead to high levels of vulnerability are not consciously attended to during the meeting.

CHAPTER #4. Collaborative Processes

2. *Recorder*: Producing a single, coherent set of notes from the meeting is essential, and assigning someone responsible for note-taking is a must for any successful team meeting. This role can also help support the facilitator, using the completion of the notes in a well-designed notes template as a mechanism for remaining true to the established agenda.

3. *Timekeeper*: The timekeeper plays an important role to remind the team when to move on to the next section of the meeting, keeping the flow respectful to the intended design of the conversation. Having the timekeeper prompt the team with reminders in relation to time ensures that the meeting remains focused and on track.

Potential Pitfall

Although formalized administrator involvement in team meetings is incredibly critical, it is important that not all roles are held by team members in formal leadership positions. Kurtis made the mistake of trying to hold multiple roles when first introducing CTMs (facilitator, recorder, timekeeper), thinking it would be beneficial to allow staff to focus on the conversation. However, it would have been much more valuable for the overall team development to distribute those roles, in time, to other members of the team and expect that everyone would engage in the variety of roles to build overall team capacity. Dispersing the roles (and in time, having different team members assume different roles) is an important consideration for all meeting structures.

In Chapter 5, we will further explore the infusion of other roles that can help meeting focus and efficiency, particularly in relation to the CTM.

Celebrations

Although the time dedicated to celebrations need not be extensive, it is a vital consideration to setting a positive tone to any meeting and placing focus on the impact that the individual and team efforts have on student success. Cassandra Erkens (2008) reminds us,

In a professional learning community, we also lead by cheering. We celebrate small wins along the way, attending to cultural impact and organizational values as we determine what and how to celebrate. The role of celebration cannot be taken lightly, especially as we nurture risk-taking and challenges to the status quo. (p. 44)

Celebrations create short-term wins (Reeves, 2009), which energize people by giving them a taste of victory (Kanter, 2004). Take a moment to consider which students would typically become the subject of collective celebrations. In our experience, our most at-risk or struggling students usually take the spotlight at the onset of the meeting, recognizing the small victories the team is achieving. Consider something as simple as "Darnel chose his own book for independent reading." "Marcy understands the basic concept of factoring." or "Michael has gone four days without a single altercation during break time." Such affirmations can give hope to the team to continue their efforts, even while realizing that these celebrations do not signify that the work is done. Instead, they provide collective energy to keep going, knowing that their efforts are making a difference for students.

However, merely identifying a celebration and moving on is missing an opportunity to surface successful practices. The key to the celebration discussion is uncovering *what we did that led to that success*. "Teachers' confidence in their peers' competence increases when they hear about each other's successes. In addition, knowledge about one another's work grows through sharing success stories" (Donohoo, 2017, p. 69). Over time, this builds high levels of collective efficacy across an organization, as we engage team members in every conversation to reflect on our collective practices that have led to success. This is where we can also turn our attention to the identified strengths and interests of a learner, to help potentially provide a path forward to leverage what a student can do well, in order to attend to a current struggle. Celebrations are not a "nice to have"—they are an essential process that generates momentum to continue moving forward to often envision innovative ways to provide the support needed for our students.

Focus on Action

We have all had the experience of completing a meeting, feeling as if much was said but little was accomplished. Pfeffer and Sutton (2000) note five barriers to using knowledge well. Their first barrier addresses the experience of talk becoming a substitute for action. This mistake equates *talking* about something to *doing* something. We hold meetings to discuss problem solutions—we might even write reports about actually doing something—but we never do much at all. Our products may include meetings, conversations, mission statements, and reports, but potentially not progress. In these examples, conversations become a substitute for action.

Consider an all too common experience when meeting to discuss the emergent needs of students. Students' names are raised for discussion, but the result is a litany of anecdotes and "war stories" related to the student, identifying multiple layers of the problem but failing to move toward action. As Fullan (2013) reminds us, "talk in the absence of action is *almost meaningless*" (p. 77).

Sometimes, this "talk" can manifest itself in a focus on blame rather than on productive next steps. Often a group's natural inclination is to identify problems being discussed as student-related (Sharratt & Fullan, 2012), and staff may find it "easier to put the burden on students rather than examine our own practices more closely" (Love et al., 2008, p. 351) or to direct attention to the parents. Blame can even be directed at previous teachers or inefficiencies in the school or greater educational system.

But blame is both fruitless and negative. Not only does engaging in blame stall progress, but by the end of the meeting, everyone feels less than productive. By ensuring that a conversation always moves toward, "So then what do we *do*?" we can place the focus on our response rather than dwelling on the cycle of blame. Simply stated, our collaborative efforts must assume an action-focused mentality. As we stated earlier, discussion is not sufficient. We need to be consistently driving to the aforementioned question, "What are we going to do?" if we truly want to see our collaborative efforts make a difference for students and staff.

Heath and Heath (2017) contend that "action leads to insight more often than insight leads to action" (p. 117). We could not agree more.

In the Field

At Crestwood School in Medicine Hat, Alberta, Canada, tent cards are present during team meetings, with one side reminding participants of the driving question, "So what are we going to do?" and their team norms and purpose of the particular meeting reflected on the other side of the card. Both sides of the tent card are shown in Figure 4.3.

Figure 4.3 Crestwood School team meeting tent card

Source: ©2020, C. Edwards, Crestwood School, Medicine Hat Public School Division, AB. Used with permission.

The actions we take *may* not lead to the success we were intending. But by taking specific actions, we may trigger a new insight, as suggested earlier by the Heath brothers, that can lead to a next step that *could* lead

COLLABORATIVE RESPONSE

to success. We can't enter into collaborative conversations assuming that we are going to uncover the secret solution. We must enter with a "willingness to try," to commit to actions that may work, but understanding that if they don't, it may lead to a new revelation or uncover next steps not able to be discerned at the outset. Actions matter!

Collaborative Meeting Space

Walk into any classroom that values collaborative learning for students, and it is relatively easy to see that the physical space is intentionally designed to support students learning from and working with one another. Tables replace desks, or desks are reorganized into pods or cohorts of students. Anchor charts abound, co-created with students, often with clearly articulated shared commitments, norms, or rights and responsibilities displayed to remind everyone what we need to do within this shared space. Instructional materials are within reach for the teacher to assist in teaching and learning opportunities with students. Exemplars and samples adorn the walls to help provide a further layer of support for students.

So the question is how can we replicate some of these intentional classroom design elements when we consider the spaces we engage in for staff collaboration? We recognize that physical space is often at a premium in schools, particularly when it comes to adult learning. After all, spaces for student learning should take precedence. However, we suggest giving consideration to how we can purposefully design a space for effective and focused collaboration for the adults. In the event that a collaborative space for staff is not a reality, a team member could be designated to set up the space prior to meeting, attending to a number of the considerations shared below.

When intentionally designing a collaborative meeting space for team meetings, it is important to consider the following:

- *Posting of team norms*: As examined earlier in this chapter, team norms need to be articulated, revisited, and practiced regularly for teams, which is difficult to do if not visually accessible. Whether through posters, stand-up picture displays, or other means, having the norms ever-present signifies their importance and easily allows continual referencing by teams.

- *Ability to project*: We discussed earlier the value of projecting meeting notes for the entire team to view during any team meeting. Ensuring that a collaborative meeting space has the ability to project a number of resources for the team is an important consideration.

- *Posting of team goals, schedule for team meetings, and other reference materials*: Artifacts and resources related to collaborative efforts should be posted for easy access and reference. These could include team goals, team meeting overviews, a calendar of important school events, standard agendas for team meetings, and team meeting roles as well as artifacts from staff conversations.

- *Displaying of overall data*: A powerful message is sent when the direct results or intended results of our collaborative efforts are within our focus when working together. Posting generalized trends and charts from our key assessment tools serves as a constant reminder of what our data are telling us to inform and influence our conversations.

- *Intentional seating*: No matter how the space is designed for seating, it needs to be thoughtfully set up for collaboration. Team members must be able to make eye contact with one another. Access to plugins for laptops needs to be considered. If some team members are on a couch while others are around a table, that is a great situation for a casual staff room conversation but not when the collaborative time is meant to be focused and purposeful. Casual seating may send the message that participant focus is not required and may actually invite unintended disengagement. If collaboration is going to be viewed as part of the regular "work" of our staff, the seating needs to be designed in a way that reinforces how we physically engage with one another.

- *Space for written thought*: Is there a whiteboard or dry-erase space accessible for sharing ideas? Is there a flip chart available, or paper to stick on a wall, or even whiteboard walls and tables (if you're fortunate to have them) to capture group discussion and brainstorming of ideas? It is important, when collaborating, that there is a space to capture the brainstorming or sketching out of ideas that may be generated from the conversation.

In Chapter 7, we will describe the value of a clearly articulated continuum of supports and the potential value of also visualizing the interventions, strategies, and accommodations found within it in a collaborative meeting space.

Companion Website Resources

4.6. Collaborative space planning checklist: Checklist to assist in planning and refining collaborative spaces for staff, particularly in relation to work connected to Collaborative Response. It is not meant to be exhaustive, but rather a list of considerations when establishing or refining collaborative team spaces.

Although not always a possibility for schools due to space limitations, purposefully and strategically constructing a space that helps support schoolwide collaborative efforts can help reinforce and promote many of the structures and processes described in the last two chapters.

Don't Ignore the Process

Establishing the time for collaborative structures within the school is the first step, but it is critically important to attend to the processes during those structured times, as described in this chapter. When first starting out, the processes may seem over the top or not necessary in order to engage in conversations about students. However, we have seen countless examples in schools where the effectiveness of the conversations hit a plateau, and it is often because a layer of process has been skipped over. School leaders lament that team members are not committed to the collaborative processes but have not engaged in regular review of team norms to help reinforce the way we agree to behave and engage with one another during the meetings. Team meetings are not time-efficient, but they have not determined a timekeeper role to help keep the conversation on track. In time, we want the collaboration to go to a deeper level of examination, questioning, and challenging our current practices—but this becomes difficult if we have not intentionally constructed processes that help us arrive at high levels of trust, vulnerability, and productivity. As stated throughout this chapter, process matters!

Process is absolutely vital when we engage in CTMs with our teams. Chapter 5 will now dive into the processes specific to this critical layer of Collaborative Response.

Collaborative Team Meetings

CHAPTER #5

Teachers talking about their students is not earth shattering. In schools we visit, we hear teachers conversing about students all the time. In the staff room, after school, during breaks, and on the weekend, teachers are continuously sharing strategies, asking other teachers about specific students, and sharing their frustrations and successes. Red flags go up when we *don't* hear such conversations.

When children are not the center of teacher conversations, the culture differs. In such schools, conversations revolve around adults— needs of staff members, problems with parents, complaints about administration—and the list goes on. We particularly worry when schools follow an unspoken rule that teaching and learning conversations will not happen in the staff room or outside of classrooms. We believe that teachers *should* talk with each other about their students, and we believe that these conversations should be edifying (or at the very least provide opportunities to work through solutions). Teachers absolutely need to talk to each other in this increasingly challenging and complex profession.

When, how, and to what end we talk about our students is critically important. Although *informal* conversations about students throughout the school can indicate a staff working together to support one another and support their students, these conversations alone are not enough. Conversations revolving around the needs of students in the classroom need to be formalized and purposeful. They need to happen regularly; they need to be focused; and they need to lead to positive actions. In other words, they need to become a part of the school's "way we do things." As we have noted earlier, reshaping school culture is key. The regular, focused, purposeful conversations about student learning are truly at the heart of the collaborative team meeting (CTM).

When reflecting on the layering of collaborative structures outlined in Chapter 3, it is not unusual to see most schools with some versions of collaborative planning time, school support team meetings, and case consult team meetings. The missing and critical layer is the CTM. If Collaborative Response is the vehicle for providing a schoolwide response for individual student needs, the CTM is the engine that drives it. These ongoing, collaborative meetings not only provide sources of support, action, and response for student learning, but they also provide opportunities for teacher support within a model of distributive coaching. In time, the examination of students drives a deeper conversation related to classroom practice and the explicit support classroom teachers can provide for their students. This chapter will explore considerations for these meetings, investigating the various elements and ideas inherent within them

COLLABORATIVE RESPONSE

and what makes them unique and different from the other layers of teams. Before we dissect them for further examination, let's visit a CTM in action.

As you read through the vignette, reflect on the following questions:

1. Who is involved in the meeting, and what role do they play?
2. How often do these meetings occur during the school year? How can they be embedded into the school's timetable?
3. How is the meeting process formalized to place direct focus on student needs?
4. How does effective facilitation move the discussion from students to effective practice?
5. How is information shared and collected related to individual student supports?

A Collaborative Team Meeting at Focus Junior High

Irene, the principal at Focus Junior High, is having another busy day. This week, CTMs are happening in her grades 7 to 9 school, with six different team meetings scheduled over the next three days. These are the second set of CTMs happening this year, with the first set happening at the end of September. Now, in the final week of October, the school year seems to be flying by!

Irene has cleared her schedule to ensure that she is a part of each team meeting. Not only is she personally involved in each CTM, but she also facilitates them. She is planning to slowly release this responsibility, but for now, her involvement as facilitator is purposeful. In only the second year of implementing these meetings, she needs to continue to communicate, both through her words and, more importantly, through her actions, that these meetings and their focus on supporting students, as well as their building of collective teacher practice, is the primary work to be done in the school. Staff know that only critical emergencies are considered higher in priority than these meetings over the next three days.

Today, five minutes away from the first meeting of the day, Irene is busy in the conference room ensuring that the CTM record template is projected for all participants to view and the keyboard is out and ready for the recorder. She has the visual display board set up, showing the names of the 80 eighth-grade students on little recipe cards stuck neatly to a trifold science fair board, arranged in tiered categories. Today, the team assembled are responsible for approximately half of the eighth-grade population. Tomorrow, the other eighth-grade team will assemble. Because this conference room is used for parent meetings as well on other days, the transportability of the boards is still a necessity. The plan is to move to a digital version of these visual displays, to eliminate the need for the bulky physical boards and allow continued development of ongoing student profiles. This task has already been added to the evolving "to-do list" for the school's Collaborative Response, as they constantly look at revisions and improvements to their current model.

On the table are copies of the school's current continuum of supports that is going through yet another revision following the school's last professional learning day, where they infused in a number of accommodations they had learned about during a recent "Teaching for Trauma" workshop. The table also includes a number of role cards, including facilitator, timekeeper, recorder, and interrupter, as well as some question prompt pages that Irene is intending to introduce for the first time today to start getting the team more engaged in probing the practices of their colleagues during the conversations.

The bell rings and, over the next two minutes, the eight chairs are quickly occupied. Each participant arrives with a data overview page, including the progress monitoring data from the past month, which was placed in mailboxes on Monday morning. Each team member also has some notes jotted onto the pre-meeting organizers, which they know they are required to bring. She takes a moment to pull up the team norms and reviews them quickly with the team. Irene suggests that today they will practice their norm of "we will question for clarity and understanding" and hands out the question prompt pages to her team. She asks that during the course of the meeting, each team member strives to ask at least two questions of their colleagues from the list of questions from the page and that they will determine at the end of the meeting how they did. After taking a moment to determine who will take on the roles of recorder, timekeeper, and interrupter, which have now become ingrained in the team meeting process and do not need review, she asks if everyone is ready to get started.

Each meeting starts with celebrations, and team members are eager to share some of the exciting progress being made by eighth-grade students related to the academic engagement of students, the focus of their school, and subsequently for these meetings. A number of teachers draw attention to the progress being made in the students' individual portfolio development, which is no surprise to Irene. This year, teams have designed a collaborative goal and priority around the development of online student learning portfolios to increase student ownership of their learning, so it is great to have the teachers paying particular attention to progress being made in this area.

One paraprofessional involved in the meeting remarks, "Desirae is showing excitement and asking really relevant questions during our current social studies focus on economics!" Such an accomplishment is huge for a girl who previously had little interest in anything to do with social studies. Irene probes a little deeper, asking what the team thinks we did to bring about this change? It is identified that connecting the economics unit to different

(Continued)

(Continued)

industries, such as fashion and gaming, has really engaged a number of students. Another staff member suggests that the specific modeling of questions to ask has also really had an impact on Desirae. Irene smiles, joins in the congratulations, and watches as the recorder dutifully records notes in the CTM record, which is projected for all to see.

As the timer for 10 minutes goes off, Irene ensures that the team is ready to move along. Irene asks, "Who should we start with today?" One teacher consults her pre-meeting organizer and offers Raheem's name. She notes that Raheem is becoming increasingly distant in mathematics, refusing to engage in conversations, and completing little in class. One of the teachers jumps in, drawing attention to her question prompt page to ask, "Why do you think the student is struggling in this area?" The teacher responds back with uncertainty, although she notes that the current supports she has been using, such as daily agenda reviews and the key vocabulary guide, seem to have made little impact. Another teacher notes that he has noticed Adam in her classes needing to understand the "why" of what he is learning or he seldom engages. The teacher admits that this could be what is happening, as she hasn't really been as cognizant about discussing why certain math concepts are important for students beyond the classroom. Irene suggests that "Connection to why for learning" be the key issue to focus on, and the teacher agrees that that could be the case.

Irene then asks the other team members to reflect on their students and determine any others where "Connection to why for learning" may also be an issue. The team collectively determines another six names to add to their notes, including Adam.

Irene then shifts the conversation, asking the team to begin soliciting ideas for how they could make connections to the "why" for learning for students. During the conversation, the team is highly engaged, sharing a number of ideas from their own classrooms and using the questions from their prompts page to dig deeper with their colleagues. At one point, a science teacher shares that he uses an organizer with his students where they have to brainstorm for particular concepts about how that concept could be applied in a real-world setting. The other teachers ask if they could receive a copy of that organizer, and the recorder assigns the action of "Share real-world connection organizer" to the teacher, asking if she could include a due date of this coming Friday. The conversation continues, as a paraprofessional suggests "Personal conversation with the student," a Tier 2 support currently listed on one of the school's continuum of support placemats that have been passed around the team.

After a few minutes of brainstorming, Irene turns her attention to the teacher who initially brought up Raheem, asking if there is any support or idea suggested during the conversation that the teacher can commit to trying in their classroom. The teacher responds that she is going to try the idea of checking in with Raheem using a 1-2-3 scale that had been suggested by Darcy, with 1 being "I'm not sure why I'm learning this" and 3 being "I know

CHAPTER #5. Collaborative Team Meetings

why I'm learning this." The action is noted in the meeting records. Irene then goes around the table, asking teachers who identified other students what they are planning to take on as an action to support their identified student. One teacher remarks, "I like the 1-2-3 check-in idea but I'm just thinking now I could do that through an online response program on my Smartboard, to gauge understanding for all students. I think I'm going to try that!" Each teacher commits to an action and timeline connected to the student they identified. However, one teacher adds, "In relation to Arman, I think there are some other factors getting in the way of him engaging in class." He asks if Arman could be added to the agenda for an upcoming school support team meeting for that team to dig a little deeper. The recorder makes a note, and Irene adds into the notes a chance to meet with the teacher prior to that meeting to collect some additional information. A paraprofessional, who does a morning strategy group, suggests also adding Arman to her list as it may be a way to make an additional connection for him that may be helpful. The group agrees and adds it to the notes, with an additional action that Jackie will add Arman to the next school support team meeting and send home a parental update regarding his inclusion in the morning strategy group. Darcy stands up and moves the recipe cards of all students discussed to the "Tier 2" category on the visual display board, with Arman's name being placed under "Tier 3."

The meeting continues. At one point, Irene engages one of the teachers who has been less vocal today, asking if they had a question they could ask from their page in relation to a student conversation. As students are discussed and actions put into place, recipe cards move on the board to recognize changing levels of support for students. It is encouraging to see one student move down a tier, because Alexander was not only experiencing success in the morning strategy group but in other areas as well. The progress monitoring data definitely supported the growth being observed by those working with him! The team quickly celebrated as Alexander's card was moved from "Tier 3" to "Tier 2" on the visual display board, and they coordinated which Tier 2 classroom strategies should remain in place over the next four weeks. It definitely was atypical to see movements being made in that direction on the board in only October.

The timekeeper interrupts saying that they only have 5 minutes remaining. Irene redirects the conversation to determine if there were any team tasks that could be taken away from today to be accomplished in the team's next collaborative planning time. One teacher suggests that they would like to see what the classroom response system that was mentioned in the Raheem conversation looks like. The team also suggests that it would be great to have common criteria for what engagement should look like in the classroom, co-created with the students. The recorder documents both these potential team tasks in the notes. Irene quickly reviews the staff list of responsibilities and ensures that each participant knows their "to-do list" before leaving the meeting. They then take a moment to celebrate that the challenge of two questions each was easily accomplished. Irene playfully suggests that she will let the other eighth-grade team know tomorrow of this team's accomplishment prior to their meeting!

(Continued)

(Continued)

Before leaving, the recorder prints 11 copies of the notes. Eight copies are for those present and an additional three copies are printed for the teachers who instruct students in this particular eighth-grade cohort but are not involved in this team. This had been an area of concern for the teachers last year, but with the refinement of the structures, the meetings can be highly productive to respond to student needs and subsequent teacher practice without everyone who teaches the cohort in attendance for the meeting, a situation that is just not possible when timetabling. One teacher is assigned the task of meeting directly with those three teachers to explain what had been discussed and the support agreed to be put in place. The individuals depart, and Irene closes the visual display board, returning it to her office, and collects a seventh-grade board, with the purpose of bringing it back to the room to prepare for the next meeting on the schedule. She makes a mental note that the continuum of supports placemat was only explicitly referenced once during the course of the CTM. Maybe it needs to become a specific role for a future meeting?

Starting Steps

For many staff members, seeing a CTM in action can help them understand what it looks like and the substantial shift away from a generalized, oversimplified understanding that it is a meeting where we talk about students. There are a large number of sample CTMs found in the Collaborative Response Samples and Resources section on the http://jigsawlearning.ca website, as well as in the following Companion Website Resources.

Companion Website Resources

5.1. Collaborative team meeting playlist: A number of sample CTMs have been collected in a YouTube playlist and are accessible through the Companion Website.

5.2. Collaborative team meeting observation organizer: Observation template to help focus attention on particular key features while observing a CTM in action.

Substantial Shifts

In the vignette, there is a visual team board present, with student cards being moved as a result of the conversation. We have discovered that the visual team board is an important element of the process in time but not necessary when first introducing CTMs. In fact, they make more sense when schools have infused data and evidence, and continuum of supports components into their process. The visual team board will be further discussed in Chapters 6 and 7, where it really solidifies its value in relation to identifying student entry levels based on data and evidence and visualizes the tiering of *supports* for students, not the students themselves.

Although not explicitly stated by Irene in the vignette, the cornerstone for these meetings is a culture of acceptance, respect, and trust, which must be developed and nurtured over time. This culture ensures that the learning community can effectively work together to share strengths and expertise. The team approach asks questions focused on specific, relevant, and meaningful information about students while working together to collect data and discover solutions. This conversation then shifts to the sharing, adoption, and transformation of classroom practices in a safe space where every individual has something to offer. Teachers no longer work in isolation but are provided a foundation for successful collaboration and effective professional growth, which at the heart is improved student learning. Ownership is fashioned as the stakeholders work purposely to improve; they are motivated, committed, and involved. CTMs become an avenue for teachers to fulfill their moral purpose. As Reeves (2009) states, the "message is 'You are so valuable and worthy, our mission is so vital, and the future lives of our students are so precious, that we have a joint responsibility to one another to be the best we can be'" (p. 11). We work together to support each other and our students.

Establishing Collaborative Team Meeting Structures and Processes

As demonstrated in the vignette, the CTM needs to be highly structured, follow clear processes, and ultimately be focused on what we can be doing in our classrooms to support the identified needs of the students. When considering the layers of collaboration, the CTM should be considered the arena where a conversation about an emerging need arises to engage the collective expertise of the team, prior to the movement of a student to subsequent school support or case consult team meetings. In time, the conversation *initiated* by a student need becomes the mechanism to engage in a deeper examination and discussion related to transforming classroom practice.

When establishing and then refining the structures and processes integral to the CTM, the following considerations need to be taken into account:

1. Maximum adult involvement
2. Focus and timeline for meetings
3. Pre-meeting processes
4. Defined roles
5. Team norms
6. Meeting agenda and notes
7. Celebrations
8. Focus on key issues
9. Action focused

These considerations are not sequential but rather highly interrelated as the pre-meeting processes help individuals arrive ready to discuss celebrations and key issues, help ensure the meeting agenda and notes align to the focus for meetings and ensure action-focused responses are captured, and so on.

Companion Website Resources

5.3. Reflecting on collaborative team meetings template:
To be utilized to reflect on CTM structures and processes, to help determine potential next steps or areas to focus on.

Substantial Shifts

The infusion of the "key issues" process for CTMs has been a critical learning and has had a monumental impact on the focus and purpose for the conversation. Prior to this infusion, teams would come together focused on an individual student but often become overwhelmed with the multiple variables affecting success (several of which may be out of our collective locus of control, a concept explored later in this chapter), with several team members potentially less engaged in the conversation if not teaching the particular student being examined. The infusion of the key issues in relation to a student not only allows multiple students to be attached to the conversation to engage more team members, but also allows the focus to be placed on the *issue* rather than the student, with the ability to more productively unearth supports at the classroom level that could be considered. The "key issue" process will be discussed later in this chapter, but its infusion has dramatically changed the focus for CTMs, and it is also connected to the layers of team meetings concept explored later in the book.

Maximum Adult Involvement

We know that "no teacher can possibly possess all the knowledge, skill, time and resources needed to ensure high levels of learning for all his or her students" (Buffum et al., 2009, p. 51). However, schools have traditionally operated within this premise, leaving teachers in isolated classrooms, working tirelessly to meet the expansive needs of an increasingly diverse population of students. In Collaborative Response, it is not enough that teachers alone come together to participate in CTMs. These meetings must involve as many staff members as possible to maximize the exploration and infusion of different ideas and perspectives to stretch everyone's collective thinking and to engage a broader network of adults aware of their responsibility in supporting students in the school. This group could include, but is not limited to, the following:

- Classroom teachers
- Administrators
- Special education coordinators
- Learning support/specialist teachers
- Coaches (literacy, inclusion, etc.)

- Paraprofessionals/educational assistants

- Counselors (social workers, family–school liaisons, etc.)

- Liaison workers (First Nations, Hutterite Colony, etc.)

- Indigenous cultural advisors (elders and knowledge keepers)

- District or external specialists (speech language pathologist, occupational therapist, behavioralist, psychologist, etc.)

- Any other staff members who can provide insights/supports to the group of students that are the focus of the CTM. Who these staff members are may depend on the focus chosen for the team. (For example, if social-emotional learning is the school focus, counselors are critical to that discussion but may not be an ongoing part of the team if literacy is the focus.)

Although participation will be highly contextual and specific to each school and potentially each meeting, the old adage "two heads are better than one" definitely applies. The diversity of thought and approach that comes with maximum staff involvement is critical. This diversity provides both multiple perspectives and a greater base of individuals who can help provide various responses. Over time, this group continues to build capacity within the school. It is also interesting to note that "collaborative cultures lend support but also contain powerful peer pressures" (Fullan, 2006, p. 64). Essentially, working together in CTMs can raise the quality of everyone's performance related to *all* students and their continuous growth. Collaboration also carries accountability and that's a good thing.

According to Surowiecki's (2004) *The Wisdom of Crowds*, the "many" are smarter than "the few." Surowiecki believes that teams work best when there is *cognitive* diversity. It is not just the smartest people; it is the outliers who can make a difference. Surowiecki's work suggests that more diverse groups, even when they don't always contain the "smartest people," will, when conditions are right, consistently make *better* decisions than groups filled with *only* the smartest people.

What this means for CTMs is that teams composed of only classroom teachers may defer to a narrow instructional point of view, particularly if those professionals lack the trust to question and engage in difficult conversations. In addition, one of the main reasons why conversations can be difficult is because people are afraid of looking "inept" or "out-of-step" with those people around them—again, going back to the human comfort of similarity. What CTMs can enhance is an acceptance and celebration for on-task, first-draft thinking—creating a space where all ideas are invited and considered. Such first-draft thinking can take the seed of an aberrant idea and grow it into something of pedagogical substance.

Our experience is that most really good teachers have come to rely on and perfect a small handful of pedagogical strategies, which they use over and over again. But what happens if one of these strategies does not work with a particular student? Here is where another teacher's strategies *might* prove helpful. In a CTM, "teachers focus on each other's strengths and the knowledge each brings to the table" (Stoehr et al., 2011, p. 74).

However, that scope is expanded when including other staff members in the conversation. Although each school context will bring with it different challenges and not all roles can be represented in the manner detailed below, striving for maximum adult involvement adds to the dialogue of the CTM. It also enhances the feeling of responsibility for students within the collaborative team and the school. In time, conversations begin to revolve around *our* students, not the students in someone else's classroom or those students who become the sole responsibility of the special education department. Let's examine the value of five particular staff groups in the CTM: administrators, assistants, counselors, special education coordinators/teachers, and specialists or other external partners.

Administrators: Administrators, whether principals or assistant principals, play a valuable role in CTMs in a number of different ways.

1. Participating in these meetings focused on student needs and pedagogical responses speaks loudly about what is truly most important in the school. Administrators who set the myriad of other responsibilities aside to roll up their sleeves and actively participate in these meetings show true commitment to collaborative efforts and a laser-like focus on student needs and responsive classroom practices. In addition, Robinson, Lloyd, and Rowe (2008, as cited in Fullan & Quinn, 2016), who conducted research on the impact of school principals on student achievement "found that the most significant factor—twice as powerful as any other—was the degree to which the principal participated as a learner with the staff in helping to move the school forward" (p. 54). Working alongside the team to share strategies to support learners can have a tremendous impact for students, staff, and the overall school community.

2. The meeting is yet another opportunity for administrators to continue to communicate key messages for the school and the priority placed on student growth and progress. "When the administrator is actively involved in adopting the model and sends the message through ongoing meetings and discussions that it is a school priority, there is a greater chance of success" (Haager & Mahdavi, 2007, p. 260). Administrators who are truly part of the "we" galvanize and recognize the efforts of each staff member.

3. Involving administrators in CTMs can provide an additional level of response when planning and coordinating supports for students. Picture the following scenario, related to addressing student behavior:

Team Member 1 (teacher):	"If we could take those three students together for ten minutes after lunch recess, we could debrief recess and discuss what positive choices they made when playing with other children."
Team Member 2 (paraprofessional):	"I'm supposed to be in the grade 5 class right after recess but they typically take about ten minutes for independent reading time following the break. I'm sure it would be all right with the teacher if I were a little late. The only problem is that I have supervision at the other end of the playground during the lunch recess and it would be difficult to maintain that supervision and then dash to catch those three students at the other end of the school after recess."
Principal:	"No problem—I can make a supervision adjustment to put you at that end of the school during lunch recess. I'll take care of it and email you the adjustment."

Administrators have the ability to recognize and make these adjustments and macro-level revisions, which can be tremendously beneficial when problem solving to determine creative and responsive interventions and actions to support students in the CTMs. Imagine the previous dialogue without the administrator involved in the meeting. So many more things would have to happen. Someone would have to take the responsibility of making the request to an appropriate administrator, who now does not have the background information involved leading to the request. The whole process adds another level of bureaucracy and time to put what should be a simple action in place.

4. Perhaps the most important reason for administrative involvement in the meeting is the knowledge a principal or assistant principal gains about students, staff collaborative efforts, individual teacher instructional responses, and other vital information directly related to the most fundamental purpose of the school's existence—student learning. As a principal who participated in all CTMs, Kurtis was able to gain an intimate understanding of students in the school as well as how staff worked together to meet those complex needs in the classroom. Classroom observations, walk-through processes, reading report card comments, or ongoing conversations with individual teachers and students could not have provided the same depth of knowledge and understanding that participation in CTMs assured. Administrator involvement is critically important in CTMs.

Getting Started

When first starting with CTMs, consider having the principal (or other designated administrators) serve as "facilitator" for the meeting, as Irene did in the vignette that opened this chapter. Because we know that "the principal's presence signals that the work being done is important and teachers perceive this as an acknowledgement that their efforts are being recognized and appreciated" (Moller & Pankake, 2006, p. 80), playing this important role at the onset of establishing these meetings sends a powerful message. In time, this role can (and should) shift to other team members as capacity is developed (a concept further explored in this chapter). However, when an administrator serves as the leadership model for how schools collaboratively address and work to meet students' needs, the importance of these meetings is amplified.

Paraprofessionals: Whether referred to as educational assistants, support staff, or paraprofessionals, noncertified staff working with students have an important role to play in CTMs and in the resulting supports established for students. Paraprofessionals provide a valuable voice, often not accessed when discussions are left solely to groups of teachers and administrators. These staff members often work very closely with students daily and, even when designated to an individual student or small group of students, can offer a different view of student strengths and needs that adds another layer of understanding to the discussion. Often, these individuals provide alternate perspectives and can be valuable resources when determining how best to respond to student needs. It also adds another group of individuals who are aware of and committed to student success.

When noncertified staff are recognized as valuable voices around the table, that recognition also positively affects their efficacy in the school and increases another level of commitment to doing all they can to support all students, not just those with whom they have the most contact. We often share in workshops with schools how, during the course of one CTM, we were discussing the need for continued sight word practice for a small group of students and an educational assistant spoke up to remark, "All those kids are at the school early every school day. I could come fifteen minutes early to do a small group sight word practice with them daily as a way to start their day!"

Although coming to school early was not a job expectation or a request that would have been placed on any individual, it became an effective support activity for those students. With an administrator involved in the conversation, it was an easy next step to make arrangements that still honored the contractual terms for the assistant's employment. It also demonstrated the level of commitment our assistants had to playing meaningful roles on the team and doing all they could to ensure the success of *our* students.

Counselors: The role of counselor, social worker, or family liaison varies wildly based on school and jurisdictional definitions; but when we speak about counselors, we refer to those individuals who work closely with students and families on issues typically outside the locus of classroom control but that greatly affect student learning. In our definition, counselors are often connected to outside agencies that support students and families and ultimately work to ensure classroom success regarding the social and emotional needs of those students. These individuals often bring alternate views of students and insights that may not be known to those working with students most closely in the classroom to CTMs. Often, they may have historical understandings of students and families that provide valuable insights into root causes and appropriate supports for students. Typically, they help bridge outside-of-school (when needed) supports and provide a greater knowledge of students' classroom learning. Most important, they can also be suggesting universal instructional responses that may benefit not only students being targeted, but other students as well.

Special education coordinators/teachers: The lack of a consistent definition of a counselor role pales in comparison to the range of job descriptions related to special education or inclusion in schools. Traditionally, a resource room or special education teacher may have held this seat at the CTM. Teachers in this role in traditional schools may not have had much experience working inclusively in classrooms. They may have worked with students in a pullout model of support and provided the premise for coding students for funding. They may have worked with teachers to build individual student program plans or provide specialized assessments. Essentially, they were the teachers for the "special education students," and often, their roles involved working in conjunction with classroom teachers; but depending on the school culture of support, that role might not have been necessarily collaborative.

The role of a special education coordinator, specialized teacher, learning coach, learning support teacher, inclusive facilitator, inclusion coach, or whatever the role title may be looks vastly different today. These roles work in classrooms with groups of students in partnership with classroom teachers. They are working collaboratively with teachers to differentiate lessons and provide support for inclusive instruction that benefits all learners. They are essentially both supporting students and teachers. Their work requires a set of working relationships within the school that rely on support, trust, and credibility. Teachers in these roles require professional credibility with colleagues, especially in school cultures where teachers traditionally close their doors to focus on isolated teaching practices.

A great way to begin building credibility and trust for individuals in these roles, as well as pave inroads to working with teachers in classrooms, is through involvement in CTMs. Our teachers with specialized training can suggest alternative instructional strategies, volunteer to enter classrooms for support, arrange external supports and assessments and a myriad of other provisions, and focus on ways to support children. Involving our traditional special education teachers in these meetings brings the following benefits:

▶ The focus is placed on students, not teachers. It becomes far less intimidating for a specialized teacher to enter a classroom when focused on the students and their identified concerns and not the teacher's instructional practices. However, focus on instructional practices inevitably becomes an intentional outcome of student-focused conversations.

▶ Classroom teachers see these colleagues as truly committed to the best interests of students, which in turn builds trust in the collective.

▶ Classroom teachers hear about the impact the learning support role may be having on students in other classrooms and the support they are providing. Often, guards are dropped when success is witnessed in other colleagues' classrooms.

▶ Support for teachers can be differentiated, knowing that not everyone adopts practices at the same pace. Although it may take a little longer to develop trust and acceptance with some staff members, that patience will pay relational dividends in the long run.

Inclusive supports provided by a specialized learning teacher role may be a smooth and painless transition for some schools. However, for schools where this shift is greater, the CTM can be a great venue for specialized teachers to begin building credibility and establishing their role as one that supports the learning needs of *all* students, a pillar of establishing equity for all students across the school. However, the specialized learning teacher does not need to be viewed as the fount of all instructional expertise for students requiring additional support. In a CTM, all team members can assume a coaching role, as the situation warrants. This broadening of the concept of learning coach becomes a type of *distributive coaching* in schools as different individuals adopt coaching roles with colleagues based on particular students or instructional strategies being explored. In this sense, everyone can be an expert and simultaneously be prepared to assume the role of learner in some situations or coach in another. In this distributive coaching environment, the formalized coaching role is not diminished but enhanced as expertise is organically extended throughout the staff team.

Specialists/external partner members: Often, the extenuating needs of students, particularly in relation to occupational therapies, speech therapies, mental health, and other areas, can fall outside the expertise of teachers and other staff members in the school building. Tapping into external expertise can be of tremendous benefit when continuing to build the professional capacity of the team and responding to the needs of students.

Involving targeted specialists is not a novel concept for schools, specifically in programming for students with exceptional needs. However, traditionally, this involvement was focused on the needs of individual (and typically coded) students and resided in the case consult team meeting layer proposed in Chapter 3. Through involvement in the CTM, these specialists can suggest universal strategies and supports that can have an impact on a greater number of students and simultaneously add to the collective classroom strategies teachers might employ. The greatest benefit can be for students with needs lacking the severity to, at least in the past, receive this level of service and support, but who can still benefit greatly from less-intense, inclusive examination of supports at the classroom level. As with other roles, the voice of the specialists and other members of external teams can only add to the richness of conversation and subsequent actions. Of course, accessibility to those specialized roles can be a deterrent in being available to attend these meetings.

Potential Pitfall

Access to specialized support roles during CTMs can be highly advantageous to strengthening the universal practices in classrooms, especially in the case of Speech Language Pathology, where much of their work is highly connected to foundational instructional practices for teaching reading. While it is extremely beneficial to have specialized supports attend CTMs, there are also some cautions and considerations.

When asking an external partner to join your CTMs, ensure that they understand the purpose and function of the meeting. Specialists in these roles inherently focus on individual students. It is advantageous to specifically share your expectations for their involvement, focusing on strategies that would support many students and not targeting supports of any one student.

School staff are often familiar with external providers as they have likely had previous experience with various team members in problem solving in regard to specific individual students. In having this prior relationship, school staff may expect and perhaps even anticipate that the specialists at the table are there to provide the answers. In this case, a prior conversation with the team to understand their role as participant rather than expert will support the conversations to proceed in the intended format.

In the Field

As a former principal in an elementary school, Kurtis and his team supported a distributive coaching model by recognizing the expertise every staff member brought to the conversation and finding ways to provide time for that collaboration to occur. It was not unusual for Kurtis or the learning support teacher to cover a teacher's class to allow an opportunity for one teacher to observe or learn from another colleague in the school. Providing time for professional learning and distributive coaching was accomplished through attendance in CTMs and recognizing that tapping into the diverse expertise in the school raised the professional capital available to ensure student success.

Of course, one of the greatest benefits to ensuring maximum adult involvement in CTMs is the collective knowledge that can be accessed and shared regarding universal classroom practices and supports (later referred to as Tier 1 and 2, as described in Chapter 7). Bringing diverse perspectives and equally diverse skill sets to the table can result in instructional innovations or possibilities perhaps not imagined when participation in the meetings is limited. However, there is a tipping point. Too many individuals around the table can be problematic, as opportunities to provide voice become limited and, as a result, disengagement increases. Our general rule of thumb is a CTM is optimal when it involves 3 to 5 teachers, with additional roles that ensure that overall participation does not exceed 8 to 10 people. Once teacher participation extends beyond 5 and overall participation extends beyond 10, conversations lose their rigor and the examination of practice becomes much more surface level. The bigger the team, the more likely for members to disengage or to not be able to collectively agree on next steps.

Starting Steps

Some schools, when first introducing CTMs with staff, have purposefully established larger groups for the meeting initially, with the intention of communicating key features through the experience of participation. Although this is highly effective when first learning about the structures and processes for the CTM, leaders must be cognizant that the large groups are shifted over time to smaller teams as we've described, to truly attend to the examination and reimagining of universal classroom practices. Although a larger group may be valuable for collective awareness of students across the school, it is important to remember that this is not the *purpose* of the CTM. If the collective awareness and discussion of students for a large group is important for your school, infuse it as another layer of collaboration for school teams such as a 15-minute "student awareness" item on the staff meeting agenda. However, that practice in time should not be mislabeled as a CTM.

Focus and Timeline for Meetings

Chenoweth (2009), in an article for *Phi Delta Kappan,* shared her findings about schools that succeed even when challenged with high-poverty, high-minority demographics. She believes that two common facts bolster student achievement: these are "reduc[ing] teacher isolation by providing time for teachers to work and learn together" (p. 41) and ruthlessly organizing around "helping students learn a great deal" (p. 39). Time for teachers to work and learn together is central to Collaborative Response, as was discussed in Chapter 3. However, Chenoweth's second tenet requires further examination. Although we would argue that every school aims to help students learn a great deal, perhaps the most critical concept in this statement is contained in the phrase "ruthlessly organizing." CTMs must ensure, in time, that team members "ruthlessly organize" around a common focus.

Effective organizations, including schools, establish a few "big ideas" or overriding principles that unite people in the pursuit of a shared purpose, common goals, and clear direction (Tichy, 1997). Schools need to narrow their focus, determining few or even one "core goal" for the organization. Once those core goals are established, these goals become the focus for the CTMs and the alignment of areas of focus for collaborative planning, as previously described in Chapter 3.

The core goal(s) established by schools focus on skills and understandings most central to student success. Literacy is often at the heart of this focus for many schools, particularly at the primary or elementary level. In fact, "One thing that high-performing schools uniformly do is establish literacy as their primary pursuit" (Reeves, 2007a, p. 237). We know that kindergarten literacy achievement can predict high school graduation (Hanson & Farrell, 1995); that nearly three-quarters of students who are poor readers by the end of third grade continue to be poor readers through ninth grade (Francis et al., 1996); and that increased time is needed to remediate a student with poor reading skills in later grades (Hall, 2008; Juel, 1988; Lyon & Fletcher, 2001).

Obviously, early reading success is key to later student success. However, literacy proficiency, specifically reading, is also a significant focus for junior and senior high schools. Tovani (2004) reinforces this point, "One critical concept embraced by both researchers and literacy specialists is that learning to read doesn't end in the elementary grades. Reading becomes more complex as students move into middle and high schools" (p. 5). Hence, literacy is typically a common goal focused on in schools and subsequently in the CTMs.

However, literacy may not be the primary focus for all schools. We have worked with schools that have placed their attention on numeracy proficiency. We have encountered high schools focused on student engagement. Many schools, particularly when attending to the realities brought about by the COVID-19 pandemic in 2020, have placed focus on student wellness or social-emotional learning and working to develop self-regulation skills for students. Regardless of the school's improvement goals, the CTM essentially becomes the space where we suggest

CHAPTER #5. Collaborative Team Meetings

students not likely to see success in that area and then use that as a jumping-off conversation to determine adjustments or additions to our classroom practice, build collective capacity, and identify areas of further learning that help contribute to progress in our improvement priorities.

In the Field

At Savanna School, a small K–12 school in northern Alberta, Canada, staff are divided into two teams for their CTMs, one involving elementary teachers (division 1–2) and the other with junior and senior high teachers (division 3–4). The school has established an annual timeline of focus areas for their CTMs, based on areas of focus for their school. The overview document, shown in Figure 5.1, shares the focus for each scheduled team meeting throughout the 2018–2019 school year.

Figure 5.1 Savanna School team CTM schedule (2018–2019)

DIV	DATE	TIME	FOCUS	STUDENT ACTIVITY
No students	Aug 31 2:00 pm		Procedures, norms, etc	
Div 1 & 2	Sept 26 period 5/6	12:24-1:45	Literacy	
Div 3 & 4	Sept 26 period 7/8	1:45-3:08	Literacy	
Div 1 & 2	Oct 24 period 7/8	*2:00-3:08	Numeracy	
Div 3 & 4	Oct 24 period 5/6	12:24-1:45	Numeracy	
No students	Nov 21 after school 1 hr		Literacy/Numeracy	
Div 1 & 2	Dec 12 Period 1/2	8:55-10:16	Social Emotional Learning (SEL)	
Div 3 & 4	Dec 12 period 3/4	10:16-11:37	SEL	
Div 1 & 2	Jan 23 period 3/4	*10:30-11:37	Literacy	
Div 3 & 4	Jan 23 period 1/2	8:55-10:16	Literacy	
Div 1 & 2	Feb 20 period 5/6	12:24-1:45	Numeracy	
Div 3 & 4	Feb 20 period 7/8	1:45-3:08	Numeracy	
Div 1 & 2	Mar 14 period 1/2	8:55-10:16	SEL	
Div 3 & 4	Mar 14 period 3/4	10:16-11:37	SEL	
Div 1 & 2	Apr 24 period 5/6	12:24-1:45	Literacy/Numeracy	
Div 3 & 4	Apr 24 period 7/8	1:45-3:08	Literacy/Numeracy	
No students	May 17		Year end wrap up	

*elementary students have recess directly before this time, so the period is 15 minutes shorter than the others.

Source: ©2020, T. Sauder/C. Young, Savanna School, Peace Wapiti Public School Division, AB. Used with permission.

It is important that "leaders in sustained successful organizations focus on a small number of core priorities, stay on message, and develop others toward the same end, making corrections as new learning occurs" (Fullan, 2011, p. 30). As leaders, our role is to ensure that all oars are rowing in the same direction and, by participating in the CTMs, school leaders ensure that this focus remains true.

Starting Steps

When first initiating CTMs, school leaders play a critical role in keeping the meeting aligned to the identified focus area. Without this focus, meetings can go off on multiple tangents, lacking clarity and cohesion, frustrating staff, and leading to little action for students. As processes are established and a solid system of support is developed around a focus, meetings will become more efficient and collaborative. In time, team meetings may be expanded to take a broader view of individual student needs (a wider variety of focus areas). However, starting with a broad scope will most likely not bring positive results. When first initiating collaborative meetings, focus must be placed on process and purpose.

Pre-Meeting Processes

Nothing halts the progress and intentionality of a CTM more dramatically than asking, "So who should we talk about?" and team members need to take a moment to review their class list before coming up with a name to initiate the discussion. When this happens, it is rarely data informed and quite possibly reactionary. The same student names are raised. Students being attended to in other team meeting structures are identified. We need to ensure that team members come to the CTM ready, with students preidentified, connected to the focus for that particular meeting, and with some initial thought given to what they know about the learner and the connected key issue they intend to bring for collaborative examination.

The utilization of a pre-meeting organizer for teachers can help ensure that CTMs are focused, efficient, and intentional, with teachers engaging in thought prior to the collective conversation.

> **Companion Website Resources**
>
> **5.4. Pre-meeting organizer:** This simple pre-meeting organizer requires teachers to come ready with four students in mind for the CTM, in relation to celebrations, students of concern, and a student requiring enrichment or challenge. When using this template or a variation, it is important to think of it as notes for the teacher for the discussion. They are not intended to be submitted, nor should they have extensive details, becoming onerous work for a teacher prior to the CTM. A print copy with quick jot notes is all that is needed, as the resulting conversation is much more powerful.

Three overarching reminders are important when introducing pre-meeting organizers (or a variation) to the CTM structure:

1. *Keep it simple*: It is critical that the organizer is brief, limiting the amount of information needing to be included or the workload required to complete it prior to coming to the meeting. This is not a referral form. Infusing too much information can actually have a negative impact on the key issue discussion, described a little later, as the focus can become too specific in relation to an individual student. Remember, the conversation that *results* from the prework is what is vital. The organizer is essentially only to help prep for that conversation. If your pre-meeting organizer includes a rich examination of an individual student, it is likely best to be used as a pre-meeting organizer for a school support or case consult team meeting.

2. *Keep it to teachers*: Although we want maximum adult representation in the team meeting to add to the diversity of the discussion, it should be the role of the classroom teachers in the meeting to come ready with the students to be discussed. As we'll explore later, other student names can arise during the conversation to target our attention, and these can come forth from any team member. However, the pre-meeting organizer should remain a responsibility of the classroom teachers in attendance.

3. *Keep the number of students limited*: Although the number of students discussed in the team meeting can grow through the conversation, and the supports and differentiated classroom practices affect entire classrooms of learners, it is valuable to keep the number of students identified in the pre-meeting organizer reduced. Quality trumps quantity when engaging in the discussion

COLLABORATIVE RESPONSE

related to the students' needs. In fact, it is highly probable that the meeting will not address the identified needs for all the students that are brought forth by teachers through the pre-meeting process. What is important is that a teacher has a predetermined response when asked the question, "So who should we focus on next?"

Defined Roles

In Chapter 4, we discussed the importance of roles in all collaborative meeting structures. The two most critical roles when first introducing CTMs in a school are the facilitator and the recorder.

Other roles can then be introduced to the CTM structure, either at the onset or over time, as the need for other roles becomes apparent. We have found that starting the CTMs with a determined and intentional number of roles is incredibly beneficial to the overall process. It is always easy to "phase out" some roles when no longer needed for the team meeting while introducing other roles when they become important.

Table 5.1 documents a number of variations for roles that we've observed in a variety of schools.

Table 5.1 Collaborative team meeting role overview

POTENTIAL ROLE	DESCRIPTION	NOTES/CONSIDERATIONS
Facilitator	Responsible for ensuring the flow and direction of the meeting. Ensures that structures and processes established for the meeting are honored	• Keep focused on determining action, rather than extended discussion • Return attention to being data informed • Promote inquiry through questioning and engagement of all team members
Recorder	Responsible for recording student notes and actions in the appropriate notes document	• Ensure that discussions have an attached action with assigned staff member and completion date • Ensure that all team members receive a copy/have access to the team notes
Timekeeper	Responsible for ensuring overall meeting efficiency and attendance to time	• Keep the team consistent to determined time allocations (for celebrations, student discussion, end time, and other structures) • Ensure awareness of end time for the meeting
Interruptor	Responsible for ensuring conversations remain focused and directed toward action	• Ensure that the role is clearly understood by all team members • When discussion is leading away from action, interrupt to say, "Yes, but what are we going to do?"
Cheerleader	Ensures that a positive tone is maintained for the meeting, with attention paid to student strengths and interests	• Consider interjecting or holding up a role card (or other signal) when a conversation deviates to negatively frame a student or their needs • Ask questions to determine student strengths or interests when unsure

CHAPTER #5. Collaborative Team Meetings   109

POTENTIAL ROLE	DESCRIPTION	NOTES/CONSIDERATIONS
Continuum curator	Attends to the continuum of support to review and offer suggestions for supports when discussing students	• Valuable to consider assigning this role to a teacher early in their career • Consider adding any additional strategies, accommodations, or interventions discussed to the continuum
Data investigator	Constantly reviews the data source(s) to help determine students to discuss or key issues to focus on	• Role can be broken up into multiple roles (someone attending to gradebook, someone looking at log entries, etc.)
Norm analyst	Ensures that the norms for the meeting are being honored throughout the team meeting	• Determine an appropriate response that can signal when a behavior is deviating from the norms • Suggest a norm to focus on for the meeting • Report after the meeting how the team did in respect to honoring the norms

Companion Website Resources

5.5. Team meeting role cards: Developing role cards that can be assigned to team members is a great way to let the team know what role each member is playing during that particular meeting, as well as provides team members adopting those roles information regarding what their particular job entails (with a description of the roles on the back of the card). In addition, table display stand templates and multiple samples are available at http://jigsawlearning.ca

From the Field

At Pat Hardy Primary School in Whitecourt, Alberta, Canada, role cards are used at team meetings, with unique role names established, as shown in Figure 5.2.

Figure 5.2 Pat Hardy Primary School team meeting roles

Norming Norman

Review norms at start of meeting.

Optional: Remind the group what that norm would look like (or not look like) if following it.

"What if" Willard

If a problem arises, offer up a suggestion.

What if we . . .

Clarifier Clara

Make sure others are heard by clarifying when necessary if there seems to be confusion.

Positive Polly

Help find the positive during difficult conversations.

Tommy Timer

Help to refocus the discussion and keep us on time. Time the sections of the meetings.

Rhonda Recorder

Record the information into the Collaborative Response software or on paper.

Action Annie

Write down (in point form) the action list to review at end of meeting; include the action and person responsible as the meeting takes place.

Leader Lenny

Lead the meeting.
Follow the agenda.

Source: ©2020, M. Moon, Pat Hardy Primary School, Northern Gateway Public Schools, AB. Used with permission.

ClipArt Source: PresenterMedia

Team Norms

We have suggested that the establishment of team norms is important whenever teams are coming together to engage in meaningful conversations. In the case of CTMs, they are absolutely vital. Essentially, they define the "rules of engagement" that we agree to adhere to during our discussions.

CTMs are intended to place focus on the classroom practices we are employing to support students and, in time, require us to examine what could be some very deeply held instructional beliefs for teachers. This requires maintaining high levels of respect for the work currently occurring in the classroom while remaining open to possibly new approaches or innovative thinking in order to meet the needs of identified students. As a result, CTMs have the potential to be fraught with mistrust; rigidity to what has worked in the past for *most* students; fear of exposing practices not having substantial impact; and recognition that unfamiliar interventions, strategies, and accommodations may need to be employed that really push our professional boundaries. Team norms must not only be specifically designed for these meetings, but must also be continually reinforced and practiced over time. It is through this process that we can collectively arrive at high levels of trust, vulnerability, and openness to new ideas throughout the school.

Getting Started

As discussed in Chapter 4, it is advantageous to develop a set of common norms for CTMs for all teams. This ensures consistency across the school, particularly as individual staff members potentially engage in multiple team meetings.

It is also beneficial to wait until after an initial CTM to construct the norms specific to this collaborative structure. Because the focus and purpose of these meetings may not be something staff members have previously experienced, team members may need to experience one or two of these meetings before being well equipped to reflect on norms that could be used to guide their effectiveness and set expectations for how we act or behave when engaged in these collaborative conversations.

Having a team norm such as, "We will remain open to new ideas and possibilities when it comes to our classroom support for students" may serve as a reminder if only displayed and casually referenced at the onset of the CTM. However, that may not be enough to truly bring that norm to life over subsequent meetings. We want to take an opportunity to explicitly practice and reflect on that norm. Consider the following directive provided by a facilitator following a cursory review of the team norms:

So today, let's focus on our norm, "We will remain open to new ideas and possibilities when it comes to our classroom support for students." Let's strive to have every teacher agree to two actions they will take, in connection to identified students, that they are not currently employing in their classroom. Then at the end of the meeting, we will each give ourselves a personal rating on a scale of 1 to 5 of how you felt you did in relation to that norm and be ready to share why you gave yourself that rating.

In this scenario, we are articulating specific measures that we will take during the course of the meeting to reinforce and explicitly practice a particular norm. Done once, this may not have immediate impact. But employing this practice over time begins to have influence and truly brings the norms to life for the team. Engaging in this explicit reinforcement would be next to impossible if the team norms were not already established, to serve as a reference point for "practicing" effective collaboration.

Companion Website Resources

5.6. Reinforcing norms compilation video: Video showing clips from three different CTMs, where different facilitator strategies are being employed to reinforce established team norms.

5.7. Strategies for deepening norms: A collection of ideas and strategies for deepening norms throughout the school and specifically in CTMs, collected from school leadership teams in Medicine Hat Public School Division in Alberta, Canada.

Meeting Agenda and Notes

The intentional design of a CTM is absolutely critical to its success. Without a solid and clearly communicated agenda in place, the process can digress into "a time to talk about kids," which may yield some benefits but not to the depth truly intended for the CTM. This is not like any other meeting. It is specifically orchestrated to use the student experience to not only identify and reinforce individual and collective efforts that are making a difference for students, but to also share and, in time, critically examine what is happening in the classroom and specific actions staff members intend to take to build on current practices.

In an effective CTM, a great deal of conversation takes place, determining current strengths and struggles for students, potential classroom practices to explore, and the responsive actions to be taken. The purpose of the team meeting notes can be twofold. The first obvious purpose is to document the meeting, particularly the actions to be taken in relation to each student.

The second purpose relates to how the meeting record is utilized during the meeting. We encourage teams to visually display the notes as they are being created, using digital projectors or collaborative online tools. This visual display effectively provides a focus for the meeting, reminding participants of the process to which we need to adhere. Furthermore, it allows collaborative agreement for the actions to be taken, as team members visually confirm what is recorded as the meeting progresses. The meeting record can also be a visual organizer that aligns with the formalized process for the meeting, as established in the meeting agenda and notes template shared below. In this template, the visual record clearly organizes the process, moving from celebrations to identification of a student with a key issue, other students with the similar issue, possible classroom practices or supports to be considered, and then the actions each individual (or the team) intends to take as a response. Time is also identified in relation to each section of the meeting.

Companion Website Resources

5.8. Collaborative team meeting agenda and notes template: This is a template to be modified for CTMs, with infusion of the agenda and time designations. Includes space for recording all elements discussed in this chapter as a comprehensive notes document.

Schools and districts may also wish to investigate WeCollab as a digital solution for team meeting notes, which includes many more features to fully support Collaborative Response across a school as well as a district. Further information can be found at http://jigsawcollaborativesolutions.ca

Following CTMs, these records should be posted digitally for all team members to access in a secure space. We have also known schools to print copies for the team members to organize their next steps following the meeting.

With this in mind, a suggested basic agenda would look like this:

5 Minutes: Review norms, establish roles

10 Minutes: Celebrations

40 Minutes: Key issues discussion

10 Minutes: Additional students

5 Minutes: Review of tasks, team tasks, and closure

The optimal time frame for a CTM is 45 to 90 minutes. With anything less than 45 minutes, it is typically difficult to engage in the level of depth, discussion, and brainstorming critical for the CTM process described in the following three sections. If engaging in a purposeful, focused, and challenging conversation, the CTM can be mentally exhausting. Going longer than 90 minutes is likely going to extend beyond the mental stamina of most participants, if truly engaged in hard conversations. Focusing on the three procedural elements of celebrations, key issues, and actions, the CTM can shine a targeted light on classroom instruction, strengthen collective efficacy, and establish meaningful next considerations for instructional practice to have an impact on the identified needs of students.

Celebrations

Consider the following interplay from an example shared earlier in relation to the importance of celebrations:

Team member A: "I would like to celebrate Darnel, who finally was able to choose his own book for independent reading last week!"

Facilitator: "That's excellent! So what have you done that you think may have led Darnel to choosing his own book?"

Team member A: "Hmmm . . . well, I guess I've been modeling how to choose a best-fit book for independent reading."

Facilitator: "Excellent! What does that look like in your classroom?"

Team member A: "I teach the students to turn to a random page of a book they are interested in and try reading. If they encounter five words that they struggle with in a half-page, I have them consider a different book. I've got a poster of it as a reminder near my classroom library."

Team member B: "Would I be able to get a copy of that poster?"

As demonstrated in the short vignette, three things are happening during this celebration:

1. *Identifying a specific success*: Getting very specific on the success is important during the celebrations (i.e., "Darnel chose his own book for independent reading" rather than "Darnel is improving so much since the start of the year"). Although an overarching celebration like "I've been so impressed with the work ethic of all the students in my AP Chemistry course" can be positive, narrowing down to specific student successes is important. It not only helps the team see success through the experience of a single or small group of students, but also sets the stage for the conversation about what we did that led to that success.

2. *Active listening and questioning by the facilitator*: The role of the facilitator is critical to helping the team uncover what we did, or what the individual teacher did, that potentially led to the student's success. This process does a number of things. It prompts the team member to reflect on specific actions and classroom practices that may be having an impact. This builds a sense of efficacy, that what we are doing, even if it may seem minor, is making a difference. The facilitator questioning also openly shares different classroom practices, approaches, or actions being taken that could provide an "aha" moment for others in the room, revealing our instructional toolboxes for all to see. In time, this questioning skill can be replicated throughout the whole team, with any team member inquiring about what the others are doing that is leading to success for students.

3. *Sharing of successful practice*: The uncovering of individual and collective practice is the primary intention of the celebration process. Although starting off positive sets a good tone for the overall meeting, the explicit identification of actions that are having success uses the student celebration as a mechanism to articulate what is working in individual classrooms or collectively across the school. That sharing can identify practices that other team members may not have considered or are not aware of what particular practices look like.

By focusing on student celebrations and unpacking what we did that led to that success, the meeting sets the stage for a discussion around classroom practices and, over time, contributes to an overall strengthening of collective efficacy across the entire team. What we are doing is having an impact. How can we continue to replicate these small successes across the entire student population?

Focus on Key Issues

Substantial Shift

Focusing on the key issue in relation to students has been an absolute game changer and transformed the CTM to *truly* focus on classroom, universal practice, using the student experience as a way to initiate a conversation. It has allowed teams to be assembled that may not need to know every single student being identified and discussed, leading to more effectiveness of the CTM process, particularly at the secondary level. It has enhanced the sharing and collective ownership of issues being addressed and led to tighter levels of team cohesion. Although schools were certainly finding success with CTMs as we had described them in the past, a focus on key issues has taken it to an entirely other level!

Let's start by examining what a conversation about students could look like *without* a focus on a key issue and the subsequent process we'll describe.

Team member A:	"I'd like to talk about Saralynn. Although she has learned a number of comprehension strategies, she is still not accessing them regularly in her reading. I've been sending home some practice books at her level, but her parents never seem to do anything with them. Her writing is also far below grade level. Whenever we start a writing assignment, she becomes distracted and then starts to distract others. I'm really worried about her, as it seems she's falling further behind on a daily basis."
Team member B:	"I taught her brother who was like that as well. Have you tried talking to Saralynn's dad about the reading activities? I found him to be really helpful for her brother Bradley."
Team member A:	"I've tried, but he doesn't seem receptive to helping out."
Team member C:	"Have you tried using speech to text for her writing?"
Team member A:	"I think she would become even more distracted with the technology."

CHAPTER #5. Collaborative Team Meetings

Team member D:	"Have you tried providing a checklist of reading strategies on a bookmark that she could have at her desk and check off the ones she's using?"
Team member A:	"Yeah, I could try that. I'm not sure that it will work, though, as I doubt she will be able to self-identify strategies even when she is using them."

We are positive that you have heard these exact conversations multiple times throughout your career just as we have. This is a typical scenario when a school engages in a traditional problem-solving approach. Let's dissect some insights from this interplay that would have been common prior to the introduction of the key issue process:

▶ *Multiple issues identified*: In Saralynn's case, the teacher identifies a number of things the student is struggling with, including the lack of parent support that really is outside of the teacher's locus of control (more about that in a later Potential Pitfall). As demonstrated by the responses from other team members, it is hard to focus on any single issue in depth as they are trying to address a number of concerns. In addition, by identifying multiple issues that are happening, the rest of the team really needs to have an understanding of who Saralynn is to really offer plausible solutions for consideration. This is usually not a problem at the elementary level but becomes more difficult at the junior and senior high levels, where a team could potentially interact with hundreds of students collectively, and it is highly probable several members on the team may not teach the student or possibly even know who they are.

▶ *Focus on a single team member*: In the conversation, all the focus is placed on a single teacher struggling with a student. Although the simplified interplay showed a teacher seemingly receptive to the suggestions of other team members, this may not always be the case. In a sense, the problem is owned by a single individual. This can, in some situations, lead to a number of negative outcomes. The teacher could become defensive, dismissing ideas being suggested without fully considering or even understanding what the practices look like. The teacher could be looking for someone else to "fix" the student—they've done all they can do, now it's someone else's responsibility. The teacher could become overwhelmed with everything being suggested that they should do. Other team members could become disengaged, seeing it as not their problem and waiting until it's "their turn" to talk about one of their students. Other participants may also quit providing suggestions if they feel that they are not being openly received by their colleagues. In a sense, this teacher is in the "hot seat" as others inundate with a plethora of ideas (received or not), while still other teachers are potentially disengaging.

▶ *Limited examination of classroom practices*: Although a skilled facilitator or a team that already has high levels of trust can overcome this, the interplay shows limited examination of practices or actions being suggested. Everyone is throwing out potential ideas but without the time to ask, "So what does that look like in practice?" In the most positive of cases, a teacher would be asking, "How do you do that?" or, "Can you share that with me?" In less-than-positive cases, ideas may be dismissed not because they lack validity but because an individual may not have a particular skill set *yet* that would enable the adoption of a new approach or strategy.

The oversimplified example of a conversation does illustrate an interchange that may lead to little action being determined, potential frustration for all meeting participants, and putting the cause of the struggle back onto the student. In essence, it can *reinforce* low levels of collective efficacy—that there really is little that we can do for this particular student.

Let's take a moment to step back and accept a truth. In the past, an instructional leader may be aware of students who are struggling in classrooms or, more typically, of teachers who may be struggling to support a particular student or group of students in specific areas. They observe less-than-effective practices being implemented and student needs not being attended to in a way they would like to see. The traditional response may be to engage in a conversation about instructional practices, support the development of practices through a myriad of professional development opportunities and models (albeit coaching, observations, workshops, etc.), and possibly move to an evaluation process. These conversations and teacher interventions are typically focused on the teacher and, in some cases, can be at best difficult and at worst confrontational. Furthermore, they are based on leadership hierarchies of power—the very idea we are trying to disrupt in our work.

Consider how the focus shifts from the teacher to the student, through the CTM, in this particular vignette. As you read, reflect on the following questions:

1. How does a focus on collaborative practice simultaneously honor and nudge the teaching capacity of Mr. Howard?

2. How does the structure and facilitation of the CTM reinforce a culture of professional sharing and risk-taking?

3. How do the collaborative structures bridge the classroom and special education practices within the school to build collective capacity?

Supporting Mr. Howard

Two years ago, Alice, the principal at Lincoln Memorial High School, was in a conundrum. It was no secret that Mr. Howard was in need of support in relation to some of his classroom practices. Although he was well known for the ways in which he engaged students in his high school social studies courses to dive deep into the content matter, through debates, re-creations, and different projects, he was not as proficient in supporting the needs of students who had the ability to understand the concepts being explored but had literacy gaps that made it difficult to attend to the textual resources he was using. Alice's classroom observations also supported her concerns as Mr. Howard often became visibly frustrated with students who had difficulty reading the text, which he felt "was at grade level." For these students, he struggled to engage them as they grew increasingly aware of his frustration. This had led to a number of students either dropping his courses, performing well below where they should be, or engaging in disruptive behaviors that further added to Mr. Howard's difficulty working with them.

Alice had engaged in conversations with Mr. Howard regarding his instructional practices in relation to addressing literacy gaps. Although respectful, these conversations had led to little change, nor had the observation time she had set up with another teacher in the school. Despite all her efforts, the instructional practices being suggested or initiated (both directly and indirectly by her) were having little if any impact on his instructional responses for students behind their peers in reading. In addition, Mr. Howard believed responsibility rested with either the students, who should be taking initiative to get extra reading help to improve, or with previous teachers, who failed to provide the students with the literacy skills essential for success in his high school courses. If they couldn't read what they needed to be reading, they shouldn't be in his courses! Why was the special education department not taking on more of the students struggling in his classes? Alice knew that she would need to take the next steps to move to more difficult and potentially contentious conversations.

During this time, the school was also in the development stages of establishing Collaborative Response structures and processes in their school, with the first CTMs starting. The teams had been strategically constructed to involve 4 to 5 teachers, but each teaching different content specializations. This ensured not only a mixing of subject specialists, but also a blending of teacher expertise and experience, strengths, and areas in need of growth. When constructing the teams, administration had been very intentional regarding the membership, particularly in relation to who could potentially provide support in this area where Mr. Howard was struggling. Teams also included members of the special education department.

The first time Mr. Howard brought forth a student where he determined the key issue was "unable to read grade-level text," it confirmed to him that the other teachers also identified the names of students with whom they were

(Continued)

(Continued)

experiencing the same issue (he even recognized some of the names!). He knew this must be happening as well for the other teachers and further reinforced what he felt was a need for the school to look at some further remediation programs for these students before they entered his courses.

However, the conversation turned to brainstorming about ways in which teachers could respond when students were not able to read grade-level text but had the ability to comprehend the curricular concepts being explored. An English teacher suggested the practice of digitizing the text and then using a text-to-speech application (it involved the use of a website he had never heard of before). Another teacher, who taught sciences, suggested the use of a peer to read the text (something he was sure other students would resent). Someone else interjected, saying, "What if we had a willing student read the text and record it for other students to potentially access?" A mathematics teacher chimed in to say, "What if we developed a bank of student recordings that could grow over time to supplement our text resources?" One of the instructional coaches from the special education department offered a website she was aware of that had varying degrees of text complexity that corresponded with key curricular concepts.

When the facilitator asked what action Mr. Howard was intending to take for the student he had brought forth, he responded that he wasn't sure if anything suggested would work but agreed to commit to trying to use the digitizing website that was suggested, and when Alice asked, "Do you need any help in accessing or using that website?" he respectfully declined. He needed some time to investigate on his own. However, he was buoyed by the next conversation in the same CTM, where the key issue brought forward was "difficulty engaging a student uninterested in the course content." He had a number of strategies and ideas to offer as this was an area in which he felt particularly confident! He shared how he had set up a debate, with students each receiving a card sharing the stance they had to assume during the debate. The English teacher asked if he could share the cards he used, which he made a note to send following the meeting.

Although it took time, over the next year, Alice witnessed some remarkable changes happening for Mr. Howard. In subsequent meetings, seeing that the focus was on the students, not his instructional practices, Mr. Howard began to open up. He began to implement some of the differentiated strategies being suggested in his classroom. Hearing of a colleague using a few different applications for students who lacked some fundamental literacy skills, he began to inquire about her classroom practices and began replicating them in his classroom. He also started to open up to ask questions in relation to some effective literacy practices as his colleagues began to access him for student engagement strategies.

When he started to see positive results, Mr. Howard began to seek professional learning opportunities related to strategies for students reading below grade level and, although hesitant and cautious at first, started experimenting with some differentiated text resources for some concepts he was teaching as part of his courses. As the school continually refined and developed their Collaborative Response, Mr. Howard continued to grow his instructional toolbox while taking a high degree of pride in knowing he was a "go to" for engaging students in content matter. A key moment came when Alice engaged in a conversation with Mr. Howard about his evolving literacy supports and he revealed, "I look back and now realize that I was reluctant to address student reading struggles because I didn't know how to deal with them. I think I was scared to admit I didn't know how to deal with students lacking the reading skills to access the materials I was using! However, when we started to talk about the students, I realized it wasn't about me . . . it was about kids! Although it was hard at first, I quickly realized it was a conversation about support, not about my inadequacies as a teacher."

Although this vignette is intentionally romanticized to illustrate a point, it shows the power connected to focusing on students, not instruction, through the strategy of focusing on a key issue. It provides school leaders and other team members committed to the mission that *all* students can and will learn the opportunity to address specific student needs and can open the door to examine individual and collective instructional practices.

Let's break down the steps included when shifting the discussion to a focus on key issues. Figure 5.3 shares a visual flowchart of the steps unpacked over the next few pages.

Figure 5.3 Key issues flowchart

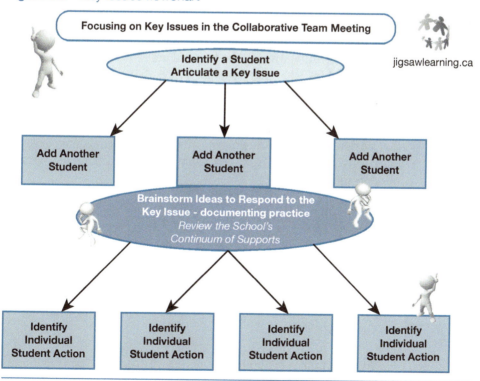

ClipArt Source: PresenterMedia

Step 1: Identifying a Key Issue Through a Student Concern

Following a review of norms and an opportunity to articulate celebrations in relation to student success, the meeting facilitator moves to asking a teacher to identify a student and a key issue they are experiencing:

> Today, I've brought Raymond to discuss, and the key issue I'd like to address is his difficulty to produce quantity and quality when it comes to writing. I know he is capable but just doesn't seem to give me anything more than a sentence or two.

The teacher has identified a student with an issue they wish to address. It is important to note that we didn't divulge a great deal of further details, or background or other information. We also resisted the urge to identify a number of concerns occurring; the identification of a single issue is focused and is about to be turned into something that we can address in the classroom.

It may seem logical to identify the key issue as "unable to provide significant writing quantity" and move forward to the next step. However, it is important to dig just a little to help determine *why* that issue may be occurring. Otherwise, the conversation may devolve into reasoning such as "the student is just lazy" or "I wish his previous teacher would have . . ." We want to delve into a key issue that will have a direct impact in the classroom. Meeting participants, led by someone holding the facilitator role, begin to ask questions to surface a root key issue that may be happening. As soon as the teacher states, "I don't think it is a case of stamina or difficulty with the physical act of writing, from what I've observed. I think what may be happening is that he struggles to get his ideas out of his head and onto paper in a way that makes sense, so he then gives up."

Now we have a key issue to address. It is important to understand that we don't need absolute proof of what is exactly happening, beyond a measure of a doubt—we just need a *hunch* from the teacher of what may be happening.

Step 2: Digging Into the Key Issue

At this point, it is vital that we *don't* turn to solutions or ideas to address the key issue for Raymond or to offer the individual teacher a myriad of possible ideas for consideration. We first need to ask the question:

> "What other students do we have that are experiencing a similar key issue?"

At this point, a facilitator turns to each teacher in the meeting to determine any other students who are struggling with the same key issue. It may not be to the same degree as what was expressed for the student who initiated the conversation, but it is important to attach other students to the conversation by name. Offering the opportunity for others in the meeting (paraprofessionals, administrators, learning support, and others) to identify additional students with the similar key issue should also be encouraged. However, it is important to note that we are only seeking names, not a subsequent story to validate the linking of another student to the key issue.

Attaching other students reinforces that the issue is not isolated to a single teacher or to a single student. Demonstrating that it is something shared by others helps foster collective trust and vulnerability, with the willingness and, in time, expectation that we need to surface areas where we are struggling and not sure where to go next. It is not a negative reflection on our teaching, but rather surfaces an area where we hope to grow and expand our toolbox, in an effort to best address the needs of our students.

Once a cohort of named students from multiple classrooms is identified as experiencing the same key issue, we take the attention *off* the students to focus on the key issue.

"So, for the key issue of struggling to express ideas in writing, what could we do to support?"

Now a beautiful brainstorming begins. Team members start to surface strategies that we are using in our classrooms. We start to ask questions such as, "So what does that look like?" We elicit the toolboxes of specialists engaged in the meeting. We ensure that our facilitator is bringing all voices into the conversation without judgment on the ideas surfaced. We use phrases such as, "What if . . ." and "I wonder if we could . . ." Here the language matters. It is a "we" conversation as we explore, not a "you should" directed at individuals.

Companion Website Resources

5.9. Team meeting discussion and question cards: This is a valuable resource to use within a CTM to generate inquiry and questions among the team. Consider handing them out to meeting participants and set a goal to use two during the discussion.

5.10. Key issues and Tier 2 supports template: Although we will focus on what we mean by *Tier 2* in Chapter 7, this template notes the key issue on which the team discussion will focus and then space to articulate the classroom practices, strategies, and potential ideas being suggested through the team brainstorm.

In the Field

At Darwell School, part of Northern Gateway Public Schools in Alberta, Canada, participants in CTMs are each given a set of discussion cards and are expected to try and use them all through the course of the conversation to help reinforce a need to deeply examine the classroom practices being proposed and the students who are being identified. A sample photograph of their cards and meeting norms from a CTM is captured in Figure 5.4.

At Corpus Christi Catholic Elementary/Junior High School in Edmonton, Alberta, Canada, teacher-generated suggestions and ideas surfaced during an examination of key issues are documented and then posted in their collaborative meeting space, to possibly be referenced later by teachers or brought to the forefront in a future CTM when the key issue resurfaces. A bulletin board from their collaborative meeting space, featuring these posters, is included in Figure 5.5.

Figure 5.4 Darwell School meeting discussion cards

Source: ©2020, L. Vardy, Darwell School, Northern Gateway Public Schools, AB. Used with permission.

CHAPTER #5. Collaborative Team Meetings   125

Figure 5.5 Corpus Christi Catholic Elementary/Junior High School key issues posters

Source: ©2020, D. Deforge, Corpus Christi Catholic Elementary/Junior High School, Edmonton Catholic Schools, AB. Used with permission.

Step 3: Returning to the Students

Once the conversation has surfaced some ideas for potential next steps and allowed an opportunity to share and examine classroom practices, we now turn back to the teachers to ask,

> For the student or students you identified, what is something you can commit to try from our conversation? What is an action you intend to take, and do you need any support to actualize it?

Now we return to the students we identified and ask the teachers individually what their action is and a timeline for putting it into place, critical to maintaining a focus on action. This process ensures that the teacher is still in control of their next steps, so that it is manageable for them, based on what they know about the student, the student's strengths and interests, their own pedagogy, and the context of their classroom. In time, these conversations become deeper, more challenging, and further refined by best practices. We start reaching further for innovative practices and start seeking out what support we need to make that happen. We hear things such as, "Can you show me what that looks like?" "Would you be able to share an example of that with me?" "Could we meet so I could understand that better?" "Is there any chance I could visit your classroom to see that in action?" or "Could we create that together to use with both of our students?"

When we focus on the key issue, surfaced through our experience with a specific student or students, we ensure that multiple students can be linked to similar key issues, increasing the overall engagement of the team. Chances are, even though we may not all teach the student who initiated the discussion, we can all identify with the key issue being surfaced and can open up our instructional toolkits to discuss an instructional response and eventually engage in a "what if" conversation to explore potentially innovative approaches to addressing the key issue being discussed. Through this process, we not only ensure a response for the students specifically linked to the key issue, but unpack classroom strategies, interventions, and accommodations that could have impact on a universal level as each individual in the room leaves with new approaches or insights to consider, with commitments to actions that, in time, start to stretch our pedagogical thinking. This approach can also surface topics or areas for further professional learning as we could shine a light on a key issue to which none of us seem to have a strong sense of how to possibly respond. This approach to professional learning is entirely influenced by the needs of our students and can create an emotional connection to the need for some further learning to help support the real needs of students being identified.

It is also important to resist the temptation to remove the student entirely from the conversation, coming to the table with a faceless key issue.

> "The key issue I'd like to discuss today is handing in assignments. I have a number of students who are not handing in assignments to me on time or in a manner that meets my written expectations."

Without a specific student in mind, it is hard to dig into a specific *why*, which leads to talking in generalities and presumptions. It also becomes harder to commit to actions or see if what we are trying is making a difference. Most important, it removes the emotional connection to why I'm willing to stretch my instructional repertoire as I'm looking for differentiated approaches that may make a difference for a human being I want to see succeed. Although the CTM is focused on key issues, it needs to be individual students who are explicitly identified by name who initiate those conversations and are specifically linked to the actions that are put in place as a result.

By ensuring that the primary focus in the CTM is shifted to key issues surfaced through an examination of individual students, we can ensure that this meeting structure within Collaborative Response places attention on the classroom-based supports and instructional practices. Essentially, we can ensure that the CTM is dedicated to the question, "So what can we do?" reinforcing a culture of response associated with high levels of collective efficacy.

Action Focused

As referenced in the previous section, a well-established CTM ensures that we are dedicated to action. The meeting is not merely a discussion or generation of ideas but carries with it a process of accountability that helps ensure that members follow through on what they suggest or propose for students as well as the instructional adjustments they plan to make based on the key issue discussion. Actions are specifically articulated in the meeting notes, with determination of the team member responsible and a date they expect to have attended to that particular action.

We've all heard the old maxim, "Talk is cheap"; however, in the case of CTMs, the opposite is true. Talk carries a cost, particularly at the expense of substantial action to support students. If the intent of a CTM is to examine and adopt instructional practices, as well as classroom-based interventions, strategies, and accommodations that make a difference to student learning, there is an obligation for reviewing the efficacy of those plans and making further adjustments. Placing an unrelenting drive toward action is critical in CTMs.

Potential Pitfall

Often, especially when first beginning the process of collaboratively focusing on the diverse needs of students, participants can become discouraged if they focus on factors largely outside of their control. In our experience, we've heard this fear manifested in comments such as, "What can we do if his parents refuse to ever read with him at home?" "You know, he's always 20 minutes late every day, missing important instructional time," "He's playing on three different sports teams—no wonder he can't complete any assignments," and so on.

When staff members place an inordinate amount of their focus on such factors, a feeling of hopelessness takes over, and we resign ourselves to "fighting a losing battle." Instead, school leaders must focus on what teachers in schools can control—after all, we typically have more than six hours a day to make a difference, which is monumental in relation to student learning.

A whole staff activity (for a staff meeting or planning day) that can help staff place their focus on what they can control is called "The Locus of Control."

- First, ask staff members to consider all the reasons for students' lack of success in schools. Think about students in their own classrooms and in others. Provide two examples, such as "arrives late to school" and "can't read the textbook," to prompt thinking (ensuring that the

(Continued)

(Continued)

   two examples include one outside of the control of the staff and one that is in control of the staff, such as the examples provided).

- Individually, in partners or in small groups, write all the reasons for students' lack of success on Post-it notes, with each Post-it note containing one reason. Allow ample time for discussion as the reasons are written. Have them keep the Post-it notes.

- Provide a large visual of two concentric circles (see Recommended Resources 5.11). Instruct staff to come up to place their Post-it notes
  - outside the circles if completely outside of the control of the school (we can't do anything about it);
  - inside the first circle if we have *some* control over it (i.e., "Student forgets homework"—we could call home to have parents help remind the student, although this may or may not be effective); and
  - inside the second circle if we do have control over it (i.e., "Student can't read the textbook"—we purchase or create an audio version).

- Group the Post-it notes into common themes or reasons to generate discussion. A follow-up could include creating a reproduction of this for staff, detailing when things are outside of our control, what we have some control over, and what is within our control. Another follow-up activity would be to have a discussion related to what we can do about those things we have some or full control over.

The purpose of this activity is twofold. First, it allows us to "let go" of things outside our control. Why waste our energy discussing or attempting to address things outside our control? Second, it highlights a number of things we *do* have control over, and these are where we should be placing our energies. Specifically, we put energy into reasons for lack of student success that are completely within our control. This activity serves as a powerful reminder to staff that we *are* in control of a great deal and can make a monumental difference once we recognize and act on what we can control.

Companion Website Resources

5.11. Locus of control visual: Graphic organizer, to be used for the locus of control activity, that allows the team to organize factors outside of our control, factors we can influence, and factors we can control and have an impact on through our individual and collective actions.

Just Do It!

In this chapter, we have outlined the CTM process and the essential elements embedded within that process. In its essence, it is about accessing and growing the collective professional capital of your staff team to best address the diverse needs of students in your school. The most valuable piece of advice we can give schools and leaders is to adopt the Nike slogan: "Just do it!"

In reflecting on the work of schools in developing professional learning communities, DuFour and his colleagues offer the same advice that applies to this collaborative work:

> Organizations that take the plunge and actually begin *doing* the work of a PLC [professional learning community] develop their capacity to help all students learn at high levels far more effectively than schools that spend years *preparing* to become PLCs through reading or even training. (DuFour, DuFour, Eaker, & Many, 2010, p. 10)

Consider Collaborative Response and particularly CTMs. Some initial conversation and work must be done prior to implementation. However, schools that experience the greatest success just jump into the water and swim. As schools work through the processes and as collaborative cultures evolve, adjustments and revisions will be made. Each school's collaborative courage becomes the ethos of the "Ready, Fire, Aim" principle. We know that there "is no perfect formula for the perfect team meeting with a perfect plan for continuous school improvement" (Johnson et al., 2012, p. 79) and that "successful change does not come from following a step-by-step manual" (Fullan & Kirtman, 2019, p. 36). All great journeys begin with a first step.

Inherent to the "just do it" philosophy is an expectation that mistakes will be made. The iterative and generative evolution of collaborative structures and processes involves constant reflection and resulting revision. This cycle has no beginning or end, and understanding that we sometimes gain more from our shortcomings than our successes can support teams in implementation. Teams also benefit from the understanding that, when our efforts don't come to fruition, we have continual opportunities to try again.

By taking that first step, it is highly realistic that not all staff members will envision the value of CTMs, which often depart from traditional teaching norms. It is important to remember that compliance may be "a necessary stage along the journey" (Williams, 2008, p. 74). As teams begin to work in these CTMs, their value will begin to be recognized. Staff will come to see CTMs as a supportive structure that carries a feeling that "we're all in this together." However, it takes time to generate such buy-in.

It is important to recognize that no amount of preplanning or additional preparation will address the time it takes to develop trust among colleagues in CTMs. Internal competition, as described by Pfeffer and Sutton (2000), can be a preexisting ingredient that initially acts as a barrier to developing trust. Although schools are similar in some ways to other organizations, they also differ. Sometimes internal competition between teachers' goals or needs undermines an organization's ability "to turn knowledge into action." Competition often is lived out by picking sides, building alliances, and overt or passive-aggressive actions that thwart others who disagree. Such competition, however it is acted out, can inhibit interdependence, trust, and loyalty—basically halting actions that openly share ideas among colleagues. In short, knowledge-sharing organizations vastly differ from knowledge-inhibiting organizations. Our goal in the last three chapters is to help schools establish the necessary collaborative structures and processes in an effort to become knowledge-sharing organizations where collaborative structures and processes might flourish.

The ethos that grounds this book is that school leadership is centered on people who do *not* compete in contests where there are winners and losers. The only winners should be children who learn. Good schools are communities of trust—not sites of scrutiny where one person's work is compared to another's. If a competitive mentality kills student engagement, it also kills teacher engagement. When first establishing CTMs, the barrier of an old, competitive culture may be a reality. However, with time, focused leadership, and unwavering attention to the needs of students, a collaborative culture will grow.

Starting Steps

Whenever new initiatives or reforms are introduced in a school, the staff team needs to see gains and achievements early. Celebrations are critical early in the process to continue to build collective momentum for the development of the model and, more important, the culture within which the model can evolve. Principals must take time to recognize and reward the accomplishments of teams as they work to support students.

One of the best ways to support the continuous focus on students is sharing celebration stories of students, finding success as a result of the collaborative actions of a team. Muhammad (2009) has advised that the "positive school cultures I observed consistently celebrated the things the school valued" (p. 106). If your school is to truly value the individual growth and success of students, leaders must continually seek and share the individual success stories that reinforce the efforts of teams that are making a difference for kids.

Collaborative Structures and Processes Missing in the Model

Early in this book, we noted that the three foundational components of Collaborative Response—collaborative structures and processes, data and evidence, and continuum of supports—are essential to the overall success of the framework. Table 5.2 describes the result if collaborative structures and processes are not established in schools striving to respond to the individual needs of students.

Table 5.2   Collaborative structures and processes not established

COLLABORATIVE STRUCTURES AND PROCESSES	DATA AND EVIDENCE	CONTINUUM OF SUPPORTS	RESULT
Not established	Established	Established	Supports established based on scores from assessment or determined by a single person. Does not take advantage of multiple viewpoints and collaborative problem solving. Knowledge of a child limited to a few and less collective accountability present. No structures to ensure collective efficacy

The "essence of professionalism is the ability to make discretionary judgments" (Hargreaves & Fullan, 2012, p. 93); as such, schools need to be structured in a way that values and uses the professional capital inherently found within its staff. If data or individual judgments are the sole drivers that determine the supports that students receive, we overlook the professional capital and collective wisdom of the group. In addition to maximizing multiple viewpoints and expertise, collaborative structures and processes effectively build group accountability, support, and trust. Collaborative structures and processes, with a spotlight on CTMs, contribute to a school culture that works together to do whatever it takes to see that its students succeed.

Data and Evidence

CHAPTER #6

Hopper and Hopper (2009) said it best when they observed, "Statistics are a wonderful servant and an appalling master" (p. 125). This statement could not align more closely with the intended use of assessments in Collaborative Response to provide *data* that, along with staff observations and intimate knowledge of students, serve as *evidence* to inform conversations and guide next steps for students. The data and evidence collected also help inform the impact of the responses that are put in place as a result. Data, in an educational context, serve as an appalling master when they are the sole determinant that dictates the direction team members need to take and the supports to be initiated for students. We certainly do not endorse this lock-step approach of "assessment result A produces response B." Rather, assessments and the data they provide are a wonderful servant that point to which students we should be talking about and guide the type of support to be considered when held up against our professional observations and relational knowledge of our learners.

Whenever we hear the term "data-driven decision making" (Taylor & Gunter, 2006, p. 3) used in school improvement discussions, we prefer to revise the phrase into "data-*informed* decision making." For us, the difference alludes to the use of data to *inform* professional conversations focused on the needs of students instead of driving them. Data provide a waving flag, indicating what we need to attend to and provide direction for an informed response.

> *Data provide a waving flag, indicating what we need to attend to and provide direction for an informed response.*

It has been observed, "What distinguishes high-performing schools from low-performing schools is the manner in which they organize, analyze, and act upon their data" (Lassiter, 2011, p. 77). Within a school's Collaborative Response, schoolwide assessments are used to paint an overall picture. The data they produce can shine a light on areas of success and areas to further address. They can highlight progress and growth being made as a school and indicate that work is still needed in certain areas or with certain subsets of students. In examining the use of data at the school level, Fullan (2013) shares that

> data can be a trifecta winner. Mere openness of results and practice can nudge people to pay attention to progress. Data are hard to avoid when they are ever present. Second, they can push people to act when others are moving forward and you are stagnant even when no one comments on the situation. And third, they can be powerful pullers when you are getting

133

somewhere and can't wait to do more, or when your colleagues
are becoming successful and you seek to understand why. (p. 78)

At the beginning of Chapter 5, we used the analogy of a motor vehicle suggesting that, if Collaborative Response was the vehicle for providing a schoolwide response for individual student needs, the collaborative team meeting (CTM) was the engine that drove it. To extend that analogy, the data and evidence we bring to our conversations serve as the guidance system that steers the vehicle, pointing out specific directions to go. They help surface specific students to be brought forward to the CTM, focusing our attention on our students that would likely realize the greatest gains with subtle shifts in classroom practice. This is a shift in our thinking that will be explored in this chapter, which has tremendous impact on the consistent building of collective efficacy across an organization.

It has been stated that without data, you're just someone else with an opinion. Although we highly value the opinion of professionals around the table, adding data enriches the conversations and ensures discussion is centered on the students who should be our focus, based on the layer of collaborative structures. If the same student (or type of student) is the center of every conversation at every layer, we stand the risk of perpetuating a general feeling that our efforts are not having an impact. We also risk missing supports for others while we spend an overabundance of time on a few. However, when the data are effectively organized, it can help us surface different students at each layer of collaboration, contributing to meeting the needs of all students while providing evidence that our work is making a difference.

When used effectively, data collected from the administration of assessments, coupled with other sources of evidence, should

1. be easily administered, scored, and organized into easily accessible visual overviews;

2. highlight which students we should be talking about specifically in our CTMs;

3. help point toward areas to be addressed for students;

4. indicate growth and guide revisions to supports currently in place; and

5. be seamlessly integrated into a school's culture of response.

This chapter will explore the key elements related to the selection, administration, and use of assessments within Collaborative Response and then explore how the data and evidence they produce are effectively organized to initiate and inform our conversations. Let's start this examination by visiting Focus Elementary to observe how data and evidence are gathered, organized, and then utilized within their school.

CHAPTER #6. Data and Evidence

As you read the vignette, consider the following questions:

1. How are the students assessed within the school's Collaborative Response?

2. How is it determined which students will be assessed?

3. Who is responsible for assessing students?

4. How are the data from the assessments disaggregated, shared, and used?

5. How do those data serve as one piece of the overall evidence being examined to inform next steps for students?

Assessments at Focus Elementary

Marquis, the learning support coordinator at Focus Elementary, takes another cursory look over the list of students to be progress monitored this week. In her role, she has taken on the coordination of the schoolwide assessment framework that has become a critical component of their school's Collaborative Response. This week includes progress monitoring, as determined by the school's annual planning calendar, and every two weeks, her Monday morning routine is similar. First, she ensures that her list of students to be progress monitored at their K–6 school is updated. Two weeks ago, she needed to go back to consult the CTM records to ensure that a number of students had been removed from the testing. This used to be done during teachers' collaborative planning time but had now been integrated into the last five minutes of their CTM as, now, teachers were used to coming ready to add or delete students from the grade-level list. This week, she knows her list is ready.

At each grade level, roughly 7 to 12 students are to be monitored, about 30% of their overall population. This number has slowly been coming down over the past two years since Focus Elementary began working on their schoolwide response process, but Marquis knows that, although she has focused mainly on celebrating her staff's continuous efforts, Doug, the school principal, is striving to see that number closer to 20%.

In their school, they are using quick reading screens to serve as progress monitoring assessments every two weeks for students the collaborative teams determine need to be continuously monitored in their reading growth.

(Continued)

(Continued)

At the primary grades, those screens focus on consonant-vowel-consonant words and reading of simple sentences. The older grade assessments are reading passages with simple comprehension and vocabulary-related questions. Three times during the year, every student in the school is screened using a reading benchmark assessment administered by a team, including herself and two educational assistants she's trained to complete the screen with students, with Doug joining in as well. In their first year, teachers administered the individualized benchmark assessments. However, they had discovered that it took a substantial amount of instructional time, with a very wide variance of administration fidelity, which affected the overall results. After they engaged in a schoolwide discussion regarding the purpose of these screens, they moved toward a team approach for administration, which was much more efficient and with higher levels of fidelity for the results. After Christmas, it will be time to do the January benchmarking with all students but that is still a number of weeks away. It is encouraging to see a number of students, even as early as November, being removed from the progress monitoring schedule by the grade-level collaborative teams.

As she does every Monday morning during a progress monitoring week, Marquis sets out grade-level bins of progress monitoring materials, which include student assessment materials and a list of students to be assessed at each grade level. During the morning, grade-level leaders will come to gather their bins. Each leader's job is to ensure that students at that grade level are assessed during the schoolwide literacy block, which happens every day right after lunch. For most leads, it will take them the first two days of the week to complete these during the literacy block, unless affected by student absences.

Progress monitoring is always completed by the same trained team throughout the year to provide as much consistency as possible. In addition to herself, it includes the team responsible for the triannual screening (two educational assistants and her principal, Doug), and it is this group that conducts all the progress monitoring for the school over the next few days. In some cases, teachers have also created additional pockets of time for the monitoring to happen. Pulling out a student for two minutes for the assessment has really become a simple task as part of the school's transformation over the past two years.

During the next two to three days, the team of four will work through their student lists to ensure that all students are progress monitored during the course of the week. As student assessments are completed, their individual assessments will be dropped back in the "completion bin" in Marquis's classroom, where she and one other educational assistant will enter scores as time allows during the week. Although she had initially questioned when she and her partner would find the time to enter the scores into the school's progress monitoring spreadsheet, it actually had become surprisingly easy to accomplish once they developed a system that worked for them.

CHAPTER #6. Data and Evidence

By next Monday, every teacher will have delivered to their staff room mailboxes updated progress monitoring scores in their data overviews for students in their grade-level cohort. These data pages are quite simple, with students ordered from lowest to highest scores and scores highlighted using a simple three-color system. All staff also have digital access to the spreadsheet to consult at any time they wish, but have been reminded that the purpose of the assessment data is only to flag students for their CTMs and be used for team analysis in conjunction with their three screening times. They are not to be considered evidence to be used in classroom evaluation and reporting. Doug and the leadership team also take the cumulative scores to analyze overall school trends, growth, and progress.

Green scores indicate students are on track; yellow indicates scores are slightly below where they should be; and red indicates students are significantly below. Over the past year, the school has really tried to focus attention typically on the yellow scores during their CTMs, leading to conversations regarding the identification of key issues related to why a student may be yellow, and then an examination of classroom practices that could be employed for students experiencing a similar key issue. Doug has adopted the slogan, "Teacher gut trumps all," simply meaning that assessment scores inform their discussions and help determine who they should talk about; but the knowledge of the staff, gained through their own classroom formative and summative assessments, will be held in highest regard. The utilization of the colors has been built into the school's pre-meeting organizer that teachers complete prior to the meeting, as they now have to indicate a yellow, a red, and a green student they wish to discuss, although the meeting is facilitated in such a way that most of the conversations are typically initiated by a yellow or green student. This has led to a significant change in the conversation and feeling of staff in relation to these meetings. Prior to the infusion of the data overviews, it felt like the meetings were about the same students over and over again, students who were now typically falling in the red scores. Staff now understood that those students were largely being discussed in the school support team meetings that she facilitated weekly with Doug and their school's family school liaison worker or could be discussed in the weekly classroom support meetings established for each individual teacher to access as needed. As a result, it was really ensuring that their CTMs could focus on students most likely to see success through subtle shifts and adjustments to classroom practice, which had made teachers more eager to engage in the conversations within their teams. It has also contributed to higher levels of equity across the school as students who may not have elicited a conversation in the past are now coming to the forefront through the intentional organization of the data. This has also included enrichment conversations, which are still very new for the school staff team.

Although it had taken time to institute their system of progress monitoring in the school, with many revisions along the way, the process now works like clockwork. What seemed a momentous task when they first initiated

(Continued)

(Continued)

the schedule of screening and progress monitoring is now just a part of how things work at Focus Elementary. Teachers actually find that they have spent less time administering assessments in the school, allowing them to spend more time on their classroom formative assessment and instruction. Additionally, their layers of collaboration are now starting to align, being very much influenced by the data focused on their key priority of reading success for their students. Marqis is excited to see what the January screening results show, as it certainly feels like their collaborative efforts are making a difference for students!

It is important to recognize that no lock-step approach exists for developing a school's Collaborative Response; instead, each school determines its own unique timeline and entry points to begin the work. When looking at the three foundational components, it is likely that schools will develop aspects of each component simultaneously. There is no formulaic method "First do this, then do this." However, we do have a targets of implementation resource discussed in the final chapter that can help schools chart a course for implementing Collaborative Response. In that resource, we recommend starting with establishing the layers of collaboration before starting to infuse data and evidence into the conversation.

It is important that schools just start talking about kids. Getting started with CTMs and then identifying and defining the layers of collaborative structures that may already exist is a vital initial step. By structuring time and processes for discussing the needs of students in different layers of team meetings, with attention paid to establishing the intent and purpose of the CTM, a culture of response begins to take shape.

When first establishing some of the collaborative structures and processes described in this text at an embryonic level (long before they became actualized in the way they are described in this text), it wasn't long before we recognized, as leaders, that some students who we knew were struggling were not being brought forth for discussion. For example, in a grade-level CTM, we could ask, "So who do we need to discuss?" Teacher A would indicate 15 of her students who were desperately in need of additional support. When the conversation turned to teacher B, the response was "my class is doing fine." Teacher C would then state that "I want to talk about Mikah," and the rest of the team would sigh as Mikah seemingly dominated the conversation every time they gathered. Spending time in each classroom told us that each of those realities simply was not the case, and when end-of-the-year summative assessments were conducted, we discovered that things were not as dire as they were expressed to be in teacher A's classroom and much worse than expressed in teacher B's. And yes, Mikah was in need of substantial support that extended well beyond the scope of just Teacher C's involvement ... but there were other students in that classroom to whom we could be turning our attention! Although a number of the processes previously described in the last chapter were not in place (including the realization of the power of shifting to key issues in CTMs), we still understood a mechanism was missing to help us determine *who* should be the primary focus for our conversations as each team member had a different understanding of the criteria to be used when selecting students for examination.

Although this example of teachers A, B, and C definitely oversimplifies our experiences, it accurately points to what we discovered. We needed a way to bring consistency to our conversations and shine a light on students who *needed* to have a spotlight shone on them, specifically in our CTMs. We essentially needed to learn to speak a common language when discussing the levels of our students and integrating data we were collecting related to students into the fold. This led to the realization of the need for data and evidence to be a foundational component for our collaborative efforts.

Substantial Shifts

Originally, this foundational component was solely referred to as "assessments" within a Collaborative Response Model, later adjusted to simply *Collaborative Response,* as discussed earlier in the text. Over time, we have discovered that simply referring to assessments was limiting in its language. Rather, assessments were only one part of the equation. The data gleaned from the assessments, when held against our professional insights and understandings, formed the evidence base on which we could respond. Data and evidence became a more effective way to describe this foundational component, an essential piece of the puzzle as it relates to Collaborative Response.

Nine key elements guide the use of data and evidence in Collaborative Response:

1. Flag students for discussion
2. Universal screens
3. Diagnostic assessments
4. Progress monitoring assessment

5. Assessment schedule established
6. Intentional organization of results for team analysis
7. Intentional organization of results for CTMs
8. Student entry levels
9. Data-informed planning

The rest of this chapter will focus on each of these key elements in detail, examining the effective, focused use of assessments, and providing teams the data necessary to assist in determining who needs support and what type of support they need as well as the evidence to help inform our individual and collective next steps.

Companion Website Resources

6.1. Reflecting on data and evidence: This reflection organizer is designed to assist schools in reviewing the key elements related to the effective use of data and evidence in schools.

Flag Students for Discussion

In Collaborative Response, the use of assessments and the data they produce serve several functions. However, the primary and most critical purpose (hence why it is the first essential element that we discuss) is that the data we are examining serve to *flag* students for discussion. In other words, we use assessment data, first and foremost, to ensure clarity regarding what we are focusing on through our collaborative efforts. Assessments provide the screen that catches struggling students, ensuring that the "my class is doing fine" scenario shared earlier cannot happen. The assessment data we gather shine a light on who should be discussed.

In some schools, assessment results function as the end of the conversation, providing the final summative evidence of student learning. In a school focused on responding to the individual needs of students, assessments function in a formative sense, acting as the genesis of the conversation. Sharratt and Fullan (2012) contend, "Data today become instruction tomorrow for each one" (p. 49). Earl and Katz (2006) also support this use of data.

> Data and statistics may provide the tools for measuring educational concepts, but the numbers are only as good as the thinking and interpretation. Data do not provide right answers

CHAPTER #6. Data and Evidence   **141**

or quick fixes. Instead, they are necessary but not sufficient elements of the conversations that ensue. . . . Interpretation requires time, thoughtfulness, reservation of judgments and open challenge of as well as support for ideas. (p. 20)

Without the inclusion of data, specifically in a CTM, conversations completely depend on the observations and thoughts of teachers about the students that team members *want* to talk about. It is entirely possible for a child to "slip through," particularly if the team is still in the process of developing professional trust or refining the layers of collaborative structures that create a space for particular student examinations.

However, when teams gather and examine assessment data, additional students surface. This focus on assessment data essentially places the focus on the student, rather than the teacher, allowing for discussions of support and instructional next steps to evolve. The point is not to cast any blame for *why* students are underperforming. Rather, it is to focus on action: "So *now what are we going to do collectively*?"

After shining a spotlight on which students need to be discussed, assessment data should help narrow the conversation by pointing to specific areas of attention. A quick examination of the assessment evidence can act as "a treasure hunt for insight" (White, 2007, p. 223), informing the conversations and potentially pinpointing specific areas of focus for response.

It is certainly true that "with the right teachers and leadership, regular tests and assessments can enliven discussions about children's learning" (Hargreaves & Fullan, 2012, p. 32). However, it is critical that assessment data enrich the discussions about student learning, not replace it. "Data can inform improvement, guide instruction, and prompt earlier intervention so no child is allowed to fall behind. But data can replace professional judgment instead of enhancing it, directing teachers' efforts only toward the tested basics, and driving them to distraction" (Hargreaves & Fullan, 2012, p. 44). Professional judgment is still at the heart of Collaborative Response, and the scores on an assessment should never replace the collective wisdom of the team, which honors the evidence we are compiling through data, observations, and professional insights and what we know and understand about a child through our relationship with them.

Hargreaves and Fullan (2012) refer to this as *professional capital*, asserting that "teachers with professional capital are not driven by data or overly dependent on measurable evidence—but they do inquire into, identify, and adapt the best ways for moving forward, making intelligent, critical, and reflective use of measurable evidence and considered experience alike" (p. 49). When data serve to flag students for discussion and help identify areas requiring further examination, collaborative efforts become much richer and more focused and help ensure that the right conversations are taking place.

Potential Pitfall

We have rationalized that assessments and the data they produce do not define students. It is important that principals heed this assertion as well when focusing on teacher effectiveness. When teachers recognize that student assessment scores are being used to summatively assess their instructional effectiveness, they are more likely to develop high levels of mistrust of their administration and start engaging these assessments as problems. For example, teachers might begin to engage in less-than-desirable activities, such as teaching to the test or finding ways to inflate scores. When data are focused on the teacher rather than the students, assessments in Collaborative Response lose their inherent effectiveness.

As we begin to understand the importance of using assessments to help identify gaps in students' learning, our next natural question is, "What is the purpose of the assessments that we are employing?"

Universal Screens

Sometimes referred to as benchmark assessments, universal screens are intended to be administered to all students and produce data that essentially should confirm what we think we already know about students. Ferriter et al. (2013) remind us, "The purpose of screening tools is not to provide detailed information about each individual student. Instead, the purpose is to quickly produce immediately actionable data about a large group of students" (p. 63). Typically administered one to three times annually, the actionable data produced by universal screens can serve several purposes:

1. They confirm what we already know about students, from teacher observations and classroom assessments. For instance, if a teacher believes that a student is proficient in mathematical operations, a numeracy screen should reveal the same conclusion.

2. They determine which students we should be focusing on. The data produced should identify which students are below the benchmark we've established in the area being assessed and need to be a focal point for further investigation and discussion.

3. They produce overall school data for analysis. Universal screening data, when examined on the large scale, can demonstrate overall progress as a school. The true power of these data is recognized when teams further disaggregate the data to

CHAPTER #6. Data and Evidence   143

determine how to further learning for those individual students who are at the heart of CTM conversations.

4. They produce data to be utilized by teams to analyze instructional effectiveness. Examining screening data can reveal what areas of instruction should be enhanced through further professional development and team coaching.

5. Universal screens can also be used to indicate entry levels as students move from grade to grade. This information can assist in transition conversations and visualization of student entry levels as students move from grade to grade and from school to school.

Potential Pitfall

One pitfall that we have seen schools fall into is "waiting for the perfect assessment." In these situations, school leadership and staff teams spend excessive time and energy seeking ideal assessment tools that fit their curriculum, student populations, budget, and a number of other factors. Unfortunately, precise fits are unlikely to happen and rather than allowing the focus to be on *how* the assessment and the data it produces are utilized, the focus is squarely placed on *what* the assessment is.

If the purpose of a universal screen is to flag students for discussion and emphasis is placed on *how* information from assessments is utilized across the school, the utopian assessment is no longer of greatest importance. Of greater importance is how will the screen align with our priority areas and can it provide us with actionable data to help fuel the conversation of "Who should we be talking about?"

We have witnessed a school that developed student surveys to gather data in relation to executive functioning skills, a priority they discerned from their ongoing observation of students and their increasing challenges. In a high school, a priority was placed on student connectivity—how many relational connections a student had—which had been determined as an indicator of student well-being. In that school, a student survey was developed to ascertain how many connections students had to adults in the building, using actual pictures of staff members in the survey to elicit who the students felt close connections with in the building. In a high school where student engagement was a priority, eight dimensions of student engagement were formulated, and then a profile for each student was developed showing a rating for the student in each dimension to help not only flag students exhibiting lower levels of engagement, but also indicate particular dimensions where they were deemed to be struggling.

(Continued)

> (Continued)
>
> During the COVID-19 pandemic, when students moved overnight to online learning, priorities quickly shifted to supporting students online in a very different educational reality. Collecting universal data related to student wifi access, parental support, and mental well-being prompted the formulation of some quick screens to gather these data. The lesson here is not to ruminate over the perfect assessment, but rather how data can be collected and organized to provide evidence related to who we should be directing our attention to.

A number of factors must be considered when implementing universal screens in Collaborative Response:

- ▶ *Clear connection to the priorities established for the school*: As discussed in Chapter 3, it is important to determine a focus or focus areas for student success, and the universal screens that are employed or developed should be clearly aligned with that focus or focus areas.

- ▶ *Efficient administration of the assessment with students*: A universal screen is not intended to be intensive or comprehensive but rather to screen students for further action. As such, it should not take an inordinate amount of time to administer. Efficiency is the key, and administration may be done through mechanisms outside of the classroom teacher, as shared in the opening vignette.

- ▶ *Ability to produce clear, coherent data for teams*: Universal screens must be able to generate data that can be easily disaggregated to give an overall picture of student achievement as well as individual students on whom to focus, which can help guide next steps. If data are to effectively inform conversations in the collaborative structures essential to Collaborative Response, they must be easy to organize and understand.

Consider a routine annual appointment as an analogy for the benchmark assessments in Collaborative Response. It serves as the annual appointment to check in with a doctor to determine your health conditions at that point in time. This is a quick analysis to determine if there are any indications or early signs of issues to which we should attend. For many students, the analysis will tell us that their overall academic health is good and that we should check again during the next overall screening process. However, for some students, data will tell us that further digging is needed to determine specific conditions and monitor changes as responses are put in place in the classroom and beyond. The next level of assessments in Collaborative Response are diagnostic assessments.

Companion Website Resources

6.2. Criteria and considerations when determining a universal screen: An overview of criteria and considerations for organizations when planning for and utilizing universal screens, also referred to as benchmark assessments.

6.3. Examining potential common assessments: Template to assist schools when considering common assessments (screens and progress monitoring) for schoolwide implementation.

6.4. Potential benchmarks/screening tools: A collection of potential benchmarks/screening tools for consideration that are being used and accessed by schools.

Diagnostic Assessments

In Collaborative Response, the next level of assessments used to inform conversations are diagnostic assessments, typically conducted in the classroom. We have often informally referred to these as "teacher assessments," since in many cases, they are the responsibility of teachers (although not in all cases). If the universal screens are comparative to an annual medical checkup, for all students to determine overall health, diagnostic assessments go deeper. Extending the medical analogy, they are the more comprehensive health tests that assist in determining the root causes of problems indicated through the screening process. They are the cholesterol, blood pressure, blood analysis, ultrasounds, and other tests done to determine a more complete picture of what is truly happening. Based on these assessments, supports and specific actions are put in place (changes in diet, exercise, medication, etc.), and then progress monitoring assessments are utilized to monitor if the actions being taken are making a difference. We will elaborate on progress monitoring shortly.

Initiating this more comprehensive level of assessment for all clients would quickly overburden the health system because there are certainly too few professionals or too little time available to ensure that this mandate is achieved. Comparatively, a school will become quickly overwhelmed if trying to ensure this extensive level of diagnostic assessment for every student. Whereas the universal screen is efficient and utilized with all students to gather quick actionable data and flag the students to whom we should be paying attention, diagnostic assessments are utilized to provide a more complete picture of specific learners, as needed, and to determine root causes of struggles that the learner is experiencing.

At this point, we need to provide a critical clarification. We are not, in any way, advocating that teacher classroom assessment should only occur for students identified as being at risk through universal screens.

Ongoing classroom assessment is integral to effective instruction, and we completely agree that "assessment is most productive when its purpose is *for* learning" (Reeves, 2007b, p. 3). Teachers must continuously engage in assessment that informs their instructional responses and guides their classroom efforts. After all, the "assessments best suited to guide improvements in instruction and student learning are the quizzes, tests, writing assignments, and other assessments teachers administer on a regular basis in their classrooms" (Guskey, 2007, p. 16). However, in Collaborative Response, diagnostic assessments, often conducted by teachers, further provide diagnostic evidence to inform conversations initiated by the universal screen. This may be a necessary step to communicate a key issue, an integral process described in the preceding chapter. If the role of universal screens is to truly flag students for discussion, the diagnostic classroom assessments being conducted by teachers bring a richer level of clarification to the conversation.

It is important to also understand that diagnostic data and evidence may be more "soft," as we need to consider that staff understandings are also greatly informed by consistent interactions with a learner. For instance, a school's universal behavior screen, such as the number of reported incidents, may provide a flag that a student is experiencing an increase in behavior-related altercations. A teacher's diagnostic "data" may then consist of observations or information collected by those who know the student best. These observations may indicate difficulties related to home or issues with bullying, for example, that cannot be gleaned from the broader screen data. Although the screen data indicate a student who needs further examination, it is a staff member's (or collection of staff members') relational information that provides the information needed to inform the next steps of response.

Potential Pitfall

An obvious question posed at this point is why are universal screens needed? Shouldn't a teacher's data, collected through their individual assessments and interactions, be enough to inform a collaborative team as to which students need supports and whether the supports in place are making a difference? These questions are valid. However, the universal screen data are critical because they ensure that students cannot slip through the cracks or go unnoticed in the collaborative conversations.

As discussed earlier, universal screens act as the common denominator across a school, directing the next steps to be taken. Relying solely on teachers' triangulation of assessments, observations, and conversations (Davies, 2020), especially in schools where common assessments are

CHAPTER #6. Data and Evidence 147

> not utilized across a grade level, is a pitfall schools can fall into when deepening the focus and conversation particularly in the CTM, as we will discuss in a subsequent section. Simply put, the inherent variability in individual teacher assessments and diagnostic data gathering is problematic when trying to ensure that no student can go unnoticed within a school community.
>
> In addition, schoolwide common screens are highly advantageous when demonstrating growth around a schoolwide goal. It is the schoolwide screens that allow leadership to examine data to determine the overall growth and success of the school in a specific target area and provide information for accountability to district and even provincial or state goals.

If universal screens flag students we should be bringing forth for conversation and diagnostic assessments help inform the next steps for specific students, how do we know that those next steps are making an impact? The answer is through the employment of progress monitoring assessments.

Progress Monitoring Assessments

Let's return once again to our medical analogy. Following the annual medical appointment (universal screens) and further investigation flagged by the screen (diagnostic assessments), health professionals consult and determine a number of actions to be taken by the patient to improve their overall health. These actions are put in place, and now the patient's health is monitored a little more closely to determine if the changes initiated are having a positive impact. Typically, these health monitors are more specific because they align with specific areas of concern (regular blood pressure tests if blood pressure was deemed to be the concern, for instance).

In Collaborative Response, this monitoring level of assessment, necessary to inform teams if supports are making a positive difference for students, is known as progress monitoring. Hall (2012) suggests, "progress monitoring sometimes is the forgotten cousin of benchmark screening." (p. 63). The cycle of collecting and examining student information to support and determine a range of supports would not be complete without the ongoing information provided through progress monitoring.

Progress monitoring allows professionals a quick look to see if the supports in place are indeed having an impact for the students. When baking a cake, a baker will test the cake before taking it out of the oven by inserting a toothpick. Even when equipped with trusted recipes and appliances, chefs could have a flop if the cake is taken out of the oven too soon. The toothpick provides quick information that allows the baker to make an informed decision as to whether it's time to take it out of the oven or if it requires further baking. The same is true of progress monitoring assessments. They provide collaborative teams with the information to determine whether further support is necessary or it's time to move on.

When determining progress monitoring tools and processes, some of the same factors apply as with universal screens. The progress monitoring assessment needs to correspond with the supports applied within the focus of the school and for individual students. If the focus is on improving student well-being, then the progress monitoring tool must provide a glimpse into what is occurring for students in relation to that area. Some progress monitoring tools and processes for data collection may be comprehensive (such as described in the original vignette that opened this chapter), whereas others are more of an informal check-in. Typically in areas related specifically to academic achievement, particularly in relation to literacy or numeracy, standardized tools may be available or developed that can provide specificity when collecting and then organizing data for examination. However, in other areas, such as student wellness, engagement, social-emotional learning, and so on, progress monitoring may be more informal, such as the use of a checklist to monitor what is happening in a classroom, a quick check-in with the student with specific questions and a determined date for that conversation, or monitoring of attendance data as an indicator of whether efforts related to engaging the student are leading to them being at the school more frequently. The simple questions to be asked are, "When we put supports in place, in relation to our areas of focus, do we have a way to check to see if what we've done or are doing is having an impact? Do we have a mechanism to tell us when we need to intensify our efforts, or scale them back due to success being determined? Do we have a way to begin saving these progress monitoring tools or processes that could be replicated for another student, specifically when the method of progress monitoring is more informal?"

The factor of administration time is also critical. This monitoring should be quick and efficient and allow staff to reflect on the current reality of students in their area of concern. These ongoing data allow data-informed conversations and individual reflections to be happening prior to the CTMs. Recall our opening vignette in Chapter 5. Team members in the CTM were able to utilize data from progress monitoring to continue to guide them as to which students they should be discussing and what areas need to be addressed for the student, informing the pre-meeting organizers they complete prior to the conversation to help focus in on specific students.

CHAPTER #6. Data and Evidence   149

Potential Pitfall

Progress monitoring tools provide a way to focus on our students in jeopardy and therefore are not used with all students. Universal screens are administered to all students, but schools must be judicious and intentional regarding which students are progress monitored. Only those where intentional supports are put in place (particularly supports considered to be Tier 3, a conversation explored in the next chapter) through collaborative team conversations should be progress monitored. If too many students are regularly progress monitored, the school system of regular assessment will be overburdened and lose its efficiency, and teachers will become overwhelmed by the number of students they may be intentionally engaging in monitoring efforts. As discussed early in this chapter, the professional judgment of the collaborative team is critical in determining which students are involved in this more frequent level of assessment. Over time, the percentage of students involved in progress monitoring should be declining.

For Collaborative Response, all three elements of universal screens, diagnostic assessments, and progress monitoring assessments have distinctive purposes, yet important roles to play. When determining next steps for students, particularly at the student support team and case consult team levels, the information gleaned from the diagnostic and progress monitoring assessments play a critical role in not only providing information vital for programming and putting in support beyond the classroom level, but also informing if those supports are having the desired impact for student growth. However, the remainder of this chapter will return to the universal screen data and investigate their purposeful collection, organization, and utilization function to have immense impact on collaborative planning; they can drastically focus the CTMs, drawing attention to a particular subset of students most likely to see measurable improvement through adjustments and refinements at the classroom level.

Companion Website Resources

6.5. Assessment planning template: An organizer to assist schools in planning for screening, diagnostic, and progress monitoring assessments, starting the conversation with tools already present within the school.

Assessment Schedule Established

A central theme integral to the sustained effectiveness of Collaborative Response is organization and structure. The development of a school-wide assessment schedule that identifies when universal screens (and potentially progress monitoring) occur is a part of that intentional organization. This schedule coordinates and plans for when assessments are administered in relation to other key school dates and establishes an assessment calendar at the onset of a school year. It also sends a clear message that these assessments are an expected part of the school's culture of response (Hall, 2012).

This assessment schedule coincides with the CTM calendar discussed in Chapter 5. After determining when CTMs occur during the course of the school year, data collection dates are strategically scheduled, so that current information is potentially available for team conversations in those meetings. Figure 6.1 illustrates a sample planning calendar from a school in January, when universal screens, progress monitoring, and CTMs were all scheduled.

Figure 6.1   Sample calendar (January)

	Sunday	Monday	Tuesday	Wednesday	Thursday	Friday	Saturday
							1
January	2	3 First day back	4	5 Staff Meeting 3:45 pm	6	7 — Staff Steering Meeting	8
	9	10	11	12	13	14 — PD Committee Meeting	15
		DIBELS Benchmarking					
	16	17	18	19	20	21	22
		Collaborative Team Meetings (Kindergarten–Jan. 13)					
	23 DIBELS Progress Monitoring	24	25	26	27	28 Staff planning day Final day of semester 1	29
	30	31 First day of semester 2					

Note: PD = professional development.

In this sample, a literacy tool named DIBELS was being used to screen and progress monitor students. Note that the two-day benchmark schedule is clearly defined, alerting teachers about when these

CHAPTER #6. Data and Evidence   151

assessments would be administered. However, the progress monitoring date is looser, expected to be administered during the identified week (in this case, from January 24 to 27). In this particular example, flexible scheduling allows the school's progress monitoring team the week to coordinate the administration of these assessments to students across multiple classrooms during a clearly defined period of time. It would be expected that all progress monitoring be completed during the course of that week.

School divisions, when engaging in Collaborative Response, can also play a role in determining universal screens to be established across all schools, with defined expectations regarding dates for administration. This systemwide approach brings further school-by-school consistency, allows consolidation of cost savings if relying on standardized assessment tools, and provides division-wide data that can be further disaggregated at the system level. Figure 6.2 shows an example of a division-wide expectation for literacy and numeracy universal screens in Peace Wapiti Public School Division in Alberta, Canada.

Figure 6.2 Peace Wapiti Public School Division screen overview

Collaborative Response Screen Overview
Peace Wapiti Public School Division

As we move forward with refining the Collaborative Response in all PWPSD schools, we are continuing with a District Plan to support Screening Protocols that look to develop a common language and approach across our District. Schools are required to follow this outline for the District Screen Plan. Schools may do additional screens in consultation with staff, school council and PWPSD Senior Administration. Any costs incurred by the additional screens will be the responsibility of the individual school.

1. **ECS Screening plan** - Some schools engaged in piloting the EYE Assessment under the direction of Karen Chrenek. Schools not participating can join in and training will be organized for September.

2. **Grades 1 to 6 Reading Assessment** - Fountas & Pinnell Benchmark Assessment
    - F & P assessments must be administered by a professional teacher.
        - Assess for the student's instructional level with the knowledge that the independent level is one to two levels below that.
        - Data is used to monitor progress, guide planning, and drive instruction.
    - Administer a minimum of one time per school year
        - Spring (May/June)
            - Spring results will be uploaded to Dossier.
            - Principal ensures spring results are passed onto and or highlighted to the upcoming teacher.
        - Fall (September/October) prior to the first report card teachers will follow the guidelines below regarding F & P assessments as needed when there appears to be a discrepancy between what the current teacher is seeing and spring F & P results from the previous year.

(Continued)

152 COLLABORATIVE RESPONSE

(Continued)

- o Students new to PWPSD schools should be assessed within two weeks if no recent F & P assessment data is available from the sending school.
- o Grade 6 students who reach **level X** will require no additional assessments into Junior High unless being recommended for special programming [K & E, Empower, etc.].
- o There is a PWPSD F&P Handbook that has been developed and will be provided to all administrators and teachers that are using this assessment.

3. **MIPI - Math Intervention/Programming Instrument** - This screen will be used for all students in Grades 2 to 10.

   Ed Tech Coaches will have all MIPI resources set up for the District each fall when they are ready for use. To set up a staff training opportunity please contact Memorese Walter or Leah Montes.

4. **Star Reading** for grades Grades 9 to 11. All **high schools** will administer the Star Reading Assessment as their Reading Screen for their students. Schools will be set up by/with the Assistant Superintendent of Curriculum and Instruction each August. Costs associated with Star Reading for all high schools will be shared between the District and Site at a rate of 50% each. Once we receive the amounts from Renaissance Learning we will communicate that out to the High Schools.

Source: ©2021, K. Elias, Peace Wapiti Public School Division, AB. Used with permission.

Note: F & P = Fountas and Pinnell; PWPSD = Peace Wapiti Public School Division.

A clearly defined and communicated assessment schedule allows teams to look forward and systematically plan for the timely administration of assessments across the school, which assists in the intentional organization of results for team analysis and CTMs.

Intentional Organization of Results for Team Analysis

Administering assessments for students is a futile and even frustrating exercise for schools if nothing is done with the data. It is not unusual for schools to be data rich and information poor. Schools must be "learning first to select data that can improve teaching and learning, and then learning how to use that data effectively for informed decision making. Numbers alone mean nothing unless we extract useful information through analyzing specifically how this data can help improve teaching and learning" (Huff, 2008, p. 212). Providing teams with usable results that are disaggregated in meaningful and clearly understood ways is vital so that data can be used to inform team conversations and the resulting actions.

Let's examine this concept of effectively organizing screening data results through a comparative vignette. As you read, recognize the frustrations that inevitably arise for teams and individual team members trying to utilize data at Information Junior High. Also note how information is provided to team members at Focus Junior High to support and inform analysis and subsequent CTMs.

CHAPTER #6. Data and Evidence

As you read, reflect on the following questions:

1. How does Focus Junior High help teachers move beyond simply looking at assessment scores?

2. How does Focus Junior High use colors to help teachers "visualize" the data?

3. How could Focus Junior High explicitly use the assessment data to inform the collaborative planning and CTM structures in their school?

A Tale of Two Schools

Information Junior High and Focus Junior High both have worked hard to establish a culture of response that includes the systematic assessment of students. Last week, all students in both schools were screened and now, one week later, the information from those numeracy assessments is being shared with teachers.

At Information Junior High, teachers receive a stack of paper in their mailboxes as well as an email to be able to access the same information digitally. For each student in their classes, they receive the four-page assessment results, arranged in alphabetical order. Each student-result package shows the overall student grade equivalent in a number of areas from the numeracy screen as well as the individual student assessment, showing responses on each question (along with the corresponding correct answer). The note attached to the stack of assessment results asks teachers to review the data and be prepared to talk about their students at the next CTM happening early next week.

At Focus Junior High, teachers receive the same stack of assessment results, but attached to the top of their stack are two simple spreadsheet overviews, which have also been sent to the teachers digitally. The first shows all the students at the grade level, listed alphabetically and showing the homeroom for each student. The spreadsheet shows all the questions on the assessment, the student's individual answers, the correct answer, and the percentage of students who answered the question correctly. It also shows overall the number of students in the grade and the percentage achieving the acceptable standard, with a simple color-coding showing incorrect answers, to help teachers visually see each student's correct response rate across all questions. The second spreadsheet shows the

(Continued)

(Continued)

same cohort of students, but now organizes the students based on their overall score on the assessment, listing them from lowest score to highest score. The scores have also been marked red, yellow, green, and blue, using a simple criterion listed at the top of the page:

Red: 0%–49%

Yellow: 50%–64%

Green: 65%–79%

Blue: 80%–100%

There is also a column titled "Key Issue" that is currently blank for all students.

At first glance, the table shows about a quarter of the listed students red, approximately another quarter yellow, and the remaining half of the students are either green or blue. The table also shows the student's score on the previous numeracy assessment, completed at the end of last year, with a color also indicated. It is interesting to note that some green students had red and yellow scores on the last screen and a few who had green scores on the last screen are now yellow.

A small Post-it note is attached reading, "Please review and bring these data overviews to your next collaborative planning time."

For data to be utilized to guide and inform conversations, they must be shared in ways that quickly "flag" students in a format easily understood by all team members. Disaggregating data for a group of students in a way that allows the assessment data to be visually accessed easily, which can then guide subsequent conversations, is necessary for schools engaging in data-informed practices.

Starting Steps

As shared in the vignette, creating data overviews does not need to be an onerous task. Using contemporary spreadsheet features, such as data sorting and conditional formatting, makes the organization and displaying of data a relatively easy exercise. At a previous school, Kurtis took on this task as the school principal as it was an easy way to gain an overall understanding of the school, as well as individual student concerns, through taking on the responsibility of organizing the data overviews to distribute to teams.

As described in the vignette, the first organization of the data is intended for team analysis. Obviously, what constitutes a team is entirely dependent on the context of the school. A large high school may engage in analysis divided by faculties or arranged by specific student cohorts (should a teacher advisor or similar construct be utilized in the school). Another school may engage in team analysis by grade levels. A smaller school may engage in division teams (K–3, 4–6, 7–9, 10–12) or primary/secondary cohorts. A very small school may investigate their entire school population as a collective team activity. Whether done collectively by a school during a professional development day, through the use of substitutes to provide release time, during scheduled collaborative planning time, or set as an expectation for the team to determine their own time to complete, a team analysis data overview abides by the following considerations:

▶ *Indication of overall student performance*: Indicating the overall student performance (i.e., percentage of students achieving acceptable standard) is an important metric to show trend data over time for a particular cohort. This information is important for the team over time, but is also important at the school or district level to indicate growth or regression for a particular cohort of students as well as cohorts in need for further examination and/or supports.

▶ *Inclusion of all students*: For effective team analysis, having all students in a particular cohort represented is important, rather than segregated into individual classrooms or cohorts. It reinforces the notion that they are all "our students" and starts to indicate particular classrooms in need of further resources. It can also potentially start to indicate the potential need for cross-classroom interventions in relation to a particular skill or concept. Although individual classroom data overviews could also be shared, the team analysis is best done if all students belonging to that team are grouped together.

▶ *Listed alphabetically*: In order to find students quickly and easily during the team analysis, students should be listed alphabetically.

▶ *Individual question results*: Including a column for each question or skill area within the assessment, with how the student responded, assists team members in two ways. The first is that it provides, at a glance, areas individual students struggled with on the assessment. The second is that it allows the team to see how the cohort as a whole did on each question. The infusion of the percentage of students correct for each question is valuable to assist with specific item analysis. By color-coding incorrect responses in each cell, it makes it very easy for a team to discern not only student struggles, but also particular areas where a cohort struggled.

In the Field

At Oscar Adolphson Primary School in Valleyview, Alberta, Canada, student data overviews use color-coding to visually help determine student progress as well as overall achievement in specific literacy skill areas. Figure 6.3 shows student data from the same cohort in November and then March, using their literacy screening tool. The overviews shown in this sample intentionally have student names removed, as it came from a bulletin board in the principal's office (and team meeting space) to illustrate the progress being made through their Collaborative Response efforts.

Figure 6.3 Literacy screen data overview

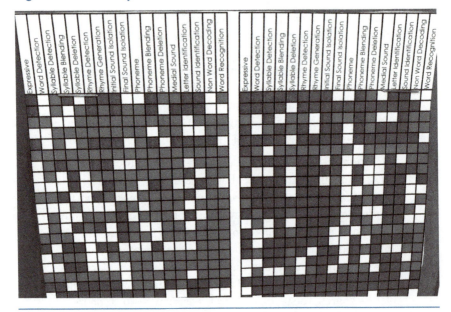

Source: ©2020, S. Howey, Oscar Adolphson Primary School, Northern Gateway Public Schools, AB. Used with permission.

Once the data analysis overview is provided to the team, it is important to have a simple yet clear process established for the team to engage in collaborative analysis, with a focus on next steps and the transference of said data into a format designed specifically for the purpose of the CTM. Asking teams four fundamental questions is a powerful way to inform their overall team response, connect it to individual teacher actions, and then use the data to help determine specific students to bring forth for collaborative conversations:

1. What strengths are indicated in the data?
2. What areas of concern are indicated in the data?
3. What are some possible next steps for your team to explore to attend to those areas of concern?

4. Who are the students, with a related key issue, to explore at an upcoming CTM?

The first three questions can help inform collaborative planning and can be directly integrated in team planning guides, as shared in Chapter 3. The fourth question relates to how the data now can have a substantial impact on the CTM conversation, effectively reinforcing the purpose of this integral collaborative structure.

Companion Website Resources

6.6. Team data analysis template: Organizers for teams to use when attending to the aforementioned four questions for team data analysis, with space to begin reflecting on students for further examination, along with an associated key issue.

Intentional Organization of Results for Collaborative Team Meetings

Whereas the data overview for team analysis needs to show information that ensures a deeper level of analysis for the purpose of individual and overall instructional response, the data organizer developed expressly for the purpose of the CTM is intentionally less detailed. Take a moment to reflect on the data overview sample in Figure 6.4.

Figure 6.4 Collaborative team meeting data overview sample

COLLABORATIVE RESPONSE

As shown in the sample, which depicts a simple overview sharing two sets of key data (overall student achievement reporting and attendance) identified as key indicators linked to the school-established priorities of student academic success and engagement, we can now start to quickly identify students for our collaborative conversations. Some key considerations inform the development of a data overview for the CTM.

▶ *Inclusion of all students*: Similar to the data overview for team analysis, the data overview for the CTM should also include all students for the particular team, reinforcing the ongoing mantra that "they are all our students." In the case of CTMs that include teachers engaging who are teaching a widely varied set of students (often the case for large high schools, where team membership is not determined by student cohorts, but by diversity in teaching assignments), a single data overview may not be used but rather the pre-meeting organization criteria that are described a little further on in this section.

▶ *Students listed highest to lowest, by key data measure related to the focus of the* CTM: Where the team analysis data overview listed students alphabetically, the CTM data overview shows students organized from lowest to highest (or vice versa), by the key measure being used to inform that meeting's focus (as described in Chapter 5). This allows us to very quickly see the subsets of students toward whom we wish to turn our collective attention.

In the Field

At a large regional high school in New South Wales, Australia, student data overviews are created for years 7 to 12, including all students in that particular year. As shown in Figure 6.5, this overview (with student names removed) includes key assessment data from a number of sources in a single document, with color-coding that allows easy organization for CTMs, depending on the focus for the meeting.

CHAPTER #6. Data and Evidence

Figure 6.5 Data overview for a large regional high school in New South Wales

Source: ©2020, J. Silcock, NSW, Australia. Used with permission.

> ▶ *Color-code criteria established*: As shown in Figures 6.4 and 6.5, the development of criteria to allow student scores to be color-coded is essential for the data overviews. Although this may mean a workout for a school's color printer, the color is instrumental in two ways. First, it helps quickly draw attention to students whose scores are telling us something. A student went from green to yellow—what is happening there? A student went from yellow to blue—yahoo! Now, what did we do that led to that success? The color allows us to engage in these individual reflections and team discussions much more easily than having to pore through numbers or letters. Second, it can help determine *which* students become our primary attention during the CTMs. This has an immense impact on the focus of the conversation, a realization that we will expand on shortly.

▶ *Indication of key issue (optional)*: Infusing an area directly for a key issue can be an activity for teams or individuals during the team analysis process to help determine one area we could affect, as seen in the data, that could become the focus for conversation in the CTM. This process allows us to "analyze, then aggregate" (Rose, 2016, p. 69), looking at the individualized needs of the students and then synthesizing into an area where we feel we can start or where we would have the greatest impact through classroom responses. Although the infusion of the key issue is not essential if it is integrated into the pre-meeting organizer, it can be a solid reminder in the data overview that can help guide our collective focus when engaging in student conversations.

Integration With Pre-Meeting Organizer

The color-coding on the data overview becomes fundamental when now using the data to directly influence the focus and conversation in the CTM. Without the infusion of data, when we ask teachers, "Who would you like to talk about," the focus can often go to those students requiring the highest levels of support, often with complexities that require support beyond the classroom. It can feel that the conversation revolves around the same subset of students and, often, students who are already the center of attention in other collaborative layers within the school, such as the school support team meetings and case consult team meetings. When we look at our data overviews, these students are often the ones who are "red" (using the color-code criteria referred to earlier). Even with substantial shifts, interventions, strategies, and accommodations at the classroom level, it may feel like we're making little progress, effectively turning our CTMs into spaces where it can feel like efforts are not having the impact we would like to see or the continued focus on a small group of students.

However, shifting our attention in the CTM to students where the data show "yellow," we do two things:

1. We shift our attention to students who may have been hiding under our collective radar, who have not typically drawn our investigation. It surfaces students we may not have been discussing in the past.

2. We identify students who are close to where we would like to see them, in relation to our area of focus, and may only need some additional supports or instructional shifts in the classroom in order to see success.

This shift in focus, accomplished through effective utilization of our data sets, can have a phenomenal impact on the CTM conversation. All of a sudden, the examination and adoption of subtle shifts in classroom practice can yield greater impact that we may not see when focusing

CHAPTER #6. Data and Evidence

solely on the students significantly below our established standards. This shift leads to building higher levels of collective efficacy in the CTM, as we start to see the conversations focused on the classroom making a difference for the students we are identifying. The paradox in thinking is that although we have shifted our focus in the CTM to students close to achieving success (we have sometimes referred to these students lovingly as our "bubble kids," ones right on the bubble between success or potentially dropping lower), we are engaging in conversations about classroom pedagogy that will still have, over time, impact on not only our highest-need students but *all* students. Often, the suggestions being put forward for students are universal, meaning that although they are intended to have specific impact for the students being discussed, they are applied broadly to a whole class and can benefit a much wider student population.

Having the integration of data right into the pre-meeting organizer for the CTM is a powerful next step for schools. As shared in Recommended Resource 6.8, asking teachers to come prepared with a yellow, a red, and a green/blue student (as determined in the data overview), a meeting facilitator can direct the conversation to focus primarily on the yellow students while also infusing a conversation about enrichment by focusing on the green/blue students, who the data say are already performing where we would like but who we know can further extend their learning.

Shifting the CTM to focus on a specific subset of students is guided by two general but powerful assumptions:

▶ We can assume that the students most often coded as red *likely* are having their needs examined and responded to within other layers of our collaborative structures in the school. Often, these are students requiring specialized programs and program plans, who can certainly not have their needs attended to solely in the CTM. This may not always be the case, which is why we still want to have some latitude in our CTMs to surface key issues initiated by these students (which is why professional judgment should always accompany what the data are saying). However, as a general rule of thumb, we can assume that these students are being discussed within other collaborative structures in our school.

▶ We can assume that with some small shifts in our instructional practices or infusing some additional interventions, strategies, and accommodations at the classroom level, we can witness emerging levels of success for the students who are close or need to have enrichment extended to deepen their learning.

Infusing the data purposefully to shift the focus in our CTMs can have a substantial impact on our culture of response and the critical role practices at the classroom level have in relation to that response. Through this, we can ensure that we are attending to the needs of students but doing so through a set of structures and processes that have intentional focus on honoring and extending classroom practices across the school.

> **Companion Website Resources**
>
> **6.7. Data overview template:** Template for developing data overviews for CTMs, including instructions for completion and how to sort the data based on the focus for the team.
>
> **6.8. Data-informed pre-meeting organizer:** Organizer for teachers to complete prior to the CTM, with explicit determination of students based on data results.

Student Entry Levels

Organizing our data and evidence through color-code criteria can affect the ongoing examination of students, as well as inform transition processes, as students move from grade to grade and from school to school. This includes the infusion of visual team boards, used when examining students at all levels within a school or potentially across a district. As mentioned in the vignette in Chapter 5, a visual team board can assist school team members in viewing the progress of students in relation to the supports being accessed as well as determine a student's entry level when first coming into a new grade.

Student entry-level criteria help determine a common understanding of the level at which students are entering a grade level in a specific area of focus. It is intended to utilize a simple color system, and once established, the entry-level criteria can be used

- to determine the color of student cards/entry levels on visual team boards;
- to determine which students should be focused on when planning supports and/or classroom instruction for teachers who may not be familiar with the incoming students;
- to support transition meetings as students move from grade to grade; and
- by other grade levels to determine targets to be aiming for when planning forward.

In preparation for students to move to a new grade (which may mean feeding into another school), collaborative teams examine the student data and evidence collected to determine student entry-level criteria. The principles shared in relation to establishing color-code criteria previously apply in this context. Schools (whether through leadership or more preferably, through a collaborative process) determine the criteria that would make a student red, yellow, or green (or blue, if looking at coding students

CHAPTER #6. Data and Evidence   163

achieving beyond expected end-of-grade criteria) as they transition out of a particular grade. Teachers or teams of teachers then examine their student data and evidence to determine the student entry level, as they prepare to move to the next grade, just a natural extension of the work of data analysis already discussed.

Companion Website Resources

6.9. Student entry-level criteria template: Template to assist schools in setting common student entry levels based on assessment data and evidence.

The visual team board then can be utilized by a team throughout a school year to remind them of the entry level of students coming to them but then become a visual throughout the school year that shows the flexing of supports being accessed at each tier (a concept explored in Chapter 7). This visual can serve as a powerful reminder of the growth being seen by students during the course of the year and then evidence to fuel celebrations for teams when a student who came to them "red" leaves their classroom "green."

In the Field

When the seeds that would later grow into Collaborative Response were initially planted, the visual boards were simple. Using trifold science fair boards at each grade level, basic student cards displaying only student names were affixed with Velcro, able to be manipulated between three basic categories on each board—maintain, watch, and concern. The maintain category represented students currently experiencing varying levels of success in the classroom setting. The watch category represented students who were either beginning to exhibit struggles or who were transitioning from the concern category. The concern category reflected students who would not meet grade-level expectations without the intervention of the team. Because the school just needed an organizer to guide the team meetings that were beginning to evolve, these boards served the purpose of placing students at the forefront.

As the school's Collaborative Response continued to evolve, two subtle adjustments were made to the team boards, as shown in Figure 6.6.

(Continued)

(Continued)

Figure 6.6 Sample visual team board

The first adjustment was categories for the board that reflected the tiers of support that aligned with the school's ever-evolving continuum of supports. Rather than the broad "maintain, watch, concern" categories, the student scoreboard now displayed the support tier each student was currently placed within, reflecting the highest tier of support currently being accessed. This is a topic that will be further explored in Chapter 7.

The second adjustment was the use of colored student cards. As data and evidence were introduced to flag students for discussion, colored students' cards indicated the entry level of students, as determined by assessments. When colored cards were first introduced, the colors were based on a common, schoolwide end-of-grade literacy benchmark assessment. The color of a student's cards reflected their performance on that benchmark assessment and served as the starting place for conversation as students entered the next grade. The colors represented the following:

　　Red: more than a grade level below

　　Yellow: less than a grade level below

　　Green: at or above grade level

　　Blue: at or above the 90th percentile on the assessment

Although this overdependence on a single assessment did not reflect the long-term vision of the school related to the use of data and evidence to inform professional judgment, it served as a starting place to begin discussions at each grade level.

As the framework continued to evolve in the school, the colors came to represent the student's level of achievement, determined collaboratively by teachers and informed by multiple literacy measures (including standardized assessments, teacher assessments, and other "soft measures" such as library circulation and student reading attitude surveys). The colors then reflected the four standards of the school's student literacy profile:

Red: not yet meeting grade-level expectations

Yellow: approaching grade-level expectations

Green: meeting grade-level expectations

Blue: exceeding grade-level expectations

Visually, the colored cards added another important aspect to the CTM. Staff could celebrate seeing red and yellow cards that were moving to less-intensive tiers of support (and it was very gratifying to see a red student card reside in the Tier 2 category on the visual boards) as well as recognize the urgency that accompanied seeing a green or blue card moving up the tiers of the continuum.

There are now digital solutions, such as WeCollab, that can be used for digital team boards, which automatically move students to the tier that best corresponds with the supports that are attached to their student profile and identify colors based on student data. To learn more, visit http://jigsawcollaborativesolutions.ca.

Data-Informed Planning

A final value associated with the collection, organization, and utilization of data and evidence in Collaborative Response is its use to inform strategic planning efforts, all the way from the student to potentially district priorities. Within a school, two other uses bear examination, as introduced in Chapter 3.

1. *Informing collaborative planning*: The examination of student data and evidence, particularly in relation to annual data sets, can inform team planning and help determine the explicit areas of focus for the team. Student data can provide the evidence of whether our efforts achieved the desired outcomes for students and our own learning.

2. *Informing schoolwide planning*: The ongoing analysis of trend data sets can help inform progress being made as well as

elicit next steps or directions to be taken. However, the use of color-coding of data can add one further element to examining impact that can really speak to the efforts of the staff team and the connection to Collaborative Response efforts. By looking at student movement on the color scale, it can make the data directly related to the student and make schoolwide data really applicable for staff team members. For example, by stating "we had 28 students enter grade nine at yellow and 10 students enter at red. Through our efforts, we now have 8 students entering the next grade red and 21 students entering yellow. Due to our efforts, 9 students have come up to grade level moving into grade 10!" This explicit focus on individual students, rather than "we had 72% of students enter at grade level and now we're up to 79%," creates a more student-focused organization of the data, which can personalize the impact of our collective efforts, and allows us to effectively put a face on the data. For more on this topic, please see Hewsons and Parsons (2013).

Furthermore, utilization of data and evidence in Collaborative Response creates a clear through-line from the response for individual students, to the impact on team collaborative planning, to its impact on schoolwide planning (and potentially to inform district-level strategic planning). This flips and then aligns the strategic planning model, where the individual student conversations drive the greater school improvement planning efforts.

Using Data Effectively Takes Time

We have argued that the use of assessments and the data they produce must be about the student, not the number (see Hewson & Parsons, 2013). Rather than placing attention on the scores, assessment data need to focus on what we do with that data and place the conversation squarely on students. Hargreaves and Fullan (2012) remind us, "In the end, it's important to be informed by the evidence, not numbed by the numbers. . . . Make evidence human and inclusive, and it becomes a powerful strategy for building professional knowledge of one's students and professional motivation to serve them better" (p. 173). Building knowledge around students and ensuring a collective drive to take action to support them is truly the goal of assessment utilization in Collaborative Response. However, it should not be expected that schools, when first establishing assessments or even consolidating the assessments already used in isolation, will collectively know what to do with the evidence generated. Using data effectively takes time.

Starting Steps

Establishing universal screens in schools can create a collective sense of urgency and provide data to ignite the initiation of Collaborative Response. We have worked in and with schools that perceived little need to examine and collaboratively respond to the needs of students—their students overall are doing just fine. In these situations, the limited data available suggest no need for change to traditional structures and practices. However, as White (2007) suggests, "The purpose of these data is to build support for necessary changes in professional practice with evidence that will satisfy the skeptics" (p. 213). Universal screen data can provide what White calls persuasive data and reveal a subset of students who are in need of attention.

It is important to note the evolutionary process involved when a school begins to refine its use of data and evidence. Even limited data, examined by a collaborative team, powerfully shine a light on the students we need to discuss and areas to be addressed in their growth and development. However, it takes time for high levels of professional trust to be established before data can truly bring about change in classroom practice and schoolwide response.

"Collaborative data analysis is not about pointing fingers at teachers with nonproficient students. It is about trusting in the collective wisdom of the team to collaboratively bring about high levels of learning for all students" (Huff, 2008, p. 209). This level of trust in the team will not happen naturally nor should we wait for it to be in place before establishing common assessments and examining the data. It will continue to evolve as teams engage in analysis and response. Although it is true that "data almost always point to action—they are the enemy of comfortable routines" (Schmoker, 1996, p. 33), sophisticated use of data and judicious implementation of assessments as held up against staff's relational knowledge are part of the natural growth of Collaborative Response.

Potential Pitfalls

It is important to heed Hargreaves and Fullan's (2012) advice: "If we are so busy analyzing data that we have less time to be with the children, then we are getting sidetracked down the wrong path" (p. 172). It is important that leadership reinforces the primary objective of data and evidence, which is to flag students for discussion, leading to professional action. The focus must be continuously placed on the action—"So what are we going to do?"—rather than excessive analysis and examination of data sets and growth charts.

Data and Evidence Missing in the Model

Once again, we return to our three foundational components of Collaborative Response to note what we observe when data and evidence are absent.

Table 6.1 Data and evidence not established

COLLABORATIVE STRUCTURES AND PROCESSES	DATA AND EVIDENCE	CONTINUUM OF SUPPORTS	RESULT
Established	Not established	Established	Conversations about the needs of students lacking data to inform—based primarily on observation or assumptions. Limited ability to determine the impact of formalized supports. Lack of consistency in determining students in need of collective response

Data and evidence are vital components to essentially ensure that we (1) focus on the right students in our CTMs and (2) know what we are focusing on when turning our attention to those students. Although teacher professional judgment is absolutely critical and highly valued, it cannot be the sole determinant in a school's systematic response model to determine which students are being addressed and how we are addressing their needs. Assessment data can also inform schools in regard to the effectiveness of both individual supports and interventions and the overall impact of their Collaborative Response. Data and evidence provide and refine the overall focus of Collaborative Response.

Continuum of Supports

CHAPTER #7

Teachers want students to succeed. In our experience working in schools, teachers and the school leadership team work hard for their students and employ a myriad of strategies and additional supports when they experience a student struggling. However, employing that varied set of strategies and supports is a diverse variable across individual classrooms in schools and largely depends on individual teacher factors, including experience, professional learning, teaching philosophy, and time. Moreover, schools as organizations typically provide a number of supports to help students beyond individual classrooms, which can also vary greatly from grade to grade and classroom to classroom.

Individual islands of excellence exist in schools in relation to classroom instruction, and the response when a student struggles is typically placed at the doorway of those individual classrooms and with individual teachers. As discussed throughout this text, Collaborative Response provides a schoolwide system for identifying students in need of collective examination, and the continuum of supports component directly answers the question, "So, now what do *we do*?"

In the introduction, we discussed the fundamental differences between envisioning Collaborative Response and tiered systems of support, such as response to intervention (RTI) and multitiered systems of support, and have surmised that these two approaches, although sharing a number of commonalities, are not synonymous. The work that we've engaged in to articulate a continuum of supports (see the Substantial Shifts that follow) most certainly arose out of the work in RTI and the development of a pyramid of interventions. During the early years of this work, we examined many renditions of a pyramid of interventions as we wrestled with how this simple idea, also used in other contexts such as health and medicine, could be used to affect student learning and student success. Our examinations led us to numerous samples from clearly mandated and compliance documents to practical functioning visuals. Our compelling questions driving our examination were how were these documents developed, how were they used, and most importantly, how did they impact student success? We also struggled with how they could be organized and documented to support and extend conversations throughout the layers of collaboration, as we've been exploring throughout this text.

Substantial Shifts

When considering the breadth of our learning as we've engaged with educators at both the school and district levels, we've come to realize that a shift from pyramid of interventions to continuum of supports was not only preferred but necessary. It has become increasingly apparent that referring to this foundational component initially as a pyramid of interventions was very limiting and, in some cases, misleading. A shift to a continuum of supports is critically important for two key reasons.

First off, we have come to understand that interventions are only one of the kinds of support that we can consider when determining the most effective responses for our students. However, we discuss that in addition to interventions (which have a very specific definition), we can also consider a multitude of accommodations and strategies when determining next steps for students. Referring to what we can consider as *supports* is much more broad and certainly more applicable than referring to every response we could take as an intervention (which further clouds the definition of what an intervention truly is). Referring to the myriad of responses as supports is a better way to approach the conversation around the multiple ways in which educators respond to the needs of their students.

Second, a pyramid suggests a hierarchy, moving up or down tiers. It can set rigid definitions between types of supports that students need to progress up a pyramid and assumes that a student needs to fail before gaining access to more intensive levels of support. We have also found that its existence is so closely tied to tiered systems of support structures that it clouds some fundamental differences between those approaches and Collaborative Response. A *continuum* is more fluid, suggesting that we consider supports across a continuum to best support a student, *effectively organizing the supports rather than the students*. We often repeat this statement when engaging with educators: we tier the supports—not the students! This negates the mindset of a child needing to fail in order to "move up" to the next tier. Instead, we proactively determine which supports on the continuum will best meet the needs of the child at that point in their learning, understanding that all students benefit from universal practices and that all students, at different times, may need more intensive levels of support in different areas within their educational experience.

The *system of supports* has been identified as "one of the biggest progress challenges—and frustrations—that school leaders and teachers face. At the end of the day, it is just a really, really complex thing to do." (Ferriter et al., 2013, p. 69). The complexity comes in as we attempt to create a comprehensive method for providing support with intensifying needs while also addressing the unique nature of students themselves. This cannot be boiled down to a simple algorithm of Student + Intervention = Success but rather requires an intensive understanding of the supports available, coupled with the expertise required for those supports, as well as a working relationship between teacher and student that allows informed judgment as to whether a support will be successful or not.

Typically represented through the use of tiered levels of response, a school or district's continuum of supports is manifested as a visual representation of the response to the critical question of a professional learning community, as posed by DuFour et al. (2004): "How will we respond when students experience initial difficulty so that we can improve upon current levels of learning?" (p. 3).

This points to the idea that different students require different levels of support (which also does not remain static as a child grows, develops, and learns), and schools are responsible to ensure that they are structured to guarantee that this flexible support happens, not leaving it to the unilateral discretion of individual teachers. Just as every student is unique, we could also apply the same assumption to each teacher in the building, knowing that each has levels of expertise in varying areas that enable them to create unique circumstances in each classroom based on their strengths and competencies. The creation and utilization of a continuum of supports attempts to establish common, consistent, research-based practices that will exist in every classroom, regardless of expertise while still protecting a teacher's autonomy for making decisions in their own classroom.

Although there is no prescriptive organization that must be adhered to when developing a continuum of supports, there are essential elements in relation to a continuum's development and utilization within Collaborative Response. We will explore these key elements in this chapter. Although we believe that schools need this organization and the specific strategies, accommodations, and interventions articulated within their continuum, schools are also highly contextual, and how the elements play out is unique to each school.

Nine key elements align to determine, define, and organize as well as implement a continuum of supports in Collaborative Response:

1. Honor current practices in areas of focus

2. Articulation of tiers of support

3. Articulation of interventions, strategies, and accommodations

4. Development of a menu of supports
5. Intentional utilization in team meetings
6. Refinement of Tier 1 instruction
7. Inform professional learning
8. Connection to visual team board
9. Alignment with collaborative structures and processes

The rest of the chapter will focus on examining each of these elements in detail, describing how schools engage in the work of

- identifying the current unique and common practices as well as the expertise that exists in each classroom across the school or district;
- determining interventions, strategies, and accommodations;
- developing an organizational framework for their supports; and
- continuous refinement of their continuum, all in an effort to systematically ensure that all students can succeed.

The continuum of supports rests on the belief that "combining targeted, strategic intervention with improved general classroom instruction leads to greater student success" (Vaughn et al., 2007, p. 24).

Companion Website Resources

7.1. Reflecting on a continuum of supports: Template that serves as a self-assessment tool to assist in determining current realities and provide direction when developing a continuum of supports in Collaborative Response.

For a school's continuum of supports to be a functional and valuable structure to guide flexible support for students, the increasing instructional intensity as a student accesses supports at each tier must be present. For high levels of learning to be the constant for our students, the continuum must ensure that instruction and time are intensified for students who need the most support.

Honor Current Practices in Areas of Focus

All schools differ. They serve different students, families, and communities. They are staffed by unique individuals. They are guided by different cultures of practice and underlying philosophies. They serve communities with wide ranges of cultural beliefs, practices, socioeconomic realities, and language dialects dependent on each family in each home. Even schools with similar grade configurations, populations, and student and staff demographics will not be mirror images of one another. Louis (2008) reminds us, "All schools are in a sense similar, but they are populated by students and teachers who bring with them variable talents and preferences, and they are embedded in communities with differing demands and needs. Place matters, and the people in the place matter" (p. 52). As a result, the continuum of supports developed at each school will be unique to the context of that school.

The initial development of a continuum of supports does not need to be rocket science. In the spirit of simplicity described at the beginning of Chapter 2, a continuum of supports can initially be thought of as a collection of best practices already being employed in classrooms by individual teachers and across the school, although perhaps not in a highly strategic manner. The key to successfully implementing a continuum of supports is striving to ensure a common understanding across the school and then effective, intentional implementation of resources to support a higher number of student needs, aligned to certain key areas of focus.

Determining an Area of Focus for a Continuum of Supports

Successful organizations establish strategic planning processes to focus on priorities that they will target. This planning typically involves leadership in that organization who worked with their staff teams and various stakeholders to set priorities and then establish corresponding targets and action plans that guide the work of their staff to arrive at their desired outcome in relation to those priorities.

From the priorities comes an area of focus on which to guide the establishment of a continuum of supports, recognizing that this process may occur after you've already commenced your collaborative team meetings (CTMs). As earlier described, establishing and initiating CTMs will engage the mechanism for providing a response for student needs, and the fundamental desire to answer the question, "So what are we going to do?" will serve as the impetus for the creation of a continuum of supports.

Active participation for staff in the development of establishing a focus area as well as designing a continuum of supports is critically important to the overall success of the framework. As with any attempt to adopt new practices, the degree to which that new practice is implemented in meaningful ways is directly related to teacher involvement in determining, developing, and initiating the practices.

Potential Pitfall

While it may be efficient or would save staff time for a district group, or a small group of teachers in a school to engage in the work of developing a continuum of supports to share with others, it is not ideal to the acceptance and utilization of the continuum of supports. In simple terms, the process is more important than the resulting product. It is the messy work of creating a continuum of supports that serves as the genesis of a collective desire to share and explore other classroom practices and student supports. Ownership and understanding of the greater purpose is only achieved through the act of creation.

A continuum of supports will attend to the uniqueness of an individual school when it is developed by staff in that school and will provide opportunities to

- identify common practices used in the school;
- identify unique strategies used in some classes and the expertise that exists in terms of leading those unique practices;
- clarify and define practices that are only familiar to some teachers;
- identify areas of professional learning; and
- identify gaps within the practices that require investigation and exploration to strengthen those gaps.

When first establishing a school's continuum of supports, it is important to first determine what supports are already in place, focusing on what the school already has, rather than what it does not. Schools already have a number of practices happening that have not traditionally been viewed through the lens of a continuum.

In the following Starting Steps, we describe a process for initializing a continuum of supports that will provide you with the content to begin to articulate the answer to the question, "What do we do when a student struggles?"

Starting Steps

In workshops and presentations, we have argued that discovering a school's existing supports need not be convoluted or complicated. By following the simple workshop design detailed below, schools can begin to envision their own continuum of supports, specific to a focus area.

The process below is intended for leadership and teaching staff; however, depending on your support staff and their involvement within student learning, it may be advantageous to include them in this activity. Educational assistants and paraprofessionals sometimes have a wealth of ideas and strategies from working in many different classrooms and grade levels. Their understanding of the supports surfaced in this activity may be advantageous to their overall support for individual students.

Step 1: Determine the focus

As described at the beginning of this section, the focus for your continuum should be driven by the priority areas in the school. However, it can be established in a number of ways. It may be guided by an analysis of data to determine the area in most urgent need of attention. We have worked with schools whose data indicated a need to focus on the literacy achievement of students, with other schools whose schoolwide data pointed toward supports related to student behavior, and yet other schools who had clear indications through their data that their area to target was student wellness.

The focus of the continuum could also be determined by a school's current areas of strength. Clearly articulating these areas of strength helps a school gain confidence when constructing a continuum. Knowing that a number of supports are already in place can assist in developing a comprehensive continuum of supports and provide a quick win for a school before later tackling more pressing areas of concern.

Typically, this focus area is determined before the workshop, either by administration, by a leadership team, or in alignment with a school's improvement priorities.

Step 2: Engage staff in articulating what they already do in the focus area

Begin with plenty of sticky notes for every staff member. Ask the question, "What do we do in our classrooms or in our school when a student struggles in [our area of focus]?" Each individual then begins to record their ideas on individual sticky notes. It's important to emphasize recording one idea per sticky note as this will be important in the next step. This is an intensive reflection on what each individual in the school is doing to support students in the identified focus area.

Then, small groups are convened to compare lists. When common supports have been identified, they place those sticky notes on top of each other. When supports seem similar, the small group asks questions and engages in a discussion to determine if it is in fact the same support or if it is actually different and will need to be further defined to clarify. This can be done on a different sticky note or added to the original.

(Continued)

COLLABORATIVE RESPONSE

(Continued)

The small groups share with the big group to combine all supports identified, again placing common supports on top of each other. The collection of ideas are then placed on a bulletin board or poster papers, or posted on a wall in the staff room. Time is then given to review the full list of supports with further clarification requested on some posts, questions posed, and confirmations made when reviewing the piles of posts.

At this point, a school could decide to leave the lists posted for a measure of time to allow further additions to the lists or for conversations to percolate prior to proceeding to step three. We have seen schools leave the lists posted in their staff room for a number of days or weeks before returning to them for step three.

Step 3: Articulating interventions, strategies, and accommodations

As articulated in a later section in this chapter, there are differences between what should be considered an intervention, strategy, or accommodation. Using a simple "I", "S," or "A" coding for each support is all that is needed for this step.

Step 4: Organizing into eventual tiers

Step four places focus on organizing the interventions, strategies, and supports into defined tiers. Staff members are divided into four groups. These groups can most easily be defined as follows:

- best practices for all students in the classroom;

- differentiated strategies, accommodations, or interventions provided by the classroom teacher to some students;

- programs or supports provided by someone other than the classroom teacher; and

- intensive interventions for highest-need students provided by someone outside of the school.

In these groups, staff survey the lists created earlier to determine strategies, accommodations, and interventions that best fit their group's area of focus. These are written individually on large Post-it notes or slips of paper and then grouped together on a wall to visually organize current practices. For any duplications, discussion follows to determine the best fit (or to further clarify if being interpreted differently).

The collections of strategies, accommodations, and interventions become the foundation of a school's continuum of supports, to be refined, added to, and further clarified over time.

CHAPTER #7. Continuum of Supports   177

This exercise will also help point to next steps. Perhaps classroom-based best practices are collectively weak and need to be addressed. Perhaps the school overall is deficient in supports beyond the classroom teacher. This early molding of a continuum of supports also can point to coaching opportunities, capitalizing on the instructional strengths of staff in the building. If "internal expertise is of more value than what we import" (Schmoker, 2006, p. 118), this internal expertise can help improve instructional response across a school (a concept to be further explored in this chapter).

In the Field

At Peace Wapiti Academy in Grande Prairie, Alberta, Canada, high school staff members engaged in an activity similar to the one described above, utilizing Post-it notes to begin the first organization of their continuum of supports, based on what already existed in the school. One Post-it note color reflected supports related to *academic* success, whereas the other color reflected supports related to *social-emotional* success, as shown in Figure 7.1.

Figure 7.1 Initial continuum of supports at Peace Wapiti Academy

Source: ©2021, W. Gerard, Peace Wapiti Academy, Peace Wapiti Public School Division, AB. Used with permission.

Potential Pitfall

While articulating all the possible supports that a school is ensuring are accessible to all students, we sometimes see the inclusion of practices such as assessments and support plans in the development of a continuum. While these are an important part of providing a comprehensive program for individual students, neither are examples of supports. In the first rendition of the brainstorming phase, allow these practices to surface. The conversation when revising and refining the continuum is well worth the time as it provides clarity to the continuum, definition of supports, and the purpose of assessments and individual support plans.

Assessments focus on targeting areas of concern, identifying gaps or areas of development, and then may (depending on the assessment) provide strategies for targeting specific identified areas of need. For example, in a psycho-educational assessment conducted by a trained psychologist, the diagnostic information is followed by a plethora of strategies. This section of the assessment may include strategies that could be used to contribute to the continuum; however, the assessment itself is not a support for the continuum.

Individual support plans are created for specific students to address specific areas of need. These plans are intended to provide consistency in targeting goals working toward achievement and growth based specifically on what the individual student requires. Strategies are an integral part of supporting a student through an individual support plan; however, the support plan itself does not belong on the continuum.

Articulation of Tiers of Support

Typically, RTI frameworks and related systems of interventions described early in the book focus on the articulation of three tiers. It would be advantageous to explore the traditional three-tier model before seeking to hold these elements up against the four-tier approach espoused in Collaborative Response.

Stoehr et al. (2011) provide a succinct definition of what is classified as Tier 1, also known as the primary or universal tier:

> Tier 1 is the general education classroom. Within the RTI framework, it is expected that 80% to 85% of the students will be successful in this tier. The use of evidence-based core instruction is essential here, as the teacher's goal is to help as many students as possible be successful and maintain classroom placement. Differentiated instruction is crucial in planning, instruction, and assessment in Tier 1. (p. 70)

Although other researchers may suggest slight variations in relation to the number of students having their needs met at this level (Howell et al., 2008, for instance, suggest that 80%–90% of students should be at Tier 1), the underlying assertion is that quality classroom instruction matters. In fact, "Tier 1—the classroom—is crucially important" (Foorman et al., 2007, p. 45) in the overall effectiveness of any tiered system of support framework as well as the Collaborative Response we've been describing. This tier demands a significant amount of attention because the quality of instruction will affect all other tiers. When schools ensure effective instruction at Tier 1 in all classrooms, theoretically, the supports at all other levels will diminish because many student needs are addressed at this foundational tier.

Tier 2, also referred to as secondary prevention (Vaughn & Denton, 2008) or targeted intervention "can be considered the first line of intervention for students who are not at benchmark with the core instruction" (Hall, 2008, p. 66). Tier 2 provides an opportunity to target specific learning gaps and addresses them through specific interventions and "should be implemented in combination with Tier 1 strategies in order to enhance and supplement the comprehensive curriculum" (Shores & Chester, 2012, pp. 32–33). Tier 2 will target approximately 10% to 15% of the student population (Howell et al., 2008).

Tier 3, also known as intensive or tertiary intervention, generally consists of 1% to 5% of all students (Howell et al., 2008). This tier provides intensive instruction that is "relentless" and "precise" (Kavale, 1988) for students who demonstrate significant struggles despite the best efforts made through Tier 1 and Tier 2 instruction and interventions.

We need to pause to reflect on the suggested percentages relayed throughout the previous definitions. In a pyramid of interventions, a pyramid shape is intentionally designed to demonstrate the decreasing number of students accessing the various levels of support. Ideally, we should see most students accessing Tier 1, with fewer at Tier 2 and even fewer at Tier 3, which has been described through percentages. However, this conceptualization works off an underlying assumption that students can be slotted into an appropriate tier, based on the support they are receiving. As we will discuss, we believe that our goal should not be to tier the students in order for them to access the supports at that tier. We instead believe that *supports should be tiered*, leading to the need to establish an additional tier.

In this chapter, we propose a four-tiered continuum of supports that, although grounded somewhat in the three-tier philosophy, provides an additional designation that we have found allows schools to further articulate effective differentiation at the classroom level as well as focus on providing tiered supports for students.

We have discussed the value, when first establishing a school's continuum of supports focused on a particular area, of articulating and then categorizing supports that already exist within classrooms and the school overall. Sometimes it can be a meaningful collaborative exercise to determine these categories after the articulation process has happened (as shared above), essentially thematically organizing interventions, strategies, and accommodations that provide the foundation of systematic tiers of response for a school. However, most schools, when establishing the foundations for their continuum of supports, benefit from having the tiers determined in relation to the increasing levels of support, with the classroom being foundational. It is critical that these tiers of support are clearly articulated, communicated, and understood throughout the learning community, whether within the context of a school or a larger school district.

As described at the onset of this chapter, most RTI models include pyramids characterized by three tiers, with Tier 1 defined as the universal level, with quality, differentiated instruction at the core. In our work in and with schools and districts, we have found that developing a four-tier continuum of supports, with this universal tier separated into two parts, serves as an effective model to both support students and support collaborative conversations that naturally evolve in relation to instruction as well as support the ongoing capacity building for staff that is a distinctive feature of a Collaborative Response. See Figure 7.2 for an overview of this continuum, with reference to often-used language found in RTI and other related frameworks. The continuum of supports as shown below is shaped uniquely to represent the plethora of strategies that exist at Tier 2, and therefore, the shape "bulges" to show the breadth of strategies, interventions, and accommodations that could be accessed at that tier. The visual also represents a visual blending of tiers as supports could flex from tier to tier based on the teacher and the overall school practices.

Why adopt a four-tier intervention model when most conventional tiered models are built upon a three-tier model of intervention? For us, the answer is in the power of collaboration for teachers in developing the schoolwide continuum of supports and the richness of the reflection and ongoing conversation related to instructional practices we should see happening in all classrooms as well as the rich array of interventions, strategies, and accommodations we can envision employing at the classroom level.

Essentially, Tiers 3 and 4 of our model somewhat resemble Tiers 2 and 3 of a traditional three-tiered model, where students are involved in supports beyond the classroom, with supports at the upper tier of the model highly individualized and intensive, often involving support from specialists external to the school. In our four-tier model, supports at the Tier 1 and Tier 2 level resemble the instructional practice typically defined in Tier 1 of the standard three-tier RTI model. Essentially, we believe in the power of *articulating differentiation* schoolwide through designating this second tier.

As described earlier, teachers work together to define the tenets of sound classroom practice (Tier 1). Working together does not mean that all educators commit to a specific instructional approach or program in their classrooms, but it does mean that they agree on what effective instruction should look like at the classroom level. If the continuum of supports developed is specific to literacy, the school staff work together to articulate what effective literacy instruction looks like at the classroom level, for example. These powerful conversations and commitments for

Figure 7.2 Continuum of supports overview

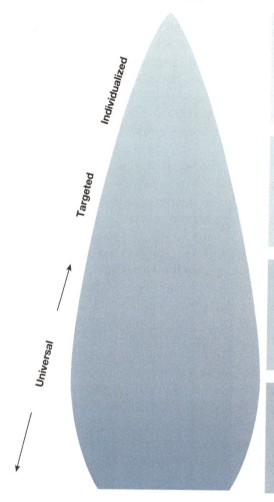

the school community become Tier 1, the instruction put in place for all students to succeed in each classroom, a conversation that evolves from the simple articulation of practices on Post-it notes.

We have defined Tier 2 as the place where teachers publicly open their "instructional toolkit" to share the differentiated approaches they utilize to support students in the classroom. For instance, it might involve more regular instruction in guided reading groups (in one school we worked at, a Tier 2 support was "daily guided reading," as students were involved in a daily guided reading experience in the classroom every day, whereas other classmates had guided reading two to three times weekly). However, small-group literacy instruction (typically coordinated in most classrooms through guided reading) was determined as a Tier 1 "nonnegotiable" across the school.

Tier 2 may involve a classroom behavior checklist system for behavior-related continuums. Whatever the focus of the supports, the organization of supports pushes teachers to share the differentiated approaches they deem most effective to develop a schoolwide repository of Tier 2 supports. Over time, Tier 2 supports are monitored for effectiveness and added to as other strategies and approaches are considered. The school ensures that the supports are articulated and teachers work together to help each other implement these supports effectively in their classrooms. In essence, Tier 2 becomes a rich array of ideas that we could be considering for some students, some of the time, but still within the domain of the classroom teacher.

The articulation of common, expected practices in Tier 1 and then the vast collection of ways in which we can provide support in Tier 2 ensures that we are doing all we can at the classroom level to provide students and teachers with a flexible list of interventions, strategies, and accommodations to consider implementing in the classroom for their students. Without solid Tier 1 and Tier 2 established in schools (through collaborative conversation, professional sharing, and ongoing revisions and refinements), Tier 3 and 4 interventions will be overwhelmed by the students in need of this level of assistance, leading to a reality that cannot be sustained over time. If we can collectively work together in schools to ensure effectiveness at the foundational levels of our continuum, we can ensure that supports at the upper tiers are most effective for the students most in need of them.

The fact that all schools differ does not mean that common frameworks or models for a continuum of supports cannot be established across schools, districts, or educational systems. There is great value in a jurisdiction establishing a common framework, with defined tiers of support to be replicated across schools. However, if a predetermined continuum of supports, with interventions, strategies, and accommodations strictly defined, is transposed on a school community, it is unlikely to have high levels of success in its adoption. After all, "Attempting to copy just what is done—the explicit practices and policies—without holding the underlying philosophy is at once a more difficult task and an approach that is less likely to be successful" (Pfeffer & Sutton, 2000, p. 24). It is important that schools determine, define, and organize their own strategies, accommodations, and interventions within each tier of their continuum before a district ever looks to compile those into a unified systems approach.

Articulation of Interventions, Strategies, and Accommodations

A next step in the development of the continuum of supports is to specifically identify what are interventions, strategies, or accommodations. All three are critical to supporting students, but each is different in its design, utilization, and potential placement in the continuum.

Interventions

Interventions are meant to effectively bridge a gap for students, provided in addition to regular classroom instruction. Three things identify an intervention and differentiate interventions from strategies and accommodations:

CHAPTER #7. Continuum of Supports

1. *Provide targeted assistance focused on a specific skill*: Unless the intervention is targeted and put in place to focus on learning a specific skill, it is unlikely to effectively address the student concern for which it is intended. As a result, it should also be able to be assessed, to determine if it is having an impact for students. We want to ensure that interventions are high impact and teaching a skill not currently in place or at a suitable level for a student. Anything but high-impact interventions are wastes of money and energy.

2. *Delivered by a highly qualified teacher or another specialist*: As interventions can be established at Tiers 3 and 4, their increasing intensity requires higher levels of training and expertise. It is not acceptable to have our least-qualified staff members providing interventions to our students in greatest need of support (although this has sometimes traditionally been the case in schools, as greater educational assistant support, potentially provided by someone not necessarily with a high degree of training, is sought for our most challenging students). For an intervention to be truly impactful, it must be delivered by an individual trained to provide that intervention with maximum fidelity.

3. *Provide additional instruction for an individual or small group*: The higher we go on the tiers of the pyramid, the smaller the intervention groups should become. Maximum gain for the majority of interventions will happen for groups of students with a size of 8 or less.

Potential Pitfall

Often, we observe schools trying to establish a plethora of interventions to support their students. We have found that schools have the greatest impact with their interventions when they focus on quality rather than quantity. Establishing a handful of proven, highly impactful interventions at each tier beyond classroom instruction at Tier 1 can ensure that those interventions receive the resources they need and keep the school focused on what works. A general rule of thumb is that schools should use a small number of proven interventions and explore a large number of potential strategies and accommodations at the classroom level (Tier 2).

Strategies

Whereas interventions will be purposefully articulated at Tiers 2, 3, and 4, potentially employed by classroom teachers, individuals other than classroom teachers, and then individuals external to the school, strategies should be articulated at Tier 2—the classroom level. Strategies do not need to meet the criteria established for interventions but should focus on "what *could* work" for students. An organization of differentiated strategies, collected from teachers and shared in the continuum of supports, becomes a valuable resource during a CTM when investigating all that could be done at the classroom level.

In a sense, this targeted collection of strategies becomes a way to further ensure that effective instruction and support exists for every student in the classroom. Even as students receive supports found within higher tiers of the continuum, the strategies at Tier 2 should continue to exist. In fact, we believe that these strategies should be more robust at Tier 2 for students currently receiving support articulated at the Tier 3 and 4 levels. A myriad of effective, proven strategies to support students at the Tier 2 level ensures that the greatest point of impact for students is found in the classroom and in the hands of the classroom teacher.

Accommodations

In its most basic definition, we put accommodations in place to help students *cope* with any gaps that may exist limiting their success. For a student who has difficulty reading text, a text-to-speech accommodation may be beneficial. For a child who struggles with attention, fidgets may be effective to reduce distractions. For students who have difficulty with basic computations, the introduction of a calculator to support may be effective.

Accommodations are an important component of any plan for student success. However, a problem exists when a continuum consists primarily of accommodations. Accommodations address gaps but are not intended to close those gaps. The inclusion of text-to-speech technologies, fidgets, or calculators will not lead to improved decoding, eliminate attention issues, or develop improved computation. Although they are a valuable part of the overall picture of support for students, they must be balanced with interventions and strategies that strive to reduce achievement gaps. Like strategies, we believe that accommodations must be organized and articulated at the classroom level (Tier 2).

Starting Steps

Once schools have articulated, defined, and organized currently utilized interventions, strategies, and accommodations into tiered groups as described earlier, the next step is delineating which specifically are interventions that would be considered strategies and which would be classified as accommodations. This organization can then be replicated into a student profile, to more easily note what is currently in place to support students and what has historically worked for students. As suggested in the earlier "Starting Steps" in this chapter, using a simple "I," "S," or "A" coding system for each support provides clarity on the essence of each support.

Just as the interventions, strategies, and accommodations found in a school's continuum are unique to the school context, those accessed at each tier are unique to a student. Our core understanding is that students need different types of supports, even at the same tier of the continuum. We can establish a menu of interventions, strategies, and accommodations articulated at each tier (more on this shortly), but then need to employ a "pathways principle" (Rose, 2016):

> This principle makes two important affirmations. First, in all aspects of our lives and for any given goal, there are many, equally valid ways to reach the same outcome; and, second, the particular pathway that is optimal for you depends on your own individuality. (p. 129)

While a lunchtime support might work effectively for one student, it may not be effective for another student. Here, the intuitiveness and professional capital accessed in the collaborative structures come into play. Together, the team comes to know which supports best fit individual students. This process eliminates the algebraic determination of interventions, where a score on a particular assessment translates into a specific intervention or support being implemented.

In our experience, such number-first interventions simply miss something all teachers come to intuitively understand—all students are unique, and the relationship a teacher establishes with a student is integral to providing the support they need. Just as the continuum must be shaped to fit the unique context of the school, the supports within the continuum also must be accessed and guided by the unique needs of individual students, as determined by the relational knowledge of collaborative teams working and interacting with students daily.

Development of a Menu of Supports

Obviously, this initial development of a continuum, which can provide the foundation for further development and refinement, is not overly scientific or prescriptive. As the continuum continues to evolve, less-than-effective practices can be replaced by more research-based supports. However, value is placed on things that are currently working in the school and collective brainstorming of staff to determine supports and interventions for their students. Programs such as the "after lunch bunch" (Cunningham & Allington, 2007) or "lunch bunch, students in 4th through 6th grade who are experiencing reading difficulties due to motivation and interest are invited to participate in this club" (Fisher & Frey, 2010, p. 9) are examples of responses aimed at supporting students through creative next steps.

The initial development of a school's continuum of supports, including articulating existing supports and organizational tiers, should not be viewed as a stand-alone event. Once established, the interventions, strategies, and accommodations must be constantly monitored for effectiveness, removed when deemed less effective (in relation to other more robust supports), and added to as the school continues to evolve and grow in how they provide for students. Hargreaves and Fullan (2012) note, "High-yield strategies become more precise and more embedded when they are developed and deployed in teams that are constantly refining and interpreting them" (p. 96). This constant refinement and interpretation is critical to sustained success in how we respond to the individual (and fluctuating) needs of students, through a school's continuum of supports.

We have suggested that implementing any new strategy should be accompanied by a system for regularly monitoring its effectiveness (Blankstein, 2004). In CTMs, when a new addition to the continuum is suggested to support an individual or group of students, it should be paired with a short-term review date to determine if it's working. Are you considering peer tutoring that uses older students to support younger students in an after-school program? Establish when the team (or a defined group) will meet to discuss whether the support is garnering the results they were hoping for. In the short term, this determination can be anecdotal; but, determining a set review date ensures two things.

First, it ensures that there is an agreed-on time, at the outset, to come back to review if a particular new practice is working (in the opinions of the team). This review may then include determining how the team will know (anecdotal, student surveys, student data, etc.), which, in time, directly links to progress monitoring. Second, it allows a defined "probation period," where the team essentially agrees to test the practice for a set period of time, rather than giving up if it doesn't go as planned the first time it is introduced for students. A formal meeting and discussion instills an institutional resilience to look beyond initial speed bumps that may (and often do) arise. In the long-term, this and all supports should have more substantial student data that inform and confirm the professional judgment of the team.

Previously in this chapter, we described the steps for the initial development of a continuum of supports characterized by the following processes:

- ▶ identify an area of focus that aligns with district/school priorities and is confirmed through data that will guide the work of the school teams;

- ▶ articulate the instructional practices that currently exist in the school in that focus area, naming each strategy explicitly to identify common practices and unique expertise that exist on the staff;

- ▶ confirm all supports as strategies, accommodations, or interventions as per the definitions described in this chapter; and

- ▶ organize the supports into tiers to define the levels within your continuum.

The next step is to determine the visual representation of your continuum of supports. This step is integral as there are a number of opportunities to articulate elements of your school culture in tandem with instructional practices and supports expressed in a visual format. This visual becomes a tool that guides the work of every team and also serves as a menu of all the possible supports that could be tried in response to the challenges teachers face day to day with their students.

Companion Website Resources

7.2. Continuum of supports template (general): Template to assist in the collection and displaying of interventions, strategies, and accommodations for Tiers 2, 3, and 4.

The menu of supports functions in the same way as a menu from your favorite restaurant. The menu describes a number of different options that can be ordered that appeal to your appetite and preference in food items and are aligned with your budget. The continuum of supports menu provides a description of the supports that could be chosen for a student depending on their personal characteristics, the challenges that they are experiencing, and the level of support required. The menu of supports becomes an integral tool to support teams in answering the question, "What do we do?"

A number of considerations should be taken into account when developing a visual representation for your continuum of supports:

- What area of focus will your continuum of supports represent?
- Will separate continuums of support for each focus area look consistent or have fundamental differences?
- Are there cultural characteristics of your school that might be included in the visual?
- What shape will be conducive to the number of supports that you have identified?
- Are there descriptions of your process that might be included?
  - When is the school support team accessed?
  - Where is teacher involvement important?
- How will you ensure easy access to revise, edit, and add to the continuum?
- How will this visual be accessed during team meetings as a menu for supports?

Figures 7.3, 7.4, 7.5, and 7.6 share samples from three different schools, at different phases of their continuum development, that reflect commonalities such as we've described, but differ in their formatting, content, and visualization. Figures 7.5 and 7.6 from Herald School in Medicine Hat, Alberta, Canada (with one figure showing Tier 3 and 4 supports and the other showing Tier 2), also includes links for staff to access for descriptions and related resources. Please note that the sample in Figure 7.4 has not undergone the process of refining Tier 1 supports into a more concise list of common expectations or core practices to be established in all classrooms, as described a little later in this chapter.

When first establishing a school's continuum of supports, as described earlier in this chapter, it is "critical that schools learn the lesson that 'best practice' in effective organizations is rarely *new* practice" (Schmoker, 2011, p. 17). The initial development of the continuum can simply be viewed as the organization of best practices that already exist within the school. The next step is *articulating* those supports, because it is probable that a teacher working right across the hallway might not know a particular strategy, accommodation, or intervention being used in a colleague's classroom.

Looking back, it now seems almost humorous the time and money we've spent in our schools for teachers to engage in professional development activities, only to return and discover that an expert was already within our school. Having a teacher recount in a staff room the great workshop they just attended and having another remark, "Oh, I did the same one a few years ago—let me know if you want to borrow any of the resources I've developed for it." really shines a light on the need for educators within a school to collectively open their instructional toolboxes and share what they are doing to support students. This articulation of interventions, strategies, and accommodations identified when establishing a school's continuum of supports is a critical step to building a sound system of next steps for students.

Although it is easy to see the value of working together to establish a continuum of supports for beginning and new staff entering the school, building a continuum of supports together also holds tremendous value for current and veteran educators within the school who learn from and share with one another. This process of identification and articulation not only opens up a world of professional sharing, but it also recognizes and celebrates the successful next steps already being employed in classrooms and across the school. So in addition to creating a menu of supports in the form of a visual for easy access, it is also valuable to articulate the interventions, strategies, and accommodations to ensure that students have access to intentional support, regardless of the classroom they are in.

Figure 7.3 Kildare School reading pyramid of supports

Pyramid of Reading Supports

Tier 4: Specialized
Intensive interventions at the Tier 4 level are individualized and determined by an individual program plan developed for the student by a collaborative team. At this Tier, outside resources, agencies, and further testing may be accessed.
- Intensive Learning Team (ILT)
- SLP, OT, PT, Mental Health Practitioners support

Tier 3: Targeted
Tier 3 interventions are supports delivered by professionals other than the classroom teacher outside the classroom. These can be designed to support students across multiple classes.
- SWAP Block: Small Group
- SWAP Block: Grade 1
- EA Support (outside the classroom)
- Confucius Teacher (outside the classroom)

Tier 2: Differentiated
Tier 2 strategies, interventions, and accommodations are provided to students in the classroom. By articulating these strategies, interventions, and accommodations schoolwide, teachers essentially collaborate to share differentiated strategies, interventions, and accommodations that work for students.
- Strategies (general, fluency, decoding/word solving, phonics, vocabulary, comprehension)
- Accommodations (classroom environment, instruction/assignments, summative and formative assessments, parent communication and involvement)
- Interventions (trained support inside the classroom)

Tier 1: Universal
Effective research-based instruction is foundational for success for students and essential when implementing school-based intervention models. Tier 1 honors and recognizes the essential work of teachers in the classroom.
- Setting a Purpose for Reading
- Reading Comprehension Strategies (Connections, Predict, Infer, Evaluate, Synthesize, Analyze/Question, Sequence/Summarize, Self-monitor/Monitor and Clarify)
- Think Aloud / Read Aloud
- Vocabulary Building
- Visual Charts and Graphic Organizers
- Responding to Reading

Menu of Tier 2 Supports

STRATEGIES

General:
- access to levelled books
- desk visuals
- Google Read & Write
- iChinese Reader
- Raz Kids
- individualized specific and immediate feedback
- scaffolding
- trained volunteers
- trained peer support

Fluency:
- duet reading
- echo reading
- paired reading with other grades
- reading trackers
- whisper phones

Decoding/Word Solving:
- decoding strategies (chunky monkey, stretch snake, tryin lion, eagle eyes, lips the fish, etc.)
- making words and sentences
- making words with a small group
- repeated exposure to individualized unknown sight words
- sight word practice

Phonics:
- explicit instruction of word families
- matching pictures to sounds (itchy)

Vocabulary:
- figurative language
- Frayer model
- personal dictionaries
- per-teaching of academic vocabulary
- synonym search and replace
- Vocabulary Spelling City
- word lists (character traits, emotions, synonyms, etc.)
- word part clues prefix and suffix

Comprehension:
- questioning (initiated and answered by student and/or teacher)
- frequent teacher check-in for comprehension
- targeted prompting
- visual supports targeted to individual
- Think-Pair-Share
- close activities
- reader's theatre
- Reference *The Reading Strategies Book* by Jennifer Serravallo to explore other reading strategies to support student's reading development

ACCOMODATIONS

Classroom Environment:
- allow breaks (set criteria, use a prescribed number of breaks, encourage breaks in the classroom)
- alternate desk (standing, table, exercise ball, etc.)
- assign a "buddy" for new environments
- extend wait time for student response understanding
- give advance notice of changes and check for understanding
- keep daily assignments posted
- physical positioning/proximity when giving directions
- posting of daily routines and reminders
- preferential seating
- preview and/or review each class lesson
- quiet space (inside/outside of classroom)
- use of a wiggle seat
- use of desktop easel or slant board
- use of fidget materials (balls, theraputty, chewelry, etc.,)
- use of noise cancelling headphones
- use of visual clock for transitions
- vary activities often

Instruction/Assignments
- allow for extended time if appropriate
- break lessons or directions into smaller units
- decrease amount (not content) of homework
- give concrete examples
- highlight text
- increase font size of reading materials
- modify the number of required problems
- pre-reading questions, focus attention on essentials
- pre-teach significant vocabulary
- provide additional examples
- provide a picture/written daily schedule
- provide clear, step-by-step instructions (oral and visual)
- provide specific and immediate feedback
- provide student a copy of the notes
- rephrase questions/student paraphrases directions
- use tactile materials (raised lines, interlined, pencil grips, etc.)
- work with a classroom partner

Summative and Formative Assessments:
- adjust test design (prompted long answer, cloze short answer, multiple choice, matching)
- advance notice of test and quizzes
- allow additional time if needed
- allow notes, word banks, or other aids during tests
- allow oral/taped tests (Read & Write Voice Notes)
- allow use of assistive technology
- alternate assessments (performance tasks)
- increase space for answers
- provide study guides and allow time for review
- reduce the number of questions
- use a scribe

Parent Communication and Involvement:
- daily agenda notes/tracking checklists
- regular email communication
- scheduled routine phone check-in

INTERVENTIONS

General:
- small group reading (guided reading)
- Confucius Teacher (in the classroom)
- EA support (in the classroom)
- one-on-one teacher support
- trained peer support
- trained volunteers

Source: ©2020, T. Jeske, Kildare School, Edmonton Public Schools, AB. Used with permission.

Figure 7.4 Kisipatnahak School behavior continuum of supports

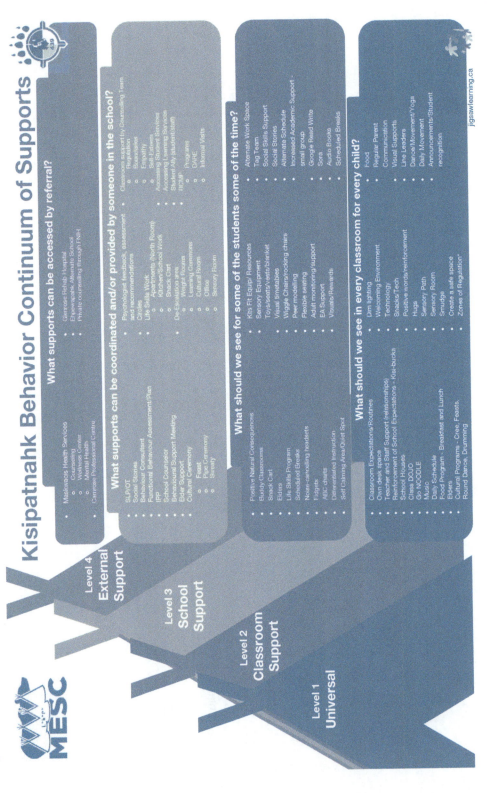

Source: ©2020, L. Ouellette, Kisipatnahak School, Maskwacîs Education Schools Commission, AB. Used with permission.

Figure 7.5 Herald School continuum of supports (Tiers 3 and 4)

HERALD SCHOOL
CONTINUUM OF SUPPORTS

Tier 4 Intensive Division Interventions - *Supports provided by someone outside of the school-based team*
(all require consultation with CST and Administration)

- Referral to the B.E.S.T Team
- Referral to Complex Communication Consultant
- Referral to RCSD AAC Specialist
- Referral and Consent for Ed Psych Assessment (based on data from Level B assessment)
- Violent Threat Risk Assessment
- School Resource Office
- Doctors Letter
- Referral for FNMI support

- Referral for additional ELL Coordinator support
- Case Conference
- Attendance Board
- Consultation with Division Psychologist
- Adult Services Transition Plan
- Consultation with Community Services: ESCD, Child & Family Services, McMann, Bridges, Disability Services, Mental Health

Tier 3 School Interventions - *Supports provided by someone other than the classroom teacher (*requires consultation with CST and Administration)

- Consult with Classroom Support Teacher
  - ☐ Student record review
  - ☐ Observation in the classroom
  - ☐ Identification of programming recommendations and strategies
- Referral for targeted supports / assessment:
  - ☐ Occupational Therapy (consent / screening tool)
  - ☐ Speech Language Therapy
  - ☐ Regional Collaborative Service Delivery *
    - ☐ Physical Therapist *
    - ☐ Audiologist *
    - ☐ Vision Consultant *
    - ☐ Deaf/Hard of Hearing Teacher *
  - ☐ Family School Liaison Worker / Counselling support *
- Tier 3 Language Arts Instructional supports: Division 1 / Division 2

- Attendance Contract
- Consistent Home Communication
- Adapted Schedule / Timetable / Learning Environment
- Levelled Literacy Intervention
- Additional Literacy and Numeracy support
- Consultative support with CST on:
  - ☐ Behaviour Support Plans
  - ☐ Medical Support Plans
  - ☐ Safety Plan (Escalation Cycle)
  - ☐ Success in School Plan (SISP)
- Create Behaviour Contract
- Possible access to additional adult support:
  - ☐ Educational Assistant (1-1, small group)
  - ☐ Early Literacy EA
  - ☐ ELL EA
- Tier 3 Mathematics Instructional supports: Division 1 / Division 2

- Success Coach
  - ☐ Whole class and small groups
  - ☐ Sensory diet in Just Right Room
  - ☐ Requires OT recommendations and must be adult directed
  - ☐ Therapeutic Listening
- Modified Programming
  - ☐ Consent for modified programming *(requires identification on report card)*
  - ☐ Life Skills programming
- Peer Mentoring
- Further assessments:
  - ☐ RRST for Grade 2-6
  - ☐ Fountas & Pinnell
- Referral for Level B Assessment *
  - ☐ Referral Form - Level B
  - ☐ Consent Form - Level B

Source: ©2020, K. Corbett, Herald School, Medicine Hat Public School Division, AB. Used with permission.

Figure 7.6 Herald School continuum of supports (Tier 2)

Tier 2 Classroom Strategies – *Targeted strategies provided by the classroom teacher* (accommodations and adaptations to programming

- Consult with the Optimal Learning Coach
- Creation of variety of learning plans:
  - ❏ Individual Support Plan
  - ❏ Behaviour Support Plan
- *Zones of Regulation* curriculum
  - ❏ Size of the Problem
  - ❏ Expected vs. unexpected
  - ❏ Social Mapping
  - ❏ 5 is Against the Law
- Structured teaching strategy - develop a visually supported work system
- Plan for transitions and changes to the schedule
- Positive behaviour strategies - classroom and individual students
  - ❏ BOATS Resource
  - ❏ Supporting Positive Behaviour (Classroom Approach)
  - ❏ Supporting Positive Behaviour (Individualized Approach)
- Strategies for supporting behaviour and social participation
- Structured teaching strategy
  - ❏ Create a visually structured environment
  - ❏ Individualized visual schedules
- Reduce visual clutter
- Focus tools (fidgets, wiggle seat, theraband).
- Individual calming bins
- Differentiated instruction based on product - give students the option of how to demonstrate their learning: recorded responses, representation other than text (visual), presentation / performance, learning portfolio's, oral response, build a diorama or model
- Read & Write Google Premium (visual dictionary, word recognition, highlighter feature)
- Provide electronic copy of the notes so the student can use text-to-speech
- Audio version of book / textbooks through Google Classroom
- App: Text compactor, Raz Kids, Starfall
- Apps for Struggling Readers and Writers - use of games during literacy stations
- Use of FM System / RedCat
- Design rubrics with students
- Tiered Products based on Bloom's Taxonomy: Tic, Tac, Toe / Learning Menus / RAFT
- Provide visual supports with verbal instructions
- Individual visual timer (e.g. sand timer)
- Tutorial sessions at lunch or after school
- Individual Conferencing - regular check-ins and check-outs

- Tier 2 Language Arts Instructional supports: Division 1 / Division 2
- Tier 2 Mathematics Instructional supports: Division 1 / Division 2
- Use First / Then language
- Plan for transitions and changes to the schedule
- Scheduled movement breaks
- Frequent breaks - provide student with a break card
- Use of highlighter when reading
- Frequent check-ins for understanding
- Assigned and flexible seating (wiggle seat, standing desk, study carrels, exercise ball, stools)
- Placement next to classroom teacher for additional support
- Strategic partnering / grouping
- Adjust lighting (light covers, lamps) and offer noise cancelling headphones or ear plugs
- Slant boards, pencil grips
- Anxiety Disorder Strategies
- Practice tests / open book tests / pre-tests to check for prior knowledge
- Regular contact with parents - individualized home communication book
- Collaborative Problem Solving - Plan B
- Social Stories
- Access to mindfulness space
- Enrichment supports
- ADHD Strategies
- Learning Disabilities Strategies
- Chunk tasks and assignments (break steps down into manageable tasks)
- Student conferencing and learning contracts
- Graphic organizers / concept maps
- Pre-teach new vocabulary and text
- Provide text at the student's independent/instructional reading level
- Have student repeat instructions to check for understanding
- Use "If" / "Then" language and provide choice
- Access to a safe place
- Chewelry
- Provide **accommodations** and **adaptations**: additional writing time, frequent breaks during assessments. reader, scribe, 10x10 multiplication chart / provide a number line, larger print, colored paper / colored overlays, ambient noise, quiet location, provide copied notes or notes in advance, cloze notes and adjusting font and font size, provide less questions but ensure the curricular content is not changed.
- Reading / Communication Buddies

Companion Website Resources

7.3. Intervention description template: This organizer can be adapted and used to assist staff in articulating specifically the interventions that are included in a school's continuum of supports. These intervention descriptions can be shared with staff and parents to ensure a clear and common understanding of interventions established in the school.

Starting Steps

The support descriptions developed are of little use if they are not accessible for staff and the school community. Consider posting them on a school website to communicate to parents the particular supports implemented for students. We have seen schools keep a binder of the pages in their meeting rooms and distribute it to teachers to ensure that they are accessible and being referred to during CTMs. We also have seen posters with strategies in the rooms where schools hold their CTMs. Posting or publishing the supports makes a public statement of commitment to supporting student needs.

Obviously, not all strategies and accommodations defined in a school's continuum necessitate a full-page description. For these strategies, it is still worthwhile to compile a list with brief descriptions, never assuming that staff or parents know what a particular strategy looks like in a classroom. Having clear articulation ensures consistency across the school and assists in the implementation (and monitoring) of supports enacted for students.

Intentional Utilization in Team Meetings

While the development and formulation of your continuum of supports has the potential to significantly affect the pedagogical practices as well as the continuity of instruction from classroom to classroom, the implementation of your menu in team meetings will actualize the practices articulated in the first steps.

Potential Pitfall

It's not enough to say that we have established a continuum of supports and we have formatted the strategies, interventions, and accommodations into a visual representation of our school's response. Sometimes schools see the development of a continuum of supports as a simple first step—and rightly so, as this is an aspect of Collaborative Response that is immediately actionable on the next School Professional Development Day. It follows a step-by-step protocol that can be implemented with relatively limited preparation or facilitation.

We have come across schools that share "we've already done that," and they have created a continuum of supports; however, it takes considerable effort to locate where the original was filed. This is an indication that the creation of the continuum was merely a professional development activity and has not been taken to the next step of application of the tool to function in team meetings. In essence, it rests in that category of the gap between knowing and doing. We have an understanding behind the creation, but it has never moved to integral implementation of the tool.

As with many other elements in Collaborative Response, the initial development and first steps may seem simplistic, but there is much to consider in the implementation of the component. So if we are trying to answer the question, "What do we do?" then the next obvious question is, "How do we use this resource?"

The first step in implementation is ensuring that the continuum of supports is available in every team meeting, from the collaborative planning team meetings, CTMs, school support meetings, and case consult meetings. Making available the plethora of supports that have been articulated by all staff members across the school when problem solving for students provides accessible strategies, interventions, and accommodations, which will greatly support the conversations about students.

Many schools use various formats to ensure that this valuable resource is available and ready to use during team meetings. Here are a few ideas that have come from schools, but there is no limitation to what is possible:

- copies present during team meetings for staff to access;

- personal copies for each classroom teacher to post in their classroom as well as copies posted in the team meeting room;

- bulletin board display in the team meeting room or staff room, including the tiers and aligned supports (such as the wall of a team meeting space at Central Elementary School in Taber, Alberta, Canada, as shown in Figure 7.7, with one side of the board sharing academic supports and the other side showing social-emotional supports);

- online document that is open and available at each meeting—perhaps even projected on a second projector in the meeting room for easy access; and

- large laminated posters that could be written on with a dry erase marker to make changes and edits during a team meeting.

Figure 7.7 Continuum of supports visual wall

Source: ©2021, C. James, Taber Central School, Horizon School Division, AB. Used with permission.

Infusion of a Collaborative Team Meeting Role

When creating the roles that will guide your collaborative teams, consider including a role for examining your continuum of supports. This individual's responsibility is to have the continuum of supports displayed in front of them, and as the discussion proceeds, this person would be intentionally bringing forward ideas from the continuum. It might sound like this: "Have we thought about trying a check-in check-out process?" or "Have we tried connecting them with a peer?"

We've engaged with schools who share that they often give the role of examining the continuum to their teachers newest to the profession. This provides new teachers with an opportunity to purview the practices of the school while exploring possibilities for their own classroom. This, of course, is partnered with the expectation that if there is anything on the list that they do not have an awareness of, they ask in a follow-up with a colleague. It also reinforces that everyone around the CTM table has a voice, and we value the suggestions and ideas from our staff members with years of experience as well as those of our colleagues just beginning their careers.

> **In the Field**
>
> At Dr. Roy Wilson Learning Center in Medicine Hat, Alberta, Canada, one of the roles at their CTM is "Captain Continuum." As shown in Figure 7.8, Captain Continuum is one of the roles identified on tent cards used during meetings, with the task of suggesting supports from the school's continuum of supports throughout the conversation.

Figure 7.8 Dr. Roy Wilson Learning Center, school meeting role tent cards

Source: ©2021, M. Kukurudza, Dr. Roy Wilson Learning Center, Medicine Hat Public School Division, AB. Used with permission.

Refinement of Tier 1 Instruction

Once the continuum of supports has been established and is functioning as an integral part of team meetings and a significant part of a school's Collaborative Response, constant refining and revision will be a natural part of the process. This work is never complete. As educators, we are continually learning and growing our practice, which in turn has implications on the growth and development of the continuum of supports.

The initial establishment of the continuum of supports begins with the step of identifying everything we do to support students in the focus area. While this is a revealing opportunity to surface classroom practice, the first round may result in a mish-mash of varying ideas. Over time, the school teams will identify practices that are no longer in use, some that are not truly impactful, and some that are the cornerstone of teaching and learning.

It is the cornerstones that are the focus of refining Tier 1 instruction. We characterize this stage as being the nonnegotiables for every classroom. Articulating what is expected, should be evidenced, and is consistently practiced in every classroom in the school assists in mitigating the educational lottery that we referred to earlier in this text. It also provides common ground for professional learning and to further enhance expertise within the school based on what is needed to support students in each school's particular context.

In sessions, we are sometimes approached by teachers and leaders with the question that if we create a common standard, will teacher autonomy be limited and the ability to engage in their craft of teaching become extinct? Our response is always a resounding no. As teachers ourselves, we understand the importance of engaging teacher creativity and the ability to design and respond to students through variations in teaching and learning, often deeply connected to who we are not only as educators but as human beings interacting with other human beings. Determining Tier 1 classroom practices provides every teacher with a common canvas on which to paint their own instructional masterpiece.

When we reflect back on our early years of teaching, we shudder when we think about how we had to piecemeal our instruction as we had significant understanding and competency in some areas (this is usually a sign of a connection made during practicum experience) and some areas we were learning day by day, lesson by lesson. We're sure that we're not alone in saying that not every aspect of teaching came with preparedness from our university courses. We would have welcomed support provided for the key components of classroom practice while still enjoying the flexibility and autonomy of creating our own classroom environment and establishing our routines and preferences within our own style of teaching. Affirmation and assurance is established when creating common Tier 1 practices across the school. It also establishes expectations that can create consistency and predictability for students as they move from classroom to classroom.

Articulating Tier 1 practices across a school, or potentially across a larger system, can be an extensive endeavor but well worth the energy. When a school or district engages in the process of describing and articulating their Tier 1 practices, certain advantages are realized in each classroom, in each school across the district:

- Commonly understood practices

- Clearly articulated expectations

- Collection of defined practices, clearly described for all

- Foundations for classroom walkthrough

- Areas to target for professional learning and growth

The process for engaging in this work loosely parallels the initial development of a continuum of supports in a school. Typically, a school or district will engage a task force, a small group of master teachers and leaders, to contribute to the decision-making in development as well as lead the implementation of the collaboratively designed model. We would recommend, if the development is occurring at a district level, that teachers from each school contribute as part of the task force to ensure that a constant flow of communication occurs throughout the development of Tier 1 practices.

COLLABORATIVE RESPONSE

Thoughtful consideration needs to be given by leaders in establishing this process. It is advantageous to create a strategic plan that will guide the work, with attention given to creation, implementation, and sustainability.

The first step is to gather tried and true practices that are being used throughout the classrooms or schools, a step already accomplished through the initial development of a continuum of supports. Then through a process of theming and attending to core research-based practices, the team articulates the core components. Although the determined labels will be different in different schools and districts, the core components most often consist of topics related to classroom environment, assessment for learning, differentiation, responsive relationships, intentional planning, pedagogy and instruction, student wellness, and so on. There are an endless number of topics that may be encompassed within this work. The end goal is to articulate those core principles that will create a foundation for teaching and learning across the school or district but still in relation to each area of focus.

Through an iterative and generative process, categories are established, and then, we begin to clearly define each category and provide exemplars, templates, or samples of effective practice as seen in the school or district, which become the tools that guide work in schools. This may be a combination of gathering samples and templates from schools and classrooms or accessing information from research to the specific creation of some tools that will guide each specific category.

In the Field

At Northern Gateway Public Schools in Alberta, Canada, the division engaged in a comprehensive, systemwide endeavor to define Tier 1 practices across all classrooms in all schools to serve as the foundation for reflective conversations, professional learning, and collaboration. The clarification of a quality learning environment included five domains of quality pedagogy (positive classroom culture, responsive instruction, intentional planning, purposeful assessment, and engaged professional) that rested on three domains within their culture of wellness for staff (physical well-being, social well-being, and mental well-being). Starting with more than 15,000 responses from teachers to the question, "What would we see in a quality learning environment?" a multifaceted engagement structure included the following:

- a steering team representing the division's learning services department and administrators from a cross-section of schools to guide the evolving work;

- a working group, consisting of membership from every school, that engaged in the work of preparing drafts to take back to schools for review and feedback, aligning with

CHAPTER #7. Continuum of Supports

> educational research with the emerging domains, developing tools for purposeful examination of domains back at school sites, and gathering artifacts of what each domain looked like in practice throughout the division;
>
> - school leadership teams that came together from across the division to engage in conversations to develop a deep understanding of each domain and develop facilitation skills and resources to engage in conversations and protocols with their staff teams regarding each domain of the quality learning environment; and
>
> - a wellness facilitator team, with membership from each school, who mirrored the work of the working group but focused exclusively on establishing a culture of wellness across all schools.
>
> Through a generative and iterative process, Northern Gateway School Division has established a systemwide understanding of what a quality learning environment should look like in every classroom but, more importantly, has reinforced a collective culture where examining and discussing classroom practice is an ongoing conversation. It provides us with yet another example of where the highly messy process is more important than the product it generates. Visit http://ngps.ca to learn more about their quality learning environment work.

One final note regarding the refinement of Tier 1. As it involves the curating and refinement of what is initially a list of a myriad of practices happening across classrooms within a school, it often means a number of the strategies and accommodations are shifted into Tier 2. Essentially, we are saying that unless we expect a certain practice to exist in every classroom for every student, it belongs in Tier 2, where it can be a consideration when it comes to supporting a student or cohort of students.

In the Field

At Nipisihkopahk Elementary School in Maskwacîs, Alberta, Canada, staff engaged in the process of refining their initial Tier 1 list of practices into eight essentials that they collectively agreed they would see across all classrooms, as shown in Figure 7.9. This meant that a number of strategies originally determined to be Tier 1 shifted to Tier 2, signifying that they may not require that each strategy be found in every classroom, but each certainly needed to be considered or tried with students before looking to engage in Tier 3 supports.

Figure 7.9 Tier 1 before and after at Nipisihkopahk Elementary School

Before:

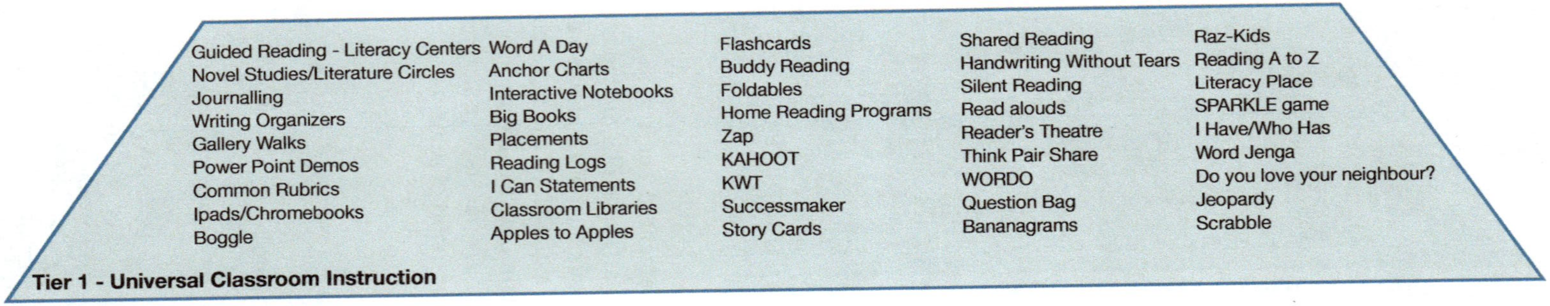

Guided Reading - Literacy Centers	Word A Day	Flashcards	Shared Reading	Raz-Kids
Novel Studies/Literature Circles	Anchor Charts	Buddy Reading	Handwriting Without Tears	Reading A to Z
Journalling	Interactive Notebooks	Foldables	Silent Reading	Literacy Place
Writing Organizers	Big Books	Home Reading Programs	Read alouds	SPARKLE game
Gallery Walks	Placements	Zap	Reader's Theatre	I Have/Who Has
Power Point Demos	Reading Logs	KAHOOT	Think Pair Share	Word Jenga
Common Rubrics	I Can Statements	KWT	WORDO	Do you love your neighbour?
Ipads/Chromebooks	Classroom Libraries	Successmaker	Question Bag	Jeopardy
Boggle	Apples to Apples	Story Cards	Bananagrams	Scrabble

Tier 1 - Universal Classroom Instruction

After:

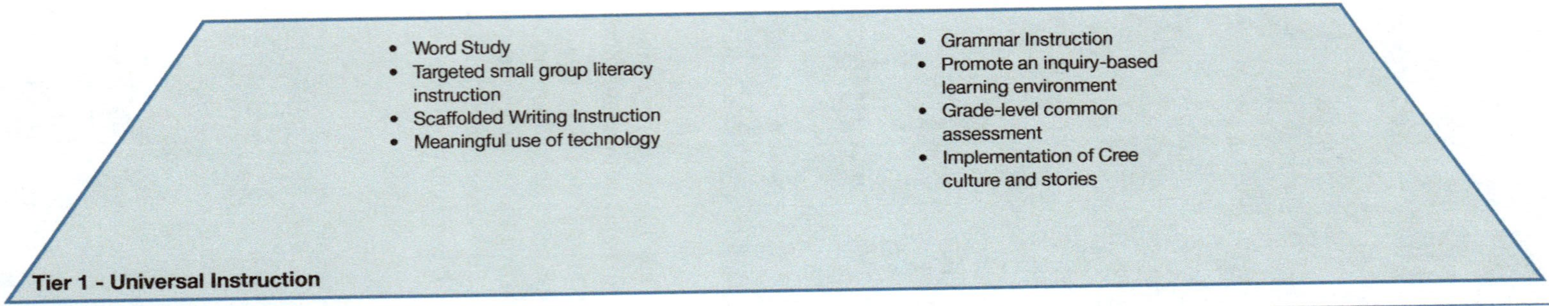

- Word Study
- Targeted small group literacy instruction
- Scaffolded Writing Instruction
- Meaningful use of technology

- Grammar Instruction
- Promote an inquiry-based learning environment
- Grade-level common assessment
- Implementation of Cree culture and stories

Tier 1 - Universal Instruction

Source: ©2021, G. Koett - Nipisihkopahk Elementary School, Maskwacîs Education Schools Commission, AB. Used with permission.

Companion Website Resources

7.4. Refining continuum of supports template: Organizer to help guide the refinement of a continuum of supports, including refining Tier 1, removing assessments and plans, and identifying interventions, strategies, and accommodations.

Inform Professional Learning

The endeavor to grow and improve our practice is an innate quality of teachers. In the very nature of the profession of teaching, the focus on learning and growing is inevitable. The challenge is not a matter of whether we engage in learning or not, as most teachers are constantly seeking relevant professional development, but rather a question of what topics, areas of focus, or areas of interest do we invest our resources of time and finances in. Through Collaborative Response and especially with the development of a continuum of supports, the areas of focus as well as the specific supports that we are engaging for students will lead to the areas of professional learning that are needed across the team. In addition, this need for professional learning is directly related and driven by the examination of student needs and key issues that may require further learning in order to provide an effective response.

For example, if the school's priority is student wellness and in CTMs teachers are consistently identifying challenges in regard to anxiety, this becomes an area to target for professional learning. When the continuum of supports has been developed and a school discovers through that exercise that there actually is a gap in the practices that they are currently engaging in regarding anxiety, it is again a confirmation that this is perhaps an area in which to invest time and resources to develop some expertise in the school to support teachers and students.

Connection to Visual Team Board

A further extension for engaging and connecting the continuum for supports is the design and use of visual team boards to represent the students that each team is responsible for supporting. This tool allows teams to ensure that *all* students have the potential of being a topic of conversation in the team meetings, reflecting not only their entry level, but now also the highest tier of support that they are currently accessing. This is essential to truly affect the equity of support in our schools. We've always envisioned this tool to function like the empty chair in the room, not just as a reminder of the student we are talking about but rather, in this instance, as a visual reference of all the students that the cohort of teachers is responsible for supporting.

202   COLLABORATIVE RESPONSE

Visual displays are powerful tools for connecting students to the conversation that takes place during CTMs as well as the other layers of collaboration. They provide concrete ways in which a cohort of students can be front-and-center in the discussion without being physically present. A visual display acts as a reminder of *every* student for which a collaborative team has committed to ensuring that their learning needs are met. It effectively ensures that all students are represented and organized in relation to the supports being put in place, forging what Sharratt and Fullan (2012) describe as the "human-emotional connection" (p. 32) that drives team members to work diligently to support students.

In the Field

As introduced in Chapter 6, the evolution of visual team boards moved from categories of "maintain, watch, and concern" to reflect two sets of information—student entry level and the highest tier of support for a learner, as defined by a school's continuum of support (Figure 6.6).

The student entry level was reflected by the color of the card and served, as discussed in Chapter 6, as an indication of what the data and evidence were telling us as students transitioned into a new grade level.

However, the categories for the board reflected the tiers of support that aligned with the school's ever-evolving continuum of supports. Through the course of the CTM discussion, student cards could be moved to the tier that corresponded with the highest level of support being implemented. Aligning team boards with the tiers of support of the school's continuum of supports allowed a visual snapshot of the number of students receiving support from each tier as well as the opportunity for celebration as student cards are physically moved to less-intensive levels of support. To learn more about digital solutions for team boards, visit http://jigsawcollaborativesolutions.ca.

The use of a visual team board serves as an organizer for the supports in place for individual students and their entry level coming into the current grade as well as a simple visual reminder of which students need to be discussed.

Potential Pitfall

The visual boards used in team meetings are intended to support the collaborative conversations about students and are not intended to label students. We regularly caution teams to take care not to use language such as, "Ben is a Tier 2 student" or "Avery is a Tier 4 student." We would respond with "Ben is Ben" and "Avery is Avery," and both of them require different levels of support at different points in time around different aspects of their learning. In fact, Ben may require Tier 2 supports in numeracy, and he may excel in reading. The use of the board and the tier described therein is a function of our response as a school team, not a description of who a child may be. Once again, it is the supports that are tiered, not the students.

In the Field

At J. S. McCormick School in Lacombe, AB, Canada, administration developed a visual to emphasize with their staff the importance of identifying a student by their name and not labeling them by tier (Figure 7.10)

Figure 7.10 Not a Tier 4 student

Alignment With Collaborative Structures

The final component for reflection in the continuum of supports is the fundamental connection between collaborative structures and their alignment with the tiers of support on the continuum. A direct correlation can be drawn between the layers of teams in the school, first shown in Figure 3.1, and the articulation of tiers of support on the continuum, now shown in Figure 7.11. As described in Chapter 3, the case consult team, school support team, CTMs, and the collaborative planning teams are clearly defined structures in Collaborative Response that align purposefully with the continuum of supports.

As seen in Figure 7.11, collaborative planning teams are dedicated to the refinement of classroom instructional practices, which are the foundation for Tier 1. CTMs focus primarily on providing differentiated support to students, as generated through the identification of key issues, which are identified as Tier 2 in the continuum of supports—classroom supports that are provided for some students some of the time but by the classroom teacher. Tier 3 supports are schoolwide supports typically provided by someone other than the classroom teacher, and the team primarily responsible for coordinating that level of support is the school support team. And finally, intensive supports that require external partners and agencies described in Tier 4 are navigated by the case consult team meetings.

When any one of the Collaborative Response structures is nonexistent or is not functioning to capacity, then the people and resources in the other layers become stretched and overwhelmed. We recognize that without intentional functioning structures, teachers have no recourse when struggling with the needs of a student but to reach out to these more-intensive teams for support.

When schools or districts have designed their collaborative structures, it is beneficial to design a visual that clearly defines each layer, their team membership, the frequency of their team meetings, their core purpose, and how and when teams are accessed for the next level of support.

In the Field

Elmworth School in Peace Wapiti Public School Division in northwestern Alberta, Canada, has created visual overviews shown in Figure 7.12, describing the different collaborative structures established in the school, when they happen, who is involved, and the purpose. The example illustrates the explicit understanding that each of the team structures serves a different purpose and will involve processes specially designed to match that purpose, posted in their collaborative meeting space as a continual reference for staff.

In Medicine Hat Public School Division, in southern Alberta, Canada, a districtwide overview, shown in Figure 7.13, has been developed to provide a framework for schools when establishing their three different layers of student-focused collaborative structures, beyond collaborative planning. Although each school will develop specific structures and processes reflective of their unique context, the expectation is that they will each have team meetings that fit within the general framework required at a systems level

Figure 7.11 Connection of collaborative structures with tiers of support

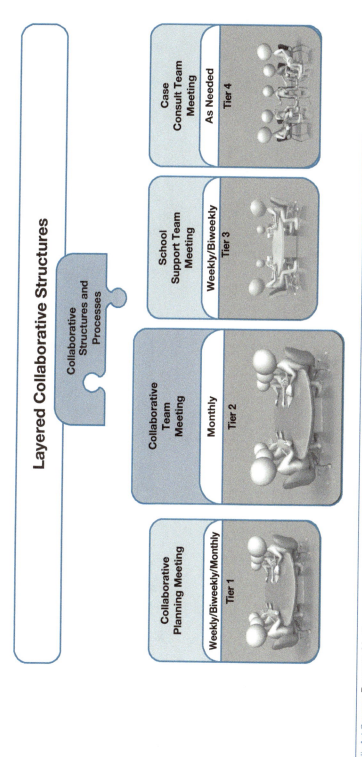

ClipArt Source: PresenterMedia

Figure 7.12 Collaborative structures at Elmworth School

Collaboration Time

Participants

ECS–Grade 4

Grade 5–9

Educational Assistants

Purpose

Organize and Plan Mentorship Hour

Plan Interventions

Review Data

Share Expertise and Strategies

Prepare for CRM Meeting

Share Resources

Develop or Improve Programs

Complete Actions

Create Team Goals

Time

Scheduled 13 times per year

1 hour each

Collaborative Team Meeting

Participants

Administration

Team A (ECS–Gr. 4) or Team B (Gr. 5–9)

Education Assistants

Inclusive Education Coach/FCSS

Purpose

Identification of Key Issues (Tier 1, Tier 2)

Focus on Classroom Strategies

Reinforce Practices Consistent With Quality Learning Environment

Review Success of Action Items Through Progress Monitoring

Time

Scheduled every 5 weeks per team

Inclusive Education Meeting

Participants

Teachers

Inclusive Education Teacher

Inclusive Education Coach

Purpose

Focus on Individual Students requiring Tier 3 (individualized supports) and Tier 4 (specialized supports and equipment)

Support Teachers with referral process, IPP process

Monitor progress of interventions

Time

Scheduled every 6 weeks per teacher

Team Meeting

Participants

Outside Agencies

Family/Parent

Classroom Teacher

Educational Assistant

Administration

Inclusive Education Teacher

Inclusive Education Coach

Purpose

Focused on communication: needs, supports, services, goals, progress

Necessitated by Inclusive Education Meeting

Time

As Needed

Success in School - 3 times per year

Source: ©2021, C. Gauthier, Elmworth School, Peace Wapiti Public School Division, AB. Used with permission.

CHAPTER #7. Continuum of Supports

207

Figure 7.13 Collaborative structure expectations for Medicine Hat Public School Division

The Collaborative Team Meeting (CTM) processes should apply to a range of teams and structures. The difference between the teams and the meetings are: focus of the meeting (e.g., groups of students vs. individual student) and the people involved in the meeting (e.g., group of classroom teachers vs. specialized services). The charts below provide guidance for the focus of each team on the continuum of supports.

Tier 1 and 2 - Collaborative Team Meeting (CTM)	Focus, Frequency, & Duration
Administrator - mandatory	• Focus on Tier 1 and 2 instructional needs of groups of students
Classroom Support Teacher (CST) - recommended	• Occur every 4 – 6 weeks/team
Optimal Learning Coach (OLC) - as invited	• Last between 20 and 60 minutes
Grade/Subject Level Teacher(s) - mandatory	
Educational Assistant - as invited	
Academic Counselor - recommended	

Tier 3 and 4 - Programming Team Meeting (PTM)	Focus, Frequency, & Duration
Administrator - mandatory	• Focus on Tier 3 and 4 instructional and/or programming needs of individual students
Classroom Support Teacher (CST) - mandatory	• Will occur more frequently than CTMs (e.g., scheduled once a week or every other week)
Specific Teachers involved w/student - mandatory	• Last between 20 and 60 minutes
Academic Counselor - recommended	
District Specialized Supports (BEST, FSLW, District Psychologist) - as invited	
Providers (OT, PT, SLP, Mental Health) - as invited	
Educational Assistant - as invited	

Tier 4 - Case Conference Team Meeting	Focus, Frequency, & Duration
Administrator - mandatory	• Focus on Tier 4 programming needs of individual students
Classroom Support Teacher (CST) - recommended	• Will be scheduled based on student needs and progress
Specific Teacher(s) involved w/student - as invited	• Typically scheduled for 1 – 2 hours
Educational Assistant - as invited	
Academic Counselor - recommended	
Parent/Guardian - as invited	
District Specialized Supports (BEST, FSLW, District Psychologist) - as invited	
Service Providers (OT, PT, SLP, Mental Health) - as invited	

Source: ©2021, C. Saddlemyer, Medicine Hat Public School Division, AB. Used with permission.

Process, Not Product

In this chapter, we have discussed the development of a school's continuum of supports as a systematic response to the question, "So, now what should we do?" The critical understanding embedded within this question is that the "we" is different from school to school and from district to district. It is important to recognize that unique characteristics within schools and districts result in diverse and dynamic approaches to establishing processes and supports to respond to the needs of students (Hoover, 2009).

Essentially, the power is in the process, not in the product. The process of determining and defining supports, organizing them into tiers, and then continuously referring to the organizational structure during team meetings is more transformational than one individual developing a continuum (or worse, copying a continuum from another school). There is definitely learning that can be transferred from one school to another and related resources can be shared, but the real power of a continuum of supports comes from the messy work of developing a school's own continuum and then continuously monitoring and adding to it as the school evolves and learns.

Continuum of Supports Missing in the Model

Again, we return to our three foundational components of Collaborative Response to note what we observe when a continuum of supports is not established in a school, shown in Table 7.1.

Table 7.1   Continuum of supports not established

COLLABORATIVE STRUCTURES AND PROCESSES	DATA AND EVIDENCE	CONTINUUM OF SUPPORTS	RESULT
Established	Established	Not established	Informed conversation about the needs of students but an unclear action plan of next steps—response inconsistent and individualized depending on specific teacher skills and may have limited impact

Developing a continuum of supports ensures that systematic responses are proactively established and students are not left to the wildly diverse range of individual teacher responses. It also helps schools achieve two outcomes that have much deeper impacts on responsive school cultures and foster a Collaborative Response mindset throughout the school:

1. The initial development is focused on a strengths-based perspective, identifying effective practices that already exist within the school. Sometimes these strengths are widely known programs most teachers are accessing for their students. Sometimes they are proven strategies buried in an individual teacher's classroom repertoire of individual responses. In either case, the process of articulating and then organizing the great things we are already doing for kids is a powerful entry point for leaders aiming to establish a continuum of supports and, more importantly, the continuous use and access of strategies, interventions, and accommodations defined within it. Through this process, leaders are essentially saying, "We do great things for students in this school! Now let's articulate what those things are!"

2. As the utilization of the continuum of supports becomes more frequent and meaningful through team meetings, the actual composition becomes fluid. Additions, revisions, and deletions just become a naturally understood process within the school as the school continues to build institutional capacity in relation to its Collaborative Response. Essentially, a continuum of supports provides structure and support to the ongoing conversations revolving around how best to support students.

A continuum of supports provides that third foundational component of a Collaborative Response, working in unison with collaborative structures and processes, and data and evidence. Let's now move into exploring some concluding thoughts to support schools as they engage in putting these pieces together!

Putting the Pieces Together

CHAPTER #8

Attempting to pull the elements of Collaborative Response together, it is valuable to once again return to Kluger's (2008) concept of "simplexity," first introduced in Chapter 2. Although the simplicity lies in the identification of three foundational components of Collaborative Response—collaborative structures and processes, data and evidence, and continuum of supports—the processes and structures inherent in establishing and sustaining each of those components, functioning in congruence with one another, are incredibly complex.

Sharratt and Fullan (2012) note, "The simple part is that you need to focus on just a small number of things; the complex part is how to make it jell" (p. 94). Greater complexity is further added when considering the process of reculturing and leading change that is inherent through these integral shifts. All three components of Collaborative Response must be attended to in order to ensure systematic and sustainable success for students. The three components of collaborative structures and processes, data and evidence, and continuum of supports are inherently reflected in Zmuda et al.'s (2004) observations of a competent system,

> A competent system requires several significant shifts—from unconnected thinking to systems thinking, from an environment of isolation to one of collegiality, from perceived reality to information-driven reality, and from individual autonomy to collective autonomy and collective accountability." (p. 1)

Leaders striving to shift paradigms related to how schools respond to students' needs not only need to "cultivate simplicity regarding the ideas that are the substance of improvement efforts" (Sparks, 2009, p. 50), but they also need to show how the threads connect to weave a systematic tapestry of response.

Potential Pitfall

It is critical to acknowledge the reality stated by Evans (2010): "No matter how much money is available, it rarely seems to be enough. Nor, it seems, are there ever enough people (or enough good people) or enough time or enough materials or enough space" (p. 25). There will inevitably be barriers, real and perceived, that echo when shifting to a collaborative schoolwide response to identify and respond to the needs of students. It is important that leaders clearly ensure an understanding of purpose and vision and then, true to the Ready, Fire, Aim mentality, work to align structures and processes to maximize the collective expertise of staff. When barriers of time, resources, and staffing are evident, that is the *most* critical time to utilize the collective knowledge and wisdom of the team to maximize and prioritize what resources are available.

We offer three final thoughts to schools, districts, and leaders working to establish their own Collaborative Response.

Acknowledge the Messiness

Change is "messy and nonlinear" (Hulley & Dier, 2009, p. 30). There is no simple step-by-step formula to follow when envisioning Collaborative Response, nor is there a checklist of "to do" items to systematically cross off. Furthermore, even if that formula or checklist did exist, there is power in the process of building one's own model.

> While other schools' experiences can be inspiring and instructive, there is a danger in a school basing its plan too heavily on a standardized model or in measuring success against progress made by other schools. Many factors—such as the specific needs and strengths of the school, available resources, level of support from district administration and the community (or lack of support), basic structures and functions in place (or missing) in the school, and the presence of competing priorities and initiatives—can make an enormous difference in determining useful and realistic goals and benchmarks of success. (Vetter, 2008, pp. 105–106)

Every school, district, and/or education authority must begin the process by building on its collective capacity and current realities, honoring the great things already alive. Our experience has been that *every* school has individual strengths and effective elements. The challenge is nesting those elements within a framework of response and then working to identify and address gaps between traditional and responsive paradigms. Transformation requires periods of uneasiness, frustration, and loss. Fullan (2001) reminds us that "a culture of change consists of great rapidity and nonlinearity on the one hand and equally great potential for creative breakthroughs on the other. The paradox is that transformation would not be possible without accompanying messiness" (p. 31).

Companion Website Resources

8.1. Targets for implementation: While there is no "to do" checklist, we have developed a targets for implementation resource that can serve as a rough road map of considerations when establishing Collaborative Response over a three-year period, with potential timelines reflective of what we typically see in schools endeavoring to embed the framework.

This messiness alludes to the principle of the Ready, Fire, Aim metaphor first described in 1982 by Peters and Waterman (as cited by Fullan, 2010). As Fullan (2013) describes it, the components consist of "ready (moral imperative and initial commitment), fire (learning by purposefully doing), and aim (consolidation, drive for more). In many cases the causal action is the reverse of what we might think logically. Instead of commitment causing action, action increases commitment" (Fullan, 2013, p. 57).

Let's break down the metaphor as it relates to staff collaboration, which is always fraught with nonlinear "messiness."

Ready: The ready phase points to the crucial work of a leader or leadership team at the implementation phase. This phase includes communicating the importance of how collaborative work can have a positive impact on teaching and learning. However, the Nike acronym "Just Do It" once again applies, because leaders cannot wallow at this ready phase. Essentially, it is critical that leaders develop "intellectual energy" (Fullan & Sharratt, 2007), generating excitement and desire to refine and improve practices. In addition to building the critical mass of followers necessary for change to take root (note that we're not stating "whole staff buy-in"), leaders at this stage need to focus on creating embedded time for staff to work together and the structures and processes within which the work will be accomplished as well as communicate starting points for collaboration (possibly even including piloting change initiatives). The ready phase essentially establishes the garden in which seeds of collaboration will grow.

Fire: Evans (2010) shares, "when the ultimate aim is a change in beliefs and assumptions, which cannot be imposed, one must often insist on a change in behavior, which can" (p. 48). The fire phase points to that change in behavior. Leaders cannot wait for total staff buy-in. Consider the following advice, again from Fullan (2011):

> Research on attitudinal change has long found that our behaviors change before our beliefs do. By behavior I don't mean aimless actions, but rather purposeful experiences. It is new experiences that generate feelings and emotions. The implication for approaching new change is clear. Do not load up on vision, evidence, and sense of urgency. Rather, give people new experiences in relatively nonthreatening circumstances, and build on them, especially through interaction with trusted peers. This sounds simple, but it can be hard to do when you are impatient for buy-in. This approach of course is entirely congruent with our fundamental stance that practice drives beliefs more than the reverse. (p. 68)

We must engage in action, working together collaboratively in teams, even if complete buy-in is not apparent. In this phase, leaders support the teams as they engage in collaborative practices. The fire phase is really about getting started and having the resolve to remember that "it's easier to act your way into a new way of thinking, than to think your way into a new way of acting" (Pascale et al., 2010, p. 38).

Aim: Nothing will go perfectly the first time staff members engage in collaborative practices. Conversations may be awkward. Trust needs to be established. Team time may not produce optimal productivity at the onset. The aim phase includes reflecting on collaborative structures, processes, and practices that staff members engage in and making shifts or "tweaks" to make these more effective. It is essential to note that learning by doing, including making mistakes, is "the most powerful kind of learning" (Lehrer, 2009, p. 54). As DuFour and Fullan (2013) point out,

> It is a heuristic process of trial and error. There is no formula to be followed that guarantees the desired outcomes. Much of cultural change involves working through complexity by finding out what is working and what isn't, and by making adjustments based on the findings. (p. 3)

Starting Steps

Consider establishing scheduled reviews when first implementing foundational components and elements of Collaborative Response. When first piloting a new assessment, determine when its effectiveness will be discussed. Schedule the third collaborative team meeting as a chance to talk about the tweaks needed to improve its effectiveness. Planning for the "aim" phase is important to ensure that the way we work together is being examined critically and constantly improving as teams grow more skilled in collaboration.

CHAPTER #8. Putting the Pieces Together

Adopting a Ready, Fire, Aim mentality is not for the faint of heart and relies on courageous, strategic leadership. Here, Reeves (2009) provides food for thought:

> This is the critical juncture in any collaborative effort. If your goal is popularity, then you are finished, and professional collaboration will meet the same fate as every other change that failed because the true standard was popularity, rather than effectiveness. If, however, you are committed to effective change, then persistence through the initial challenges to achieve the essential short-term wins will be necessary, even when that persistence is unpopular. (p. 48)

When preparing to shift school cultures from traditional isolation to more collaborative, team-oriented practices, adopting a Ready, Fire, Aim approach can ensure long-term success. Remember that "it is not inspiring visions, moral exhortation, or mounds of irrefutable evidence that convince people to change, it is the actual experience of being more effective that spurs them to repeat and build on the behavior" (Fullan, 2011, p. 52). Part of this messy experience also involves setbacks and failed actions. True learning and risk-taking cultures embrace those failures as part of the process, recognizing that "setbacks aren't permanent roadblocks but rather, signals that they need to keep learning" (Grenny et al., 2013, p. 134).

Our advice is to approach the inevitable messiness, inherent in a Ready, Fire, Aim mentality, as a team, which leads to the second final thought.

Collaboration Is Key

Throughout this text, we have relied on one fundamental truth in education: "Collaborative schools do better than individualistic ones" (Hargreaves & Fullan, 2012, p. 112). Schools that foster and support collaboration do better, and "teachers who work in professional cultures of collaboration tend to perform better than teachers who work alone" (Hargreaves & Fullan, 2012, p. 112). It is no coincidence that the first word in our framework of response is collaborative. Adults working closest to students have experience, knowledge, and talents that can go largely untapped in a traditional educational paradigm that honors (and in some cases vehemently upholds) cultures of isolationism.

However, untapped professional capacity is only the tip of the iceberg. When educational professionals work in collaborative teams, the whole is certainly greater than the sum of the parts. We have experienced time and time again that collaborative teams discover strategies and approaches for students that might have never been generated if the space, protocol, and time for student-centered conversation were not held in highest regard. Establishing a formulaic "assessment score equals resulting intervention" will *not* meet the diverse and ever-changing needs of our students and classrooms. Collaborative problem-solving at every level is absolutely essential if we truly wish to achieve the lofty goal of addressing the needs of *all* students. This focuses on a greater moral purpose, "the deep commitment to raising the bar and closing the gap of learning for *all students*" (Fullan, 2013, p. 57), which leads to the final thought we wish to leave all educators reading this text: hope.

Every Child Deserves a Team

We ended our introductory chapter with a focus on this message: every child deserves a team. Without that intrinsic organizational belief that all students can achieve success and that the promise of that success drives our collaborative efforts, restructuring schools to align with the foundational components of Collaborative Response will have limited sustainable impact. Almost four decades ago, Freire (1982) recognized that "dialogue cannot be carried out in a climate of hopelessness. If the dialoguers expect nothing to come of their efforts, their encounters will be empty, sterile, bureaucratic and tedious" (p. 80). Teachers who believe that they can make a difference in the lives of students really do make a difference (Ashton & Webb, 1986). However, "just to urge teachers to look on the bright side and be more hopeful is not enough" (Hargreaves & Fullan, 1998, p. 2). Our schools and districts must establish the climate and conditions that fan the low flames of hope, in some cases, while in others, produce a spark of hope where none may exist. Each and every child who enters our classrooms every day deserves the very best we have to offer as a team. Together we are stronger, and that strength translates to success for all children.

Truly great organizations "maintain unwavering faith that you can and will prevail in the end, regardless of the difficulties, and, at the same time have the discipline to confront the most brutal facts about your current reality, whatever they may be" (Collins, 2005, p. 13). The ultimate goal is to transform good schools into great ones and great districts into outstanding ones, who not only believe that all children deserve a team but have the structures, processes, and frameworks to reflect that ideology. Collaborative Response ensures that schools and districts are *recultured* to maximize professional capacity in meeting the diverse needs of *all* students.

References and Resources

Allington, R. L. (2009). *What really matters in response to intervention: Research-based designs.* Pearson Education.

Allington, R. L., & Walmsley, S. A. (2007). No quick fix: Where do we go from here? In R. L. Allington & S. A. Walmsley (Eds.), *No quick fix: Rethinking literacy programs in America's elementary schools (The RTI Edition)* (pp. 253–264). Teachers College Press.

Ashton, P., & Webb, R. (1986). *Making a difference: Teacher's sense of efficacy.* Longman.

Barth, R. S. (2001). *Learning by heart.* Jossey-Bass.

Bateman, D. F., & Cline, J. (2019). Current trends in preparing general education teachers to work with students with disabilities. In D. F. Bateman & M. L. Yell (Eds.), *Current trends and legal issues in special education* (pp. 23–36). Corwin.

Blankstein, A. M. (2004). *Failure is not an option: Six principles that guide student achievement in high-performing schools.* Corwin.

Boudett, K. P., & Lockwood, M. (2019). The power of team norms. *Educational Leadership, 76*(9), 12–17.

Buffum, A., Mattos, M., & Weber, C. (2009). *Pyramid response to intervention: RTI, professional learning communities, and how to respond when kids don't learn.* Solution Tree Press.

Buffum, A., Mattos, M., & Weber, C. (2012). *Simplifying response to intervention: Four essential guiding principles.* Solution Tree Press.

Chenoweth, K. (2009). It can be done, it's being done, and here's how. *Phi Delta Kappan, 91*(1), 38–43.

Collins, J. (2005). *Good to great and the social sectors: A monograph to accompany* Good to Great. HarperCollins.

Collins, J. (2009). *How the mighty fall: And why some companies never give in.* HarperCollins.

Cunningham, P. M., & Allington, R. L. (2007). *Classrooms that work: They can all read and write* (4th ed.). Allyn & Bacon.

Davies, A. (2020). *Making classroom assessment work* (4th ed.). Connections Publishing.

Deal, T. E., & Peterson, K. D. (2009). *Shaping school culture: Pitfalls, paradoxes, and promises.* Jossey-Bass.

Donohoo, J. (2017). *Collective efficacy: How educators' beliefs impact student learning.* Corwin.

DuFour, R. (1998, Spring). You won't find this on any checklist. *Journal of Staff Development, 19*(2), 57–58.

DuFour, R. (2008). Introduction. In A. G. Buffum & C. Erkens (Eds.), *The collaborative administrator: Working together as a professional learning community* (pp. 1–11). Solution Tree Press.

DuFour, R., DuFour, R., & Eaker, R. (2010). *Revisiting professional learning communities at work: New insights for improving schools.* Solution Tree Press.

DuFour, R., DuFour, R., Eaker, R., & Karhanek, G. (2004). *Whatever it takes: How professional learning communities respond when kids don't learn.* National Educational Service.

DuFour, R., DuFour, R., Eaker, R., & Karhanek, G. (2010). *Raising the bar and closing the gap: Whatever it takes.* Solution Tree Press.

DuFour, R., DuFour, R., Eaker, R., & Many, T. (2010). *Learning by doing: A handbook for professional learning communities at work* (2nd ed.). Solution Tree Press.

DuFour, R., & Fullan, M. (2013). *Cultures built to last: Systemic PLCs at work.* Solution Tree Press.

DuFour, R., & Marzano, R. J. (2011). *Leaders of learning: How district, school and classroom leaders improve student achievement.* Solution Tree Press.

Duhigg, C. (2016). *Smarter faster better: The transformative power of real productivity*. Anchor Canada.

Eaker, R., DuFour, R., & DuFour, R. (2002). *Getting started: Reculturing schools to become professional learning communities*. National Educational Service.

Earl, L., & Katz, S. (2006). *Leading schools in a data-rich world: Harnessing data for school improvement*. Corwin.

Edmondson, A. C. (2019). *The fearless organization: Creating psychological safety in the workplace for learning, innovation and growth*. John Wiley.

Ericson, A., & Pool, R. (2016). *Peak: How to master almost anything*. Penguin Canada.

Erkens, C. (2008). Growing teacher leadership. In A. G. Buffum & C. Erkens (Eds.), *The collaborative administrator: Working together as a professional learning community* (pp. 39–53). Solution Tree Press.

Evans, R. (2010). *Seven secrets of the savvy school leader: A guide to surviving and thriving*. Jossey-Bass.

Ferriter, W. M., Graham, P., & Wight, M. (2013). *Making teamwork meaningful: Leading progress-driven collaboration in a PLC at work*. Solution Tree Press.

Fisher, D., & Frey, N. (2010). *Enhancing RTI: How to ensure success with effective classroom instruction and intervention*. Association for Supervision and Curriculum Development.

Foorman, B. R., Carlson, C. D., & Santi, K. L. (2007). Classroom reading instruction and teacher knowledge in the primary grades. In D. Haager, J. Klingner, & S. Vaughn (Eds.), *Evidence-based reading practices for response to intervention* (pp. 45–71). Paul H. Brookes.

Francis, D. J., Shaywitz, S., Stuebing, K., Shaywitz, B., & Fletcher, J. (1996). Developmental lag versus deficit models of reading disability: A longitudinal individual growth curves analysis. *Journal of Educational Psychology, 88*, 3–17.

Freire, P. (1982). *Pedagogy of the oppressed*. Penguin.

Fullan, M. (2001). *Leading in a culture of change*. Jossey-Bass.

Fullan, M. (2006). *Turnaround leadership*. Jossey-Bass.

Fullan, M. (2007). *The new meaning of educational change* (4th ed.). Teachers College Press.

Fullan, M. (2010). *All systems go*. Corwin.

Fullan, M. (2011). *Change leader: Learning to do what matters most*. Jossey-Bass.

Fullan, M. (2013). *Motion leadership in action: More skinny on becoming change savvy*. Corwin.

Fullan, M., & Kirtman, L. (2019). *Coherent school leadership: Forging clarity from complexity*. Association for Supervision and Curriculum Development.

Fullan, M., & Quinn, J. (2016). *Coherence: The right drivers in action for schools, districts, and systems*. Corwin.

Fullan, M., & Sharratt, L. (2007). Sustaining leadership in complex times: An individual and system solution. In B. Davies (Ed.), *Developing sustainable leadership* (pp. 116–136). Sage.

Graham, P., & Ferriter, W. M. (2010). *Building a professional learning community at work: A guide to the first year*. Solution Tree Press.

Grenny, J., Patterson, K., Maxfield, D., McMillan, R., & Switzler, A. (2013). *Influencer: The new science of leading change* (2nd ed.). McGraw Hill Education.

Guskey, T. R. (2007). Using assessment to improve teaching and learning. In D. Reeves (Ed.), *Ahead of the curve: The power of assessment to transform teaching and learning* (pp. 15–29). Solution Tree Press.

Haager, D., & Mahdavi, J. (2007). Teacher roles in implementing intervention. In D. Haager, J. Klingner, & S. Vaughn (Eds.), *Evidence-based reading practices for response to intervention* (pp. 245–263). Paul H. Brookes.

Hall, S. L. (2008). *Implementing response to intervention: A principal's guide*. Corwin.

Hall, S. L. (2012). Using progress monitoring data. In C. F. Shores (Ed.), *Response to intervention* (pp. 63–78). Corwin.

Hanson, R., & Farrell, D. (1995). The long-term effects on high school seniors of learning to read in kindergarten. *Reading Research Quarterly, 30*(4), 908–933.

Hargreaves, A. (2009). The fourth way of change: Towards an age of inspiration and sustainability. In A. Hargreaves & M. Fullan (Eds.), *Change wars* (pp. 11–43). Solution Tree Press.

Hargreaves, A., & Fullan, M. (1998). *What's worth fighting for out there?* Teachers College Press.

Hargreaves, A., & Fullan, M. (2012). *Professional capital: Transforming teaching in every school.* Teachers College Press.

Hargreaves, A., & O'Connor, M. T. (2018). *Collaborative professionalism: When teaching together means learning for all.* Corwin.

Hattie, J. (2015). *What works best in education: The politics of collaborative expertise.* Pearson.

Heath, C., & Heath, D. (2010). *Switch: How to change things when change is hard.* Broadway Books.

Heath, C., & Heath, D. (2017). *The power of moments.* Simon & Schuster.

Hewson, K. (2013, January/February). Time shift: Developing teacher teams. *Principal, 92*(3), 14–17.

Hewson, K., & Parsons, J. (2013, June). The children in the numbers: Why aggregate achievement goals miss the mark. *Education Canada, 53*(3), 9–11.

Hoover, J. J. (2009). *RTI assessment for struggling learners.* Corwin.

Hopper, K., & Hopper, W. (2009). *The Puritan gift.* J. B. Tauris.

Howell, R., Patton, S., & Deiotte, M. (2008). *Understanding response to intervention: A practical guide to systemic implementation.* Solution Tree Press.

Huff, S. (2008). Digging deep into data. In A. G. Buffum & C. Erkens (Eds.), *The collaborative administrator: Working together as a professional learning community* (pp. 197–215). Solution Tree Press.

Hulley, W., & Dier, L. (2009). *Getting by or getting better: Applying effective schools research to today's issues.* Solution Tree Press.

Johnson, E. S., Smith, L., & Harris, M. L. (2012). Leadership perspectives on RTI. In

C. F. Shores (Ed.), *Response to intervention* (pp. 79–94). Corwin.

Juel, C. (1988). Learning to read and write: A longitudinal study of 54 children from first through fourth grades. *Journal of Educational Psychology, 80*(4), 437–447.

Kanter, R. (2004). *Confidence: How winning streaks and losing streaks begin and end.* Three Rivers Press.

Kavale, K. A. (1988). The long-term consequences of learning disabilities. In M. Wang & M. C. Reynolds (Eds.), *Handbook for special education: Research and practice: Vol. 2. Mildly handicapped conditions* (pp. 303–344). Pergamon.

Kluger, J. (2008). *Simplexity.* Hyperion Books.

Kouzes, J., & Posner, B. (2003). Challenge is the opportunity for greatness. *Leader to Leader, 28,* 16–23.

Lane, K. L., Oakes, W. P., Buckman, M. M., & Menzies, H. M. (2019). Comprehensive, integrated, three-tiered (Ci3T) models of prevention. In D. F. Bateman & M. L. Yell (Eds.), *Current trends and legal issues in special education* (pp. 23–36). Corwin.

Lassiter, C. J. (2011). Leadership for a high-performance culture. In J. Hattie & D. Reeves (Eds.), *Activate: A leader's guide to people, practices, processes* (pp. 57–90). Lead + Learn Press.

Lehrer, J. (2009). *How we decide.* Houghton-Mifflin Harcourt.

Lencioni, P. (2002). *The five dysfunctions of a team: A leadership fable.* Jossey-Bass.

Lieberman, A., & Rosenholtz, S. (1987). The road to school improvement: Barriers and bridges. In J. Goodlad (Ed.), *The ecology of school renewal: Eighty-sixth yearbook of the National Society for the Study of Education* (pp. 79–98). National Society for the Study of Education.

Louis, K. S. (2008). Creating and sustaining professional communities. In A. M. Blankstein, P. D. Houston, & R. W. Cole (Eds.), *Sustaining professional learning communities* (pp. 41–57). Corwin.

Love, N., Stiles, K. E., Mundry, S., & DiRanna, K. (2008). *The data coach's guide to improving learning for all students.* Corwin.

Lyon, G. R., & Fletcher, J. (2001, Summer). Early warning system. *Education Matters*, 23–29.

Martin, T. L. (2008). Professional learning in a professional learning community. In A. G. Buffum & C. Erkens (Eds.), *The collaborative administrator: Working together as a professional learning community* (pp. 143–157). Solution Tree Press.

Marzano, R. J. (2003). *What works in schools: Translating research into action.* Association for Supervision and Curriculum Development.

McLaughlin, M., & Talbert, J. (2001). *Professional communities and the work of high school teaching.* University of Chicago Press.

Meyer, A., Rose, D. H., & Gordon, D. (2013). *Universal design for learning: Theory and practice* (1st ed.). Cast Incorporated.

Milne, A. A. (1972). *Winnie-the-Pooh.* Dell Publishing.

Moller, G., & Pankake, A. (2006). *Lead with me: A principal's guide to teacher leadership.* Eye on Education.

Muhammad, A. (2009). *Transforming school culture: How to overcome staff division.* Solution Tree Press.

Parsons, J., & Beauchamp, L. (2011). *Living leadership for learning: Case studies of five Alberta elementary school principals.* Alberta Teachers Association.

Pascale, R., Sternin, J., & Sternin, M. (2010). *The power of positive deviance: How unlikely innovators solve the world's toughest problems.* Harvard Business Press.

Pfeffer, J., & Sutton, R. (2000). *The knowing–doing gap: How smart companies turn knowledge into action.* Harvard Business School.

Pingault, J. B., Tremblay, R. E., Vitaro, F., Carbonneau, R., Genolini, C., Falissard, B., & Cote, S. M. (2011). Childhood trajectories of inattention and hyperactivity and prediction of educational attainment in early adulthood: A 16-year longitudinal population-based study. *American Journal of Psychiatry, 168,* 1164–1170.

Pink, D. H. (2009). *Drive: The surprising truth about what motivates us.* Riverhead Books.

Reeves, D. B. (2006). *The learning leader: How to focus school improvement for better results.* Association for Supervision and Curriculum Development.

Reeves, D. (2007a). Challenges and choices: The role of educational leaders in effective assessment. In D. Reeves (Ed.), *Ahead of the curve: The power of assessment to transform teaching and learning* (pp. 227–251). Solution Tree Press.

Reeves, D. (2007b). From the bell curve to the mountain: A new vision for achievement, assessment, and equity. In D. Reeves (Ed.), *Ahead of the curve: The power of assessment to transform teaching and learning* (pp. 1–12, 254). Solution Tree Press.

Reeves, D. B. (2009). *Leading change in your school: How to conquer myths, build commitment, and get results.* Association for Supervision and Curriculum Development.

Rose, T. (2016). *The end of average: Unlocking our potential by embracing what makes us different.* HarperCollins.

Schmoker, M. (1996). *Results: The key to continuous school improvement.* Association for Supervision and Curriculum Development.

Schmoker, M. (2006). *Results now: How we can achieve unprecedented improvements in teaching and learning.* Association for Supervision and Curriculum Development.

Schmoker, M. (2011). *Focus: Elevating the essentials to radically improve student learning.* Association for Supervision and Curriculum Development.

Senge, P., Kleiner, A., Roberts, C., Ross, R. B., & Smith, B. J. (1994). *The fifth discipline fieldbook: Strategies and tools for building a learning organization.* Doubleday.

Sharratt, L., & Fullan, M. (2012). *Putting FACES on the data: What great leaders do!* Corwin.

Shores, C. F., & Chester, K. (2012). Determining appropriate research-based interventions. In C. F. Shores (Ed.), *Response to intervention* (pp. 17–50). Corwin.

Sinek, S. (2009). *Start with why: How great leaders inspire everyone to take action.* Penguin Group.

Sparks, D. (2009, Winter). Reach for the heart as well as the mind. *The Journal of the*

National Staff Development Council, 30(1), 48–54.

Stoehr, J., Banks, M., & Allen, L. (2011). *A tapestry for school change: PLCs, DI & RTI.* Corwin.

Surowiecki, J. (2004). *The wisdom of crowds: Why the many are smarter than the few and how collective wisdom shapes business, economies, societies, and nations.* Doubleday.

Taylor, R. T., & Gunter, G. A. (2006). *The K–12 literacy leadership fieldbook.* Corwin.

Tichy, N. (1997). *The leadership engine: How winning companies build leaders at every level.* Harper Business.

Tovani, C. (2004). *Do I really have to teach reading? Content comprehension, grades 6–12.* Pembroke.

Vaughn, S., & Denton, C. A. (2008). Tier 2: The role of intervention. In D. Fuchs, L. S. Fuchs, & S. Vaughn (Eds.), *Response to intervention: A framework for reading educators* (pp. 51–70). International Reading Association.

Vaughn, S., Wanzek, J., Woodruff, A. L., & Linan-Thompson, S. (2007). Prevention and early identification of students with reading disabilities. In D. Haager, J. Klingner, & S. Vaughn (Eds.), *Evidence-based reading practices for response to intervention* (pp. 11–27). Paul H. Brookes.

Vetter, J. B. (2008). A leadership team approach to sustaining social and emotional learning. In A. M. Blankstein, P. D. Houston, & R. W. Cole (Eds.), *Sustaining professional learning communities* (pp. 97–119). Corwin.

White, S. (2007). Data on purpose: Due diligence to increase student achievement. In D. Reeves (Ed.), *Ahead of the curve: The power of assessment to transform teaching and learning* (pp. 207–225). Solution Tree Press.

Williams, K. C. (2008). From C to shining C: Relational leadership practices that move teachers from compliance to commitment. In A. G. Buffum & C. Erkens (Eds.), *The collaborative administrator: Working together as a professional learning community* (pp. 73–87). Solution Tree Press.

Zmuda, A., Kuklis, R., & Kline, E. (2004). *Transforming schools: Creating a culture of continuous improvement.* Association for Supervision and Curriculum Development.

Index

action plans, 20, 31, 173
agendas, 69, 75–80, 85, 91, 110, 113
assignments, 116, 126–27, 146, 192
at-risk students, 29

barriers, 36, 62, 67, 82, 130, 212
Bateman D. F., 35
best practices, 22, 27, 125, 173, 176, 188
brainstorming, 85, 90, 114, 120

calendars, 44, 61–62, 85
Castaway Elementary, 16, 22
charts, 31, 85, 167, 189, 190, 192
    anchor, 84, 200
checklists, 85, 117, 148, 212
Chenoweth, K., 104
Classroom Support Teacher. *See* CST
Collaborative Response Model, 5, 74, 139
collaborative team meetings. *See* CTMs
color-coding, 137, 153–56, 158–59,
    160, 162, 164–66, 177, 202
Corpus Christi Catholic Elementary/Junior
    High School, 124–25
counselors, 37–38, 41, 62, 64, 73, 96–97, 100
Crestwood School, 83
CST (Classroom Support Teacher), 207

Darwell School, 124
data overviews, 89, 137, 154, 157–61
    individual classroom, 155
    literacy screen, 156
    sample, 157
    single, 158
    for students, 137
    for teams, 154
distractions, 141, 184
diversity, 4, 23, 96, 107, 158
DuFour, R., 1–2, 9–10, 22, 47–48, 61,
    129, 171, 214

Eaker, R., 2, 10, 22, 129
Edmonton Catholic Schools, 125
Edmonton Public Schools, 189
educational assistants, 38, 73, 75, 99,
    136, 183, 206–7

efficacy, collective, 1, 5, 8, 27, 30–31, 82,
    114–15, 118, 126, 131, 134
Ehpewapahk Alternate School, 190
elders, 37, 96, 190
Elmworth School, 204, 206
energy, 50, 128, 143, 183, 197
equity, 1, 13, 22, 25–27, 29, 35,
    137, 201

facilitators, 80–81, 88–89, 99, 108, 111,
    114–15, 120, 122–23
families, 25, 40, 42, 96, 100, 172–73
feedback, 60, 189, 198
fidgets, 184, 189, 190, 192
flexibility, 26, 36, 62, 67, 151, 171, 172,
    182, 190, 192, 197
Focus Elementary, 45–47, 50, 134–38
Focus Junior High, 88–92, 152–54
Fullan, M., 23, 25, 28, 96, 106, 133, 140–41,
    166–67, 202, 211, 213–16

gaps, 17, 21, 28–29, 35–36, 179, 182,
    184, 194, 201, 212, 216
    identifying, 28, 51, 142, 174, 178, 212

Hargreaves, A., 131, 141, 215–16
Heath, C., 49, 83
Herald School, 188, 191–92
highest-need students, 161, 176
high schools, 104, 119, 143, 152
    graduation, 28, 104
    large, 155, 158–59
home, 45, 91, 116, 127–28, 146, 173, 192
    practice, 19–20, 40, 55, 116, 128,
        189, 200
Hopper, K., 133
Horizon School Division, 195.
    See also Taber Central School
Howell, R., 179

Indigenous cultural advisors, 37, 96
Information Junior High, 152–54
intentional organization, 10, 137, 140,
    150, 152, 157
IPP process, 206

Kildare School, 189
Kisipatnahak School, 190

Lincoln Memorial High School, 119
literacy, 4, 20, 45, 51, 95–96, 104–5,
  121, 148, 151, 180
lunch, 16–18, 62, 67, 136, 190, 192
  recess, 98
  support, 185
  working, 67

Mamaw-Ohpikihawaso'miskawasowihtowina,
  76, 77
Martin, T. L., 20, 47
Maskwacîs Education Schools
    Commission, 190, 200–201
mathematics, 45, 54, 90
McCormick School, 203
menus, 11, 172, 185, 187–88, 189, 193
messiness, 174, 199, 208, 212–13
Milne, A. A., 15. *See also* Winnie-the-Pooh
monitoring, 136, 147, 148, 150, 186,
    193, 206, 208

Nipisihkopahk Elementary School, 199–201
norms, 45, 53, 58, 70–72, 76, 79–80, 84,
    89, 105, 109–12, 122
  schoolwide, 71
Northern Gateway Public Schools,
    110, 124, 156, 198
Northern Gateway School Division, 199
numeracy, 51, 55, 105, 148, 151, 203

Oscar Adolphson Primary School, 156
Oski Pasikoniwew Kamik School, 76–77

paraprofessionals, 26, 38, 40, 42, 64, 89–91,
    98–99, 123, 175
parents, 17, 20, 40, 83, 87, 116, 127, 192–93
  parental support, 117, 144
Pat Hardy Primary School, 109–10
Peace Wapiti Academy, 177
Peace Wapiti Public School Division (PWPSD),
    75, 105, 151–52, 177, 204, 206
PLCs (professional learning communities), 129
popularity, 32, 68, 215
posters, 71, 76–77, 84, 114, 124–25, 193
Post-it notes, 128, 177, 181.
    See also sticky notes
principals, 43, 57, 97–98, 130, 142

productivity, 70, 75, 79–80, 86
professional capital, 6, 28, 32, 103,
    131, 141, 185
professional development days,
    59–60, 155, 194
professional judgment, 6, 141, 149,
    161, 164, 168, 186
professional learning, 11, 55, 59–60, 103, 126,
    169, 172, 174, 196–98, 201
professional learning in collaborative teams, 59
profile, school's student literacy, 165
programming, 26, 28, 102, 149, 192, 207
Programming Team Meeting (PTM), 207
progress, 43, 47, 52, 59–60, 63, 89, 105–6, 133,
    135–37, 142, 149–50, 206–7, 212
  monitoring, 10, 135–39, 145, 147–51,
    186, 206
pyramids, 170, 180, 183, 189
  of interventions, 32, 169–70, 179

QR codes, 12, 24

Robert W. Zahara School, 74–75
Robinson Elementary, 17
role cards, 89, 108–9
Roy Wilson Learning Center, 196
RTI (response to intervention), 2, 27,
    32, 169, 180
  frameworks, 178

Savanna School, 105
SEL (social-emotional learning),
    96, 104, 105, 148
simplexity, 25, 33, 173, 211
SLP, 189, 207
special education, 26, 29, 37–38, 40–41,
    62, 64, 100
  coordinators/teachers, 97, 100
  department, 35, 97, 119–20
  processes, 2, 39
  students, 100
  teachers, 39, 100, 101
specialists, 35, 37, 78, 97, 102, 123, 180, 183
sticky notes, 175. *See also* Post-it notes
strategic planning, 166, 173
Surowiecki, J., 96

Taber Central School, 195. *See also* Horizon
    School Division
teacher retention, 22

templates, 11–13, 51, 61, 66, 71, 78–79, 107, 109, 113, 162, 187, 198, 201
  collaborative team meetings, 94
  data overview, 162
  intervention description, 193
  student entry-level criteria, 163
  team data analysis, 157
  team meeting overview, 61
  team planning guide, 45–46, 51, 53–54, 56–57, 77, 157
tests, 142, 145–46, 148, 186, 189
textbooks, 127–28, 192
timekeepers, 81, 89, 91, 108
timelines, 9, 63, 65, 76–79, 91, 94, 104, 125
  annual, 105
  for CTMs, 63
  establishing, 51
  individualized education plan, 65
  for meetings, 9, 94, 104
  potential, 213
  unique, 138

timers, 46, 90, 110
  individual visual, 192
  sand, 192
timetables, 61–62, 66, 92
training, 27, 35, 129, 151, 183, 189
transformation, 93, 136, 212–13
trust, 33, 70, 76, 86, 93, 96, 100–101, 111, 118, 130–31, 167

value, 32–33, 36, 84–85, 93, 97, 129–31, 134, 177, 179, 185, 188, 195
vignettes, 8, 21, 33, 88, 93, 99, 121, 135, 144, 148, 154–55, 162
visual team boards, 11, 93, 162–64, 172, 201–2
voices, 71, 78, 80, 99, 102–3, 123, 195

wellness, 40, 190, 198–99
Winnie-the-Pooh, 15, 22. *See also* Milne, A. A.
workshops, 45, 57–58, 89, 99, 118, 174–75, 188

DIVE DEEPER

We know you want every student to succeed, but it can be stressful trying to do it alone. Jigsaw Learning provides you with the tools to collaboratively create learning solutions with your team!

Kurtis, Lorna, and the rest of the Jigsaw Learning team can work with your school or district to build expertise and help you meet your goals. We collaborate to develop customized, comprehensive, and interwoven plans of support to respond to the needs of your organization.

Kurtis Hewson

Lorna Hewson

Learn more at www.jigsawlearning.ca

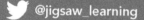 @jigsaw_learning

 JigsawLearningAB

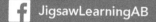 JigsawLearningAB

 Jigsaw Learning Incorporated

Helping educators make the greatest impact

CORWIN HAS ONE MISSION: to enhance education through intentional professional learning.

We build long-term relationships with our authors, educators, clients, and associations who partner with us to develop and continuously improve the best evidence-based practices that establish and support lifelong learning.